ROADMAP
TO
STARDOM

WITHDRAWN

6106

ROADMAP
TO
STARDOM

HOW TO BREAK INTO ACTING
IN HOLLYWOOD

RIF K. HAFFAR

Ameera Publishing
Los Angeles, California, USA

Copyright © 2006 by Rif K. Haffar

Rif K. Haffar is a recovering telecom executive, businessman and author. He received his early education in the Middle East and England before immigrating to the U.S. in 1978. He has a degree in television production and an MBA. His book, *Away From My Desk; A Round-the-World Detour From the Rat Race, the Tech Wreck, and the Traffic Jam of Life in America*, was published in 2002.

Ameera Publishing LLC,
Los Angeles, California, USA
www.ameerapublishing.com

Book and cover design and editing services by THE MAN UPSTAIRS

Publisher's Cataloging-In-Publication Data
(Prepared by The Donohue Group, Inc.)

Haffar, Rif K.
    Roadmap to stardom : how to break into acting in Hollywood / Rif K. Haffar.
    p. ; cm.
    Includes bibliographical references and index.
    ISBN: 0-9715451-3-8

1. Acting–Vocational guidance–California–Los Angeles   2. Acting–Vocational guidance–Handbooks, manuals, etc. I. Title.

PN2055 .H34 2006

792.02/8/023/79494   2005933913

For Tarek, Malek, Thomas, Liam & Ameera

Stars every one

★

Until you do what you believe
in, how do you know whether
you believe in it or not?

— Leo Tolstoy

☆

CONTENTS

TABLES AND CHARTS

ACKNOWLEDGEMENTS

Tracy, still lion-hearted—also very nearly lion-lunch on a recent excursion in Zimbabwe—remains a patient audience of one and a collaborator in every sense.

NaSh and Tooz, literary giants in my book, have been indispensable advisors and editors.

Victor Kruglov, my agent, a man of few words, all straight to the point.

Omar and Randa, always supportive but willing to say, "You're sure you want to use *that* word in *this* book?"

Robin, John, Elena, Olivia, and I'll-be-there-soon-Sophia, for keeping it real.

Sibel, for much-needed advice and encouragement.

Jan Bina, Jon Smet, Tim Armstrong, Ann-Marie Elia, Jenny Wilke, and the remarkable people I met as I got to know Hollywood.

And Mabel, for England, for English, for the passport.

★

INTRODUCTION

Acting is a masochistic form of exhibitionism. It is not quite the occupation of an adult.

— Sir Laurence Olivier

☆

Ah, stardom. They put your name on a star in the sidewalk on Hollywood Boulevard and you walk down and find a pile of dog manure on it. That tells the whole story, baby!

— Lee Marvin[1]

☆

☆

IT'S ANOTHER lovely day as we stroll along the Strand in the Million Dollar Slum. That's what some people call Hermosa Beach, one of a handful of coastal towns that occupy the Santa Monica Bay littoral between Malibu and Long Beach. It earned this nickname because houses and property are so very expensive yet the town is more a surfers' hangout than an upscale suburb. Hermosa has a laid-back feel. It is considered Manhattan Beach's clumsy sibling and carries none of the glitz and glamor of other area cities like Palos Verdes, Beverly Hills, or Santa Monica. It's a town where the mayor holds office hours at Java Man coffee shop every Tuesday night. People are more likely to be walking around in shorts and flip-flops than in street clothes. But it's not all small time—Jay Leno performs at the Comedy and Magic Club most Sundays. Eric "The Body" Fonoimoana, beach volleyball gold-medalist at the Sydney Olympics, lives here. The beach is one of the best and most beautiful in the country, maybe even the world. Technically speaking, Hermosa Beach is part of Los Angeles County, the country's most populous, with something like ten million people negotiating its parking lots...er...freeways.

Tracy and I have lived here for a while now and know that, even though Hollywood proper is fifteen miles to the north, showbiz people are everywhere around us.

> 1834   William Horner develops the *zoetrope* [Greek for wheel-of-life], a device that simulates action by rotating a series of images in rapid succession.

"Showbiz" and "the business," as used in Los Angeles and in this book, signify any activity that is somehow related to performing for money or acclaim or both. It is ubiquitous. Every other person we meet here is a screenwriter or producer or actor or, more accurately, wants to be one of those things. A tiny minority is actually gainfully employed in the business. In the apartment next door is *Playboy Magazine*'s 2002 Playmate of the Year, Dalene Kurtis; a good, quiet neighbor, fond of singing Olivia Newton John's "Let Me Be There." Three doors down is a burly, genial man who calls himself a producer. When we get to know each other better I learn that he hires young actresses and drives them across the border to Mexico where they perform in mud-wrestling videos. Downstairs is a garrulous sound engineer who's always dropping big Hollywood names. One day his apartment burns down and we never see him again. Within six months of moving in I've met a dozen young actors and actresses. All but one are looking for an agent.

> 1891   Thomas Edison develops the Kinetoscope, which moves film in front of a ligh and allows it to be viewed through a peep-hole by one person at a time.

Back on the Strand, as we pass the Poop Deck restaurant, two young women catch up with us, marching in step and swinging their arms exuberantly. They're in painfully abbreviated shorts. The one on the left, with the larger caboose, has "JUICY" in big, white letters dancing across the butt of hers. A hot pink whale tail peeks over her waistband. Both are wearing UGGs, those sheepskin wool-lined mukluks that are now all the rage with the hippest of the South Bay's hipperati. As they go past we overhear the following fragment of their conversation:

Bachelorette #1: I hate him.

JUICY: I hate mine too.

Bachelorette #1: It's like I don't exist, y'know? One stinking audition in two months. And that was for some dumb commercial that called for a woman twenty years older than me. I dragged my ass all the way to Glendale—two hours each way in hell traffic—for what? There must've been two hundred other girls there.

JUICY : At least you got a call. I haven't had an audition since before Easter! I called him last week—he says my headshots aren't working. Hmph! This sucks. Jim wants to go back to Indianapolis.

Bachelorette #1: No waaaayyy!

JUICY : Oh, yah. Unless I get busier real soon. I guess it might pick up in a couple of months but I can't last that long. Is this hiatus? It is, isn't it? Anyway, I'm broke and...

They stride out of earshot and we resume our own conversation where theirs had left us. We pass a large man dragging a puggle.

Showbiz is a paradox. It attracts the multitudes, particularly to Hollywood, then beats down and disillusions them. Yet still they come. After the first couple of exchanges with people who claim to be actors, producers or screenwriters, you learn that a certain degree of tact is called for in discussing their career. Better let them tell you what they've worked on recently. If you ask, you could put them in the uncomfortable position of having

> 1895   Auguste and Louis Lumiere mark the first public exhibition of projected film at the Salon Indien in Paris.
>
> 1896   Thomas Edison records the first-ever film kiss in *The Kiss*, a twenty-second short starring May Irwin and John Rice.

to explain that they are between jobs and keeping body and soul together by waiting tables or serving drinks or something else that has very little to do with showbiz. This condition is not fleeting. Even if a person were to become a working actor or model—a state that I define as acting or modeling for actual dollars—odds are they will never make enough money doing it to support themselves without moonlighting.

Putting livelihood aside for a moment, no matter if you're interested in modeling and acting for other reasons than making money, showbiz is hell. Even successful actors describe the business in terms that would discourage most reasonable people from going down that bumpy road. It's gruel-

> It is grisly yet lulling that the waiters in L.A. are waiting to be actors, that valet parking attendants have script projects, and that the kids in the mail room have board-game plans to take over the studio. There is so much scrambling, smiling readiness to be convincing. People in L.A. think in scenes and give you lines; the city is like a daytime talk-show.[2]

ing, cruel, heartbreaking, unrewarding, fickle and so on. The highs are dizzying and the lows are devastating. To succeed you must be eternally dedicated, thick-skinned, doggedly determined; able to live with constant uncertainty and prepared for depression and euphoria. Above all, you must realize that success in showbiz, the only enduring success, is doing it. The money comes and goes, fame comes very seldom and goes very quickly and in the end you're left with yourself.

So why do it? Why subject yourself to the punishment? Why not just play it safe and become an accountant or a medical worker? Why leave the comfort of a tame but reliable nine-to-five for the capricious once-in-a-while rewards of a career in acting? What is it about acting that tempted even a pre-papacy Pope John Paul II to have a go at it? Is it precisely because the thing is so tough? Are people drawn to showbiz because it is one of the few remaining desperate romantic pursuits? Are aspiring actors of today the Lord Byrons and Jack Kerouacs of days gone by, following their passions regardless of cost?

Why are *you* doing it?

Whatever your motivation, this book is a guide to the very first stage in your acting career. It provides the aspiring actor with a step-by-step roadmap to breaking into showbiz, complete with a comprehensive glossary and other essential resources. The actor who will benefit most from reading it is just getting started in Hollywood. There are several books already in print that propose to do this. *Roadmap to Stardom*, however, in addition to being a guide, includes a memoir of my own attempt to break into acting in Hollywood. I set out to discover what it takes, how things work, the ins, the outs, the vagaries and peculiarities of the business. This diary is in chapter 11. If you're the type of person who is too impatient to read the instruction booklet before assembling furniture, you may want to jump ahead to the diary. It will give you a real sense of how things work in Hollywood.

> 1905   The first movie theater opens in Pittsburgh with a showing of *The Great Train Robbery*, a twelve-minute Western.
>
> 1905   *Variety* magazine is launched.
>
> 1906   The world's first feature film, Charles Tait's *The Story of the Kelly Gang*, premieres in Melbourne, Australia.

Some of the information applies whether you are in Los Angeles or New York or elsewhere, but on the whole this book is meant for the Hollywood-bound. Also, the focus here is on TV and Film. Theater is excluded almost entirely because it is a very different beast, an even more ruthless beast, than TV and film.

> Sometimes I think the three chief products this town turns out are moving pictures, ambition and fear.[3]

My aim is not just to provide a useful work of reference for the beginning actor, but also to communicate, through my own experience of showbiz, a sense of day-to-day life in this crazy business.

Read on.

☆

1. Paul F. Boller, Jr. and Ronald L. Davis, *Hollywood Anecdotes*, (New York, William Morrow and Company, Inc., 1987), 15.

2. David Thomson, "Uneasy Street," *Sex, Death and God in L.A.*, David Reid, ed., (New York: Pantheon Books, 1992), 327.

3. Budd Schulberg, *What Makes Sammy Run*, (New York, The Sun Dial Press, 1943), 261.

☆

Chapter One

MONEY MATTERS

And ye shall know the truth,
and the truth shall make you
free.

— John 8:32

☆

Ye shall know the truth, and the
truth shall make you mad.

— Aldous Huxley

☆

☆

I N THIS book, the truth shall make you free from the delusion that you will earn a lot of money as an actor. That might make you mad but the evidence is compelling. According to Salary.com, the median salary for an actor in Los Angeles as of October 2005 is $50,543.[1] By comparison, the median salary for a nurse is $82,621. Background actors, as you might expect, earn less. This may come as a shock, considering the big bucks that some stars pull down. For example, Ray Romano was reportedly paid something in the orbit of $50 million dollars for the 2003-2004 season of *Everybody Loves Raymond*. That's a lot of scratch. By contrast, Brad Garrett, who plays Ray's on-screen brother Robert, is said to have made a paltry $4 million during that same season.[2] He was understandably distressed and renegotiated his deal. Cited for it in the *Guinness Book of World Records*, Arnold Schwarzenegger, California's "governator," was paid $30 million for *Terminator 3*.[3] Cameron Diaz was paid $20 million for *Charlie's Angels; Full Throttle*.[4] Jack Nicholson, Julia Roberts, Angelina Jolie, George Clooney, Johnny Depp, Tom Cruise and others in this league earn huge and widely publicized salaries.

Since these big stars are emblematic of the industry, we imagine that fame and wealth go hand in hand. In reality many actors who are familiar faces earn modest salaries and live middle class lives at best. The following tables, drawn from Salary.com, show a more realistic view of earnings expectations for actors today.

1909   First feature film produced in the U.S. is Vitagraph's *Les Misérables*. It is shown in four installments because, even back then, American audiences were thought to have short attention spans.

1909   Nine thousand movie theaters are in operation in the United States.

1909   The word "star" is used for the first time to describe leading men and women.

1912   Universal Pictures Company and Paramount are founded.

1912   Hungary is the world's leading producer of feature films with fourteen. The USSR is second with nine. The U.S. has two.

WHO MAKES WHAT?

In the tables below, compare actors' wages to those in less glamorous but better paying professions. The percentages in the top row indicate the proportion of individuals who earn less than the amount in the corresponding cell. For example, from the first table below we learn that 25% of actors in Los Angeles earn less than $41,651; another 25% earn between $41,651 and $50,543; the highest-paid 25% earn in excess of $61,711. *Important Note: This is what working actors earn.* If you're not working, you're not in the picture. Bada bing.

Actor/Performer Earnings

Percentile	25%	50%	75%
Los Angeles	$41,651	$50,543	$61,711
USA	$36,892	$44,768	$54,660

Nurse Practitioner Earnings

Percentile	25%	50%	75%
Los Angeles	$76,866	$82,621	$88,882
USA	$68,083	$73,180	$78,726

★

Extra/Stand-in Earnings

Percentile	25%	50%	75%
Los Angeles	$25,416	$30,834	$38,220
USA	$22,512	$27,311	$33,853

Carpet Installer Earnings

Percentile	25%	50%	75%
Los Angeles	$33,608	$40,631	$49,968
USA	$29,768	$35,988	$44,259

★

If you find the above numbers sobering, your flabber will surely be gasted by those that the Federal Bureau of Labor Statistics (BLS) comes up with. According to its *Occupational Outlook Handbook, 2004-05 Edition*:

> Of the nearly 100,000 Screen Actors Guild (SAG) members, only about 50 might be considered stars. The average income that SAG members earn from acting—less than $5,000 a year—is low because employment is erratic...Median annual earnings of salaried actors were $23,470 in 2002. The middle 50% earned between $15,320 and $53,320. The lowest 10% earned less than $13,330, and the highest 10% earned more than $106,360.[5]

WHAT WILL YOU MAKE?

So what does all this mean? The following table synthesizes the above data from Salary.com and the BLS report in terms of the probability of your earning a certain salary.

Earnings Probability Table

Annual Salary	Odds
Lower than $13,000	1 in 10
Lower than $40,000	1 in 4
Between $40,000 and $60,000	1 in 2
Higher than $60,000	1 in 4
Higher than $106,000	1 in 10

At the risk of flogging a dead nag, I'll mention again that these numbers are for *employed* actors. If you are unemployed in acting—as most actors are at any given time—you will be earning nothing! This is why the BLS reports that the average annual earnings of SAG members is $5,000, much lower than the median. Review the following definitions:

> One day, an extra who was hired for a day's work on an early sound film purposely brought a pocketful of crickets with him and turned them loose on the set when no one was looking. As a result, sound technicians spent three days trying to track down the source of the strange chirping that kept ruining their recordings. But the mischievous extra—and all the other extras—pocketed three-day paychecks instead of one when the sequence was finally finished.[6]

★ **Median Income:** The income level at the middle of the range.

★ **Average Income:** Total earnings of the group divided by the number of individuals in the group. Averages can mislead, as the following old mouthful illustrates: If your head is in the oven and your feet are in the freezer then, on average, you're comfortable.

Still, when the BLS says that average income for SAG members is $5,000, and that there are about 100,000 SAG members, we can extrapolate that the group's total earnings are $500,000,000.[7] Five hundred million bucks. Sounds like a whole lot of money, doesn't it? Now reduce this amount by the salaries of the top stars who are earning around $10 million each. Let's agree with the BLS and say there are fifty of these heavy-hitters. Suddenly the $500 million is gone and there's not a lot left for the rest of us. Catch the drift?

> Here it's different. Here every man is potentially a zero. If you become something or somebody it is an accident, a miracle...But it's just because the chances are all against you, just because there is so little hope, that life is sweet over here. Day by day. No yesterdays and no tomorrows.[8]
>
> — Henry Miller describing Europe in the thirties. He may as well have been describing Hollywood then and now.

SLIPPERY MONEY

Anyway, even if you do make a lot of it, there is something slippery about showbiz money. Why do so many stars make heaps of it and still wind up flat broke? How could a top-rung celeb like Burt Reynolds ever find himself bankrupt? Well, along with fame come various pressures that inevitably push up a celebrity's cost of living. Not long before filing Chapter 11 in 1996, Reynolds had said: "Like every American I'm having a cash flow problem right now. That's why I'm an actor, not an accountant."[9] Big houses, fancy cars, various staff to assist in managing a star's time and privacy—all these things cost money. Lots and lots and lots of it. Burt Reynolds is not alone; the universe of Hollywood celebrities who have declared bankruptcy includes an impressive constellation of stars.

> "God, this is a tough town," Kit said.
>
> "Why is it tougher than anywhere else?" I said.
>
> "Because it still has the gold-rush feeling," she said. "The gold rush was probably the only other set-up where so many people could hit the jackpot and the skids this close together."[10]

Here's a representative roster:[11]

Kim Basinger .... Oscar-winning actress

Lorraine Bracco .... Oscar-nominated actress

Gary Coleman .... Actor

Cathy Lee Crosby......... Actress-author

Richard Harris.............. Oscar-nominated actor-director

Sherman Hemsley........ Actor

Don Johnson................ Actor-producer

Wayne Newton .... Singer-actor-entertainer

Debbie Reynolds.......... Oscar-nominated actress-singer

Mickey Rooney............. Oscar-nominated actor-author

Then there's the siren call of the good life and its evil sister the fast life. Many have become famous and wealthy and gone on to impoverish themselves by living extravagantly. George Best, the brilliant Irish soccer star who played for Manchester United and passed away recently, said it best:

> 1912   Keystone Film Company is founded, first *Keystone Kop* silent movie is released. The series lasts through 1915 and includes eight films. In 2004, Carolyn Parrish, a Canadian parliamentarian, invokes the Kops' blockheaded klutziness when she describes the country's Liberal Party as "the Keystone Kops running around."

"I spent a lot of money on booze, birds and fast cars. The rest I just squandered."[12] In a few cases—though not few enough—drugs and other recreational substances play a role in the troubles of people who find celebrity and wealth in Hollywood. Among the most memorable is the late Julia Phillips, whose startling book *You'll Never Eat Lunch In This Town Again* paints a raw picture of the Hollywood glam life and how it can lead to pecuniary ruin. Robert Evans lurched down that road as well but recovered admirably. He told the story in his 1994 autobiography, *The Kid Stays in the Picture*, a fascinating look at the cloisters of Hollywood power and money. Both Phillips and Evans lived the lives of shooting stars. They fed on incredible energy, talent, and no small amount of luck. Then they flamed out spectacularly. Evans survived to see his life story made into a movie. Later he said: "I'll tell you this though, it was a lot easier watching it than living it."[13]

There are two bottom lines to this chapter:

★ BOTTOM LINE #1

Pay attention to money. After all, it's called show *business* and not show *charity*.

★ BOTTOM LINE #2

Working as an actor in Hollywood is not and must not be regarded as a path to wealth. The odds against it are monstrous.

> In 1948 [Bing] Crosby got $350,000; [Gary] Cooper got $300,000; [Errol] Flynn took home $200,000 (for only three films; and Betty Grable, still America's highest paid woman, made $350,000...The movie elite had come a long way from its first days in Hollywood when the highest paycheck in town was $5,000 a week, and that going to the only real superstar in 1913—Mary Pickford.[14]

Now you know.

If, after you've read this chapter, you still believe that this career is for you, then you must be independently wealthy, crazy fearless, or in it for something other than money. Any of these is a good enough reason.

Knock 'em dead!

☆

1. Salary.com, "Salary Wizard," October 2005, http://swz.salary.com/salarywizard/layoutscripts/swzl_keywordsearch.asp.

2. Lia Haberman, "Not Everybody Loves 'Raymond,'" *E! Online*, August 13, 2003. http://www.eonline.com.

3. Lew Irwin, "Arnold Gets $30 Million for *Terminator* Sequel," Hollywood.com, December 10, 2001, http://www.hollywood.com/news/detail/id/1098622.

4. Netscape Celebrity, "Top Ten Hottest of 2003", December 2003, http://www.channels.netscape.com/celebrity.

5. Federal Bureau of Labor Statistics (BLS), "Occupational Outlook Handbook, 2004-05 Edition," May 2004, http://www.bls.gov/oco.

6. Boller and Davis, *Hollywood Anecdotes*, 55.

7. SAG now estimates 120,000 members.

8. Henry Miller, *Tropic of Cancer*, (New York, Grove Press 1961), 150.

9. Nicola Beresford, "Money's Too Tight To Mention," *Munster Express Online*, Friday April 30, 2004, http://www.munster-express.ie/040430/opinio.htm.

10. Schulberg, *What Makes Sammy Run*, 261.

11. Celebrity Research Lists, "Noted Individuals and Corporations - Bankruptcies," October 1, 2005, http://www.angelfire.com/stars4/lists/bankruptcies.html.

12. "Birds" is British slang for "women." George Best was not, to the best of my knowledge, an ornithologist.

13. Ian Johnston, "The Kid Stays in the Picture," BBC, January 23, 2001. http://www.bbc.co.uk/films/2003/01/23/robert_evans_the_kid_stays_in_the_picture_interview.shtml.

14. Zelda Cini and Bob Crane, with Peter H. Brown, *Hollywood Land and Legend*, (Westport, CT: Arlington House, 1980), 157.

☆

Chapter Two

CROOKS

Louis: *Tu vois le mal partout.* [You see evil everywhere].

Marion: *Je ne vois pas le mal partout. Il est partout.* [I don't see evil everywhere. It *is* everywhere.]

Belmondo and Deneuve in Truffaut's *La Sirène du Mississipi,* (1969)

☆

You can fool all the people all the time if the advertising is right and the budget is big enough.

— Joseph E. Levine[1]

☆

Obviously crime pays, or there'd be no crime.

— G. Gordon Liddy

☆

☆

CAVEAT EMPTOR! That's Latin for "buyer beware!" Look, if companies like Enron and Worldcom can rip us off; if clergy can get busted for taking advantage of children; if Martha Stewart can go to jail and if our most senior elected officials can lie to us, it's a good bet that we're just not safe in this world. That's why you must have an idea what's what out there and how to protect yourself.

Your best defenses against getting ripped off are good information and good friends. Good information is easily obtainable on any number of public service and government websites. You'll find a few in this chapter and in appendix C, "Online Resources." As for friends, these are people whom you trust completely and who can play devil's advocate when you have an idea or plan of action. All the better if they are directly involved in showbiz. I had the good fortune of knowing a handful of people who lived and worked in Hollywood and were willing to advise me. Be careful, though, not to be so much in need of help that you befriend louts whose scam it is precisely to get close to you.

> 1914   First World War starts. It is called the War to End All Wars. By the time it's over, fifteen million people are dead.
>
> 1914   Charlie Chaplin debuts character of the Little Tramp. English but living in America, he is knocked by some for not going to war. Instead, his comedies bring laughter to a world sorely in need of it.

Showbiz has more than its fair share of reprobates. The situation is particularly serious because the scams are not just about taking your money. They are sometimes about enticing wannabes to do things that are illegal or immoral. The damage to lives and careers can be irreversible. These Tinseltown scoundrels prey on the young and impressionable that arrive annually in the City of Angels to take their shot at fame. Your career plan does not include being preyed upon. Be vigilant.

> "Hello, chump," he yelled, "welcome to Los Angeles, the city of Lost Angels."[2]

Unless you were raised in the Vatican and continue to live and take all your meals there, this will not be the first time you've seen the following cardinal laws:

★ If it sounds too good to be true, darn it, it probably is.

★ Never pay commission up front for an acting job.

★ Never give anyone your money before you have investigated them fully.

★ Never sign anything that you have not read and understood.

★ Protect your personal information as if it were your liver.

★ The Internet is lousy with shysters. Invest in a firewall and virus protection. This is an absolute no-brainer.

★ Never trust anyone who says you're better looking than others do. Except, of course, your mom. Her, you can trust.

Follow these guidelines and you will be a mighty tough mark, even if there is a parallel universe of hucksters and snake-oil salesmen in Hollywood. While most people in showbiz, or any other legitimate biz, are honest and hardworking and adhere to moral and ethical standards, there are some who are just plain rip-off artists. Your challenge is to sort the good guys from the bad.

> The common rules of behavior and how we deal with other human beings basically define our ability to succeed or not. Because the stakes are so high in this industry, people are not normally trusting, and you have to win their trust.[3]

Most scams capitalize on the actor's need for exposure. They understand the psychology that drives actors: *This could be my big break!* They know that you are willing to take chances and that some beginners are hungry, desperate and ambitious enough to do anything to be seen. To help you steer a safer course during your career's start-up phase, following is a list of situations that could be scams. It is neither comprehensive nor precise, since new scams are born every day, as are variations on existing ones. When all is said and done, you must rely on your own common sense, hopefully stopping short of becoming a paranoid basket case.

> 1915   Premiere of D. W. Griffith's *Birth of a Nation*. It is the first movie shown in the White House and the foundation of many still-relevant filmmaking principles.
>
> 1916   Samuel Goldfish and Edgar Selwyn form the Goldwyn Company. Goldfish changed his name to Goldwyn. When they later parted ways, Selwyn complained, "Not only did he steal a large part of my money, he also stole half of my name."

DOT.CON

There are lots of ways to flush perfectly good money down the Internet. Some are designed specifically for actors. Others do not discriminate. Following are a few favorites:

CAUGHT IN YOUR OWN WEB!

One way to part you from your money is to sell you a personal website and convince you that it will be your portal to riches. You are enticed to pay for construction and maintenance of a site on which to post your résumé and photos. You're told that casting agents from far and wide will hoof a cyber-path to your door. It sounds good but you'll find that this website becomes a lonely outpost on the information superhighway. Casting directors will not pop in to check you out. That's because they already know where to look for talent. So unless you have them to throw away, save your skins.

> 1916   Annette Kellerman (Anitia) immortalizes her posterior in posterity as the first star to appear nude, in *Daughter of the Gods*. Her costar, William E. Shay (Prince Omar), is speechless.

There is a related scam that the Federal Trade Commission (FTC) calls "web cramming." You are offered a free website for a 30-day period. Every assurance is made that you will have no obligation to buy the thing if you don't want to. Trouble is, you soon learn that the "free" offer is not at all free and that your phone bill has been loaded with heavy charges.

> 1918   Birth of Warner Bros. West Coast Studios at 5842 Sunset Blvd. Harry, Albert, Sam and Jack Warner all work there. Price of property? $25,000. Today? Don't ask.
>
> 1919   United Artists is established by Charlie Chaplin, Mary Pickford, Douglas Fairbanks and D. W. Griffith.

Many showbiz-related Internet sites are absolutely vital to the industry. For example, Casting Networks at www.lacasting.com has become a valuable mechanism for agents and casting agencies to look at and select talent. More on this in chapter 7, "Auditions."

CAUGHT IN SOMEONE ELSE'S WEB!

This is a variation on the con in the preceding section. In this case the website operator does not sell you your own website. They instead convince you to pay them a monthly fee in exchange for the privilege of listing your name and contact information and photos on theirs. The pitch is the same: you'll get casting directors by the flock calling you in for auditions. The tricky bit is that this is not technically a scam. After all, it's your decision to subscribe. Even if you relied on exaggerated estimates of your potential gain, the net result is the same: you pay for nothing. Spotting and weeding out this kind of pig in a poke calls for some careful research on your part. Contact someone else who has already used this company's services. How did they do? Were they inundated with calls? Did the phone ring even once?

1920	Rudolph Valentino, earliest movie hunk, stars in *The Sheik*.
1921	Chaplin releases *The Kid*.
1921	Fatty Arbuckle is arrested and tried for rape and murder of young actress Virginia Rappe. He is found innocent.

COMMON INTERNET SCAMS

Whether you're an actor or not, you must protect your identity and assets while using the Internet. The FTC provides the following list of the most common web scams as well as tips on how to avoid them:[4]

- ★ Internet Auctions
- ★ Internet Access Services
- ★ Credit Card Fraud
- ★ International Modem Calling
- ★ Web Cramming
- ★ Multilevel Marketing Plans/Pyramids
- ★ Travel and Vacation
- ★ Business Opportunities
- ★ Health Care Products/Services
- ★ Fake Charities

Then there's the 419 scam, which originated in Nigeria and is named after the clause in that country's penal code that deals with these frauds. And the lottery fraud, and the "lost heir" fraud. All of these propose to give you lots of money. As the con develops, fees and bribes and other expenses crop up. You are expertly bilked of your own money and never see the millions you have been promised.

There are many, many more.

REALLY CREATIVE STUFF

Half an hour ago a thirty-something man walks in and takes the easy chair in the back room at Java Man, just a few feet away from where I'm infosnacking on the net and mainlining some of the best coffee in the Northern Hemisphere. He sets up his laptop and becomes preoccupied with it until his cell phone chirps. He answers and gives the caller directions. Soon after a handsome young man in sweat pants and muscle shirt walks in. He has black, spiky, gelled hair parsed and sculpted into little cones that make his head look like a sea urchin. I'm not judging.

They shake hands. The young man sits down and hands the other guy color headshots. The latter begins to explain that he and his colleagues are producing a web romance novel type thing. This goes on for a few minutes. I can't help eavesdropping. Urchin-head asks a few questions about the production. The "producer" answers in non-committal sound bites. Then, offhand, he mentions that a fee is required for the audition and photoshoot. Urchin-head would have to pay in advance of getting any kind of gig. Why? He already has headshots. If you haven't already figured it out, this is a scam. I think he knows it too because he abruptly up and leaves. This one gets away. I'm reminded of those National Geographic videos where the springbok struggles free of the lion's clutches and cheats death. Of course in the next scene the zebra gets it. This con is more sophisticated than the previous two. Scammers might go to great lengths to set up what seems like a real production and hook you with an appeal to your sense of teamwork. Don't you want to be part of this wonderful project? Of course you do. It is amazing the lengths to which scumbags will go to defraud you. Read the *Los Angeles Times*. It exposes an unending parade of showbiz swindles.

> 1922   The first incarnation of the Motion Picture Association of America (MPAA) is founded to self-regulate the industry. Will Hays heads it. Thus comes the Hays Code which, among many other things, bans onscreen "excessive and lustful kissing."

"YOU'VE GOT THE LOOK" SCAM

Have you ever had someone tell you that you have the "look." I have. At Starbucks. I was utterly disarmed and would have swallowed the hook, line and sinker except that I was in a hurry. When I mentioned

Because of the film business, generations of very beautiful people have moved here, bred and settled. You have three generations of incredibly beautiful people living here. And in the business, people are not selected for their intelligence, depth or compassion. It's all on looks.[5]

this to a friend back at the office, she laughed and set me straight.

This scam is older than salt and almost always about selling classes or photo shoots or screen tests. Sure, once in a blue moon an agent or producer discovers people in the street. My own agent, while having lunch with me one day, excitedly left the table at Buddha's Belly and gave his card to a young woman who caught his eye as she walked her dogs on Beverly Boulevard. Remarkably, it turns out that her agent had just died and she was looking for another. Only in Hollywood! My agent is legitimate and would happily represent her. Generally, however, if you hear, "You've got the look"—beware! This con is so popular and enduring that the FTC has published a free downloadable booklet addressing it specifically: If You've Got The Look...Look Out![6] Here's an excerpt:

1923   Cecil B. DeMille releases the costliest film ever produced to that time, The Ten Commandments.

1923   Another record is set by the British film The Prodigal Son. It is four hours and forty minutes long.

1924   Walt Disney directs his first cartoon. He is twenty-three.

1924   Charlie Chaplin makes The Gold Rush.

WHAT THEY SAY VS. WHAT THEY MEAN
Unscrupulous model and talent scouts have their acts down pat. Listen carefully to read between their lines.

★ "We're scouting for people with your 'look' to model and act."
   I need to sign up as many people as possible. My commission depends on it.
★ "Your deposit is totally refundable."
   Your deposit is refundable only if you meet very strict refund conditions.
★ "You must be specially selected for our program. Our talent experts will carefully evaluate your chances at success in the field and will only accept a few people into our program."
   We take almost everyone.
★ "There's a guaranteed refund if you're not accepted into the program."
   Everyone's accepted into the program. Forget the refund.
★ "You can't afford our fees? No problem. You can work them off with the high-paying jobs we'll get you."
   We demand payment, whether or not you get work.

THE SCHOOL SCAM

1924   Metro Pictures, Goldwyn Pictures Corporation, and the Louis B. Mayer Pictures Company merge into MGM. 1924   Columbia Pictures is founded.

There are excellent acting and modeling schools that will teach you what you need to know to be more competitive in showbiz. None of these, however, can guarantee you employment, any more than a university can guarantee you a job when you graduate from there. In fact, less so. For one thing, in showbiz the odds are against you. For another, even the best training in the world could come to nothing because of lack of opportunity or dedication or stamina or because, after all, you do not have the look that employers are looking for.

1927   Al Jolson stars in *The Jazz Singer*, world's first real feature-length movie with sound. End of the silent era. In 1939 Jolson plays himself in *Hollywood Cavalcade*.

Before you enroll in any class or school or workshop, research it. Call the Better Business Bureau in your area.[7] Check to find out if the institution is accredited. The American Academy of Dramatic Arts, for example, includes the following accreditation information on its website:

> Accreditation Information
> The American Academy of Dramatic Arts is a non-profit educational institution chartered by the Board of Regents of the University of the State of New York. Academy credits are transferable to colleges throughout the United States. The numbers depend upon the amount earned, the student's choice of college, entry requirements and the desired degree.
>
> Los Angeles Accreditation
> The American Academy of Dramatic Arts in Hollywood is accredited by the Western Association of Schools and Colleges, 10 Commercial Boulevard, Suite 204, Novato, CA 94949, 415-506-0234, and the National Association of Schools of Theatre.[8]

Accreditation is independent confirmation that the school to which you are considering giving a wad of dough is qualified to teach you something. The Council for Higher Education Organization provides a website that is rich with information to help you choose a good school.[9]

There are three levels of accreditation:

★ **Institutional**: Applies to institutions of higher learning that grant degrees.

★ **Programmatic**: Applies to divisions of institutions, such as a department within a college.

★ **Specialized/Professional**: Applies to vocational schools or programs. This includes most acting and modeling schools.

Accreditation, a useful standard for institutions of higher learning, does not apply as widely to workshops, specialty schools, and other short-term programs. In these cases, compare their offering with that of other schools and check with people who have already participated. Remember, even if the acting or modeling school is perfectly legitimate, it still can't guarantee you employment.

To be fair, though, isn't that too much to ask? What if you're an awful student? What if you can't act your way out of a paper bag no matter how much instruction you receive? Obviously, different people get different value from the same course or seminar. Adjust your expectations accordingly and consider any classes you take an investment in your future; additional preparation to help you achieve your goals as opposed to a platter on which acting or modeling gigs are served.

HEADSHOT SCAM

This is often an extension of the "You've Got The Look" scam. The fact is, if you want to be an actor or model, you will need photos. See chapter 5, "Headshots," for additional information about that. However, you need to have a good sense for what a fair price is and what to expect from the photographer. Before you hire one, make sure to see their work, either online or in their portfolio. Meet them beforehand if you can. As always, your best guidance comes from a personal reference.

The headshot scam can come at you from any number of directions. A school, an agent, or a "you've got the look" slickster can pitch it. In all cases you'll be relieved of a whole lot of money in exchange for photos that may or may not get you where you want to go.

1929   First Academy Awards. *Wings* (1927) is the first and last silent film to win Best Picture award.

1929   Marx Brothers produce their first film, *Cocoanuts*. Sample dialogue:

Mr. Hammer (Groucho): You—you know what an auction is, eh?
Chico: I come from Italy on the Atlantic-Auction.

AGENT/MANAGER SCAM

Imagine a hundred people working for you. You collect a percentage of their earnings. In return, you do nothing. Sound great? Of course it does. Sound preposterous? Of course it does. This is the core of the agent/manager scam. The end game is to convince you, the struggling actor, to sign a contract with an individual who promises to help you get work. The scam works in a couple of ways:

★ They do, in fact, make an effort to get you gigs, but charge you far more than a fair percentage. A manager typically charges 15%. Anything more than that is a red flag.

★ They do nothing and expect a percentage of your earnings.

Clearly the latter proposition is worse. In both cases, however, you will be sharing your earnings with this individual. I could have business cards printed tomorrow that read "Talent Manager." I don't need a license and I am not overseen by anyone. Now all I have to do is convince talented up-and-comers like you to let me represent them. I'll draw up a contract in which you agree to pay me—ahem—20% of everything you earn.

1928   RKO (Radio-Keith-Orpheum) Pictures is founded
1928   Silent cartoon, *Plane Crazy*, is first appearance of Mickey Mouse.
1928   Warner Brothers' *Lights of New York* is world's first feature film that contains dialogue throughout. *The Jazz Singer* had been mostly a musical and contained only two dialogue sequences and a total of 354 spoken words.
1927   Grauman's Chinese Theatre opens in Hollywood with debut of DeMille's silent *King of Kings*.

Sound unbelievable? I hope so. If you find this situation highly unlikely, then maybe you will not fall prey to this kind of ploy. Chapter 6, "Agents," goes into detail on how to find the right agent or manager and what to expect in contract terms.

WOLF IN SHEEP'S CLOTHING SCAM

If you're new to Los Angeles, or possibly even to the U.S., and you're here to make a career in Hollywood, watch out for charlatans of either gender who insinuate themselves into your life and then become a liability. I know that this sounds very broad but that's because the nature of the scam is such. Choose your friends carefully wherever you are and choose them very, very carefully in Los Angeles. Mike Medavoy, Hollywood producer and studio mogul, said it well: "Friends? In Hollywood? Is there such a thing?"[10]

In the late twenties, Frank Lloyd Wright, the revolutionary designer-architect, told a group of people that in his view the "Continental Tilt" was a phenomenon which made it possible for all loose nuts in the United States to slide into Hollywood.[11]

Hollywood has a reputation for jaded inconstancy. Well, it's true. Not so much because people in showbiz are somehow less ethical or moral than anyone else. It's because that's how the system is rigged. If change and shifting loyalties are a fact of life in America, they are the essence of it in showbiz. If you're looking for a predictable, sedate state of being, try becoming a notary in Dubuque.

OTHER SCAMS

The variety of scams is bewildering. You may be offered a role with the promise of future payment that never comes. You may be asked to invest some of your own money in a film or a play. Someone might approach you with the seemingly innocuous proposition of attending a casting evening but it turns out you've been set up as a pretty face or worse, an escort. An acting instructor might ask you to demonstrate your range by seducing him or her on stage. A casting director might ask you to undress. You have to know where to draw the line. There is no way to enumerate all the ways in which you could be taken advantage of. Refer to the cardinal laws at the beginning of this chapter, use common sense and you'll be fine. Mix your courage and ambition with a healthy dose of caution and skepticism and you'll be giving yourself a much better chance of doing well in Hollywood.

Almost nothing in Hollywood is a sure bet. And if someone tells you you're looking at a sure bet, don't work with them because in the end, somehow you'll get screwed. Like the words "trust me."[12]

1929   John Gielgud, who passed away in 2000, plays Rex Trasmere in Britain's first all-talking feature, *The Clue of the New Pin*. His last film is *Catastrophe* (2000). Seventy-one years of showbiz. Now that's a career!

In the early stages of your career, most of your rights and obligations as a performer will be spelled out for you. Even the contracts you sign with your agent and manager will be boilerplate and have automatic limits and protections put in place by the California legislature as a consequence of the miserable time suffered by actors under the studio system of earlier years. However,

> A real good show-business friend is someone who, if you die, will cancel his massage appointment to attend the memorial. Maybe.[13]

as you become busier and more famous and as you begin to command higher salaries and employ a retinue of handlers and business managers, you will need a good showbiz attorney to help you navigate the treacherous waters of multi-picture deals and other fantastic eventualities.

You will find an excellent primer on these issues in *All You Need to Know About the Movie and TV Business* by Gail Resnik and Scott Trost. Both Resnik and Trost are entertainment attorneys and they dedicate at least half their book to legal and contractual issues in showbiz. What's more, they present these in a lucid and readable manner that will not leave your head spinning.

> 1929   Movie attendance doubles 1927 level to 110 million.
>
> 1929   Eastman Kodak demonstrates first film engineered specifically for talkies. This caps the career of George Eastman, who dropped out of school at fourteen but went on to patent numerous inventions and to single-handedly put photography within reach of the masses. Eastman took his own life in 1932 after being diagnosed with irreversible spinal disease. He left a note: "My work is done, why wait."

Well, not spinning much, anyway.

SCAM VICTIM ASSISTANCE

What if, despite your best efforts, you fall victim to some cunning double-cross? As soon as you suspect something, call your local police department. The following organizations can also help:

LAPD Bunco Division: 213-485-3795

Better Business Bureau: 909-835-6064

City Atty.'s Office Consumer Protection Section: 213-978-8070

L.A. County Dept. of Consumer Affairs: 213-974-1452

If you are a member of a performers union, contact them for guidance. They have staff who are familiar with these cons and can advise you.

☆

1. Joseph E. Levine (1905-1987) was a Hollywood producer whose credits include *Hercules* and *The Producers*.

2. Schulberg, *What Makes Sammy Run*, 46.

3. Alexandra Brouwer, Thomas Lee Wright, *Working in Hollywood* (New York: Crown Publishers, Inc., 1990), 11.

4. Federal Trade Commission, "Dot Cons," October 2000, http://www.ftc.gov/bcp/conline/pubs/online/dotcons.htm.

5. Donald Rawley, *The View From Babylon: The Notes of a Hollywood Voyeur*, (New York: Warner Books, 1999), 12.

6. Federal Trade Commission, "If You've Got The Look, *Look Out!* Avoiding Modeling Scams," May, 1999, http://www.ftc.gov/bcp/conline/pubs/services/model.htm.

7. http://www.bbb.org.

8. http://www.aada.org/html/degrees/hw_accreditation.html.

9. http://www.chea.org.

10. Gina Piccalo, "A Glamorous Drug, An Illness, A Very Public Battle," *Los Angeles Times*, September 22, 2004. Medavoy counted attorney Howard Weitzman among his close friends. Until, that is, Mr. Weitzman represented Dr. Arnold Klein in a lawsuit that was brought by Medavoy's wife, Irena. You'd think a man's friend would not represent someone who is suing him. As Medavoy was leaving the courthouse, someone asked him if he and Weitzman would continue to be friends, to which he issued his retort.

11. Cini, *Hollywood Land and Legend*, 20.

12. Rawley, *The View From Babylon*, 33.

13. Bernie Brillstein and David Rensin, *Where Did I Go Right?: You're No One in Hollywood Unless Someone Wants You Dead*, (New York: Warner Books, 2001), 78.

☆

Chapter Three

ROADMAP
TO
STARDOM

Everyone has talent. What is rare is the courage to nurture it in solitude and to follow the talent to the dark places where it leads.

— Erica Jong[1]

☆

If you don't know where you're going, you will probably end up somewhere else.

— Laurence J. Peter[2]

☆

☆

SHOWBIZ IS complex. Success comes when many factors are aligned; when luck, preparation, talent, money, patience, courage, determination, and who you know, gather together to make for your success—however you might define it—or your failure—also yours to define.

One thing is certain: you must have a plan. As they say, "those who fail to plan, plan to fail." This chapter puts in order the many things you must do to kick off your acting career. Your own plan

> 1930   Greta Garbo appears in her first talkie, *Anna Christie*. Her first line is, "Gif me a visky, ginger ale on the side—and don't be stingy, baby!" Her last movie, *Two Faced Woman,* plays in 1941.

may include other steps, like getting your teeth fixed or buying a car. What follows, however, is a generic enough roadmap to apply to anyone. It will help structure your assault on the shores of Hollywood.

PLAN TO BECOME A STAR

This may seem self-evident—who doesn't want to be a star?—but must in fact be a deliberate and serious decision. Why? Because it will entail considerable pain. If you haven't thought it through and made a firm determination to do it, you are unlikely to

> In the early years, furthermore, the public regarded Hollywood actors with suspicion; they were denied admission to exclusive clubs and rarely invited into fashionable homes. Apartment houses in Los Angeles frequently posted signs announcing, "NO DOGS, CHILDREN, OR ACTORS."[3]

make much headway. The odds of becoming a working actor—let alone a star—are slim; the odds of becoming a star unwittingly are minuscule. On the other hand, how nice that we live in the twenty-first century and not in the dark days of Puritanism, when things for actors were bad. How bad?

"Close upon the heels of this second [ordinance] came a third [ordinance], which declared all players [actors] to be rogues and vagabonds, and authorized the justices of the peace to demolish all stage galleries and seats; any actor discovered in the exercise of his vocation should for the first offense be whipped, for the second be treated as an incorrigible rogue, and every person found witnessing the performance of a stage play should be fined five shillings."[4]

Yikes.

MOVE TO LOS ANGELES

You could attempt stardom from somewhere else, but it won't work. For one thing, the commute to and from auditions in Hollywood would be a killer. You could move to New York if you want to do theater. Chicago has a growing media production industry. But, for TV and film, La La Land is where it's happening. Of course you'll need a few pointers on how to take on this town and chapter 4 shows you the way.

> 1931   Double features are introduced as a pastime for the masses who are unemployed as a result of the Great Depression.
>
> 1931   CBS broadcasts first seven-day-a-week regular TV schedule.
>
> 1931   Twenty-seven people, including the producer V. Frissell, die in a ship explosion during filming of *The Viking*. Largest number of deaths in the course of a film production.

PITCH

This is still America, land of the free, home of the hype. That you can act and are available means nothing if you don't aggressively advertise the fact. Chapter 5, "Pitch," is loaded with tips on getting the best possible headshots, organizing your résumé, and otherwise mustering the marketing materials. Revisit chapter 2, "Crooks," for tips on how to avoid certain scams that take advantage of your need for exposure.

> Side by side with the human race there runs another race of beings, the inhuman ones, the race of artists who, goaded by unknown impulses, take the lifeless mass of humanity and by the fever and ferment with which they imbue it turn this soggy dough into bread and the bread into wine and the wine into song.[5]

GET AN AGENT

Getting an agent and joining the Screen Actors Guild (SAG) are the two most difficult things to do in the earliest stages of becoming an actor. If you're lucky, someone you know will put in a good word for you and a reputable—or at least capable—agent will invite you in for an interview. If, like the rest of us, you don't have that much luck, you'll have to get an agent the old-fashioned way: compile a list and mail your headshot to as many members of the agent community as you can. If you look like a money-maker, you'll get a few calls and be invited to visit an agent or agency, maybe read a few lines, maybe do a monologue, and hopefully get signed as a client. Once you have an agent it's more likely though by no means a sure thing that you'll start going on auditions. See chapter 6 for the lowdown on agents.

> 1932   Mae West breaks into Hollywood in *Night After Night*. She is forty. Prior to movies, she had raised eyebrows with *Sex*, a play she wrote and directed on Broadway, which earned her a week in jail on Welfare Island, accused of obscenity. Her last film is *Sextette* (1978). So much for rehabilitation.
>
> 1932   Shirley Temple breaks into Hollywood in *Red-Haired Alibi*. She is four.

GET AUDITIONS

An audition is a test. Acting is one of the few businesses in which you are interviewed each time you show up for work. Imagine pilots having to perform a test flight before every actual flight. Or a surgeon having to prove, before each operation, that he knows what he's doing. Not only that; several other surgeons are there as well, trying their level best to outdo him. May not be a bad idea but it doesn't work that way. The fact that you have to do that in acting speaks to the wonderful variety that makes showbiz so interesting. You must audition for every job because every job is different.

> Films! That's all these girls dream about. To be film stars! They think tomorrow someone will come with a contract and then: Goodbye Pavanpul!
>
> It doesn't happen. They are young in Pavanpul and they will be old in Pavanpul.
>
> They tell you stories about girls to whom it did happen, like Nimmi, who became a famous film star. But there's been only one Nimmi, and that was thirty years ago. And in the meantime there have been hundreds and thousands of Chinars, and Baharos, and Ranis, and Nidams. And they're all still here, still waiting for the producer with the big fat contract.[6]

There are exceptions. At the bottom of the showbiz ladder you can work as a background actor without an audition. At the high end you would get jobs without an audition because you're Omar Sharif or Dame Judi Dench. There is no question about your box office draw and the producer wants you to the exclusion of anyone else. You're on the A-list. In all other cases, you must audition! Chapter 7 will tell you all you need to know about auditions, how to chase them and what to do when you've caught one.

> 1933   Screen Actors Guild (SAG) is founded.
>
> 1934   Frank Capra's *It Happened One Night* is first movie to win Best Picture, Director, Actor, Actress, and Adapted Screenplay Academy Awards.
>
> 1934   Donald Duck debuts in *The Wise Little Hen*. He stars in 128 cartoons and appears in many more. His middle name is Fauntleroy. Donald Fauntelroy Duck.

GET WORK

After going on many auditions you land a role, then another one, and another, and another. Before long you're working all the time. That's the idea, anyway. Mind you, there are many types of gigs out there. They include speaking roles, background or extra work, voice-overs, and plain old work-for-no-pay gigs that will keep you in play and honing your craft. Work is discussed in detail in chapter 8.

> If you're an actor, act! Go get experience. Do what your job is, anywhere, anytime, anyhow you can. If you're an actor, act!
>
> — *Mad About You* Director Gordon Hunt[7]

GET TRAINING

There are hundreds of acting and modeling schools in the Los Angeles area. Most are good. Some are expensive. A few are shams that operate for the primary purpose of separating you from your wampum. Some of the world's most famous actors had little formal training. Others have studied and continue to study even while enjoying some measure of success; they are constantly honing their craft. Attentive

> 1935   20th Century-Fox is established.
>
> 1935   The Czech film, *Ecstasy* (1933), starring Hedy Lamarr is blocked from the U.S. by the Treasury Department because it contains nudity and sexual situations.

readers will note that craft-honing is a recurring theme in this and other books on acting. That's because most actors—working or the other kind—spend oodles of

> 1937   Filming begins on *Gone With the Wind* at David O. Selznick Studios.
>
> 1937   Beginning of Hollywood's Golden Age. It would last through the forties.

time doing it. Don't sign up for anything until you've read Chapter 9, "Training." It will give you an overview of your options, good and bad.

JOIN A PERFORMERS UNION

Until you've been admitted to the Screen Actors Guild (SAG) or at least one of its sisters, the American Federation of Television and Radio Artists (AFTRA) or Actors' Equity Association (AEA), you will be an outlier. Sadly, even if you do get in, there is a flipside. After joining a union, you can no longer do non-union work. This immediately and effectively limits your employment opportunities. See chapter 10, "Performers Unions" for a full discussion of this very important issue.

> To be a star, yes, you have to have talent, and my God, do you ever have to be lucky, but riding alongside is this: desire. One so consuming that you are willing to piss away everything else in life. Stars have no friends, they have business acquaintances and serfs. They can only fake love on screen. But they get the good table at Spago.[8]

GET FAMOUS

Your big break arrives one quiet afternoon. You're on the couch, cradling a bowl of cheese popcorn and wistfully watching *Love Story* when the phone rings. It's your agent, giddy with glee. You've been selected from an original group of one thousand people to star in *The Mother of All Adventures*. The movie goes on to become a blockbuster and you are hurtled to international fame. There will be half a dozen sequels. Now that you're famous, how will you stay that way?

GET RICH

The money follows. With every project your compensation grows. Within the year you're a millionaire. Soon you own a manse in Beverly Hills and can't remember the last time you drove your own car or did your own shopping. Now the endorsements pile up and your adoring public sees you in your underwear on billboards all over the country.

The above "Get Famous Get Rich" scenario is unlikely. Sure, you could be one of those remarkably gorgeous and talented people who are discovered by an absurdly powerful impresario who casts them as the lead in a film that is a huge success and secures them a solid career.

Though—um—probably not.

The likelihood of breaking into showbiz that way is smaller than that of having been born with a vestigial tail. (If you have a vestigial tail and are reading this, please take no offense. It's just that the condition is rare and seems suitably metaphorical).

More likely, you will work your way up the ladder and fall off somewhere between Get an Agent and Get Auditions. Or you will eventually become a working actor who makes a living from acting but is neither very famous nor very rich.

> 1938   NBC TV broadcasts first unscheduled event, a fire on Ward Island.
>
> 1939   Bumper crop of classics is released, including: *Gone With the Wind*, *The Hunchback of Notre Dame*, *Mr. Smith Goes to Washington*, *Stagecoach*, *The Wizard of Oz*, *Beau Geste* and *Of Mice and Men*.
>
> 1939   Start of WWII. Turns out WWI, the War to End All Wars, didn't.
>
> 1939   Marks numerous TV telecast firsts, including: presidential appearance (Roosevelt), heavyweight boxing match, Major League baseball game, college football game, NFL football game.

The chapters that follow will elaborate on the Roadmap to Stardom and chronicle my own attempt to follow it. You will see: it looks good on paper but real life is not linear and logical. You may succeed in getting an agent even before you have headshots. You may join SAG even before you have an agent. You may get work without ever taking a single class. You will also realize, as I did, that talent is not the preeminent factor in showbiz success. Tenacity and stamina are. You will do better in Hollywood if you can persevere for as long as it takes. Most wannabes drop out because they run out of money, not because they can't act. The recipe for success in Hollywood includes the following ingredients:

★ Desire	★ Talent	★ Tenacity
★ Money	★ Discipline	★ Brains
★ Time	★ Professionalism	★ Training
★ Looks	★ Courage	★ Practice[9]

Early in your personal quest, you must figure out how you stack up in each of the above categories. If you're highly talented but broke, you must concentrate on finding

> Success is not final, failure is not fatal: it is the courage to continue that counts.
>
> — Sir Winston Churchill

work that provides enough money for you to live on but also time to go on auditions and get acting gigs. If, on the other hand, you're dim on talent but do not have to work for a living, capitalize on your good fortune and go on all the auditions and gigs you can. Remember: this is a multi-round game. The longer you play the more likely you are to win. In any case, the cake you bake with your unique ingredients will itself be unique and your roadmap will be as well.

☆

---

1. Erica Jong is a novelist and educator whose 1973 first novel, *Fear Of Flying*, drew raves and rants. She received the Sigmund Freud Award for Literature in 1975 so I figure she ought to know a thing or two.

2. Dr. Laurence Peter (1919-1990) is the author of *The Peter Principle*, which caught fire in the late sixties and has continued to be essential Kool-Aid in MBA programs everywhere. The Peter Principle states: "In a hierarchy, every employee tends to rise to his level of incompetence."

3. Boller, *Hollywood Anecdotes*, 125.

4. Henry Barton Baker, *English Actors: From Shakespeare to Macready* (New York: Henry Holt & Co., 1879), 29.

5. Miller, *Tropic of Cancer*, 254.

6. *The Courtesans of Bombay*, prod. and dir. Ismail Merchant, 74 min., Merchant Ivory Productions, 1997, videocassette.

7. Joel Asher, "Directors on Acting," Vol. 4, *Actors At Work Series*, directed by Joel Asher, Sherman Oaks: Joel Asher Studio, 1993.

8. William Goldman, *Which Lie Did I Tell* (New York: Pantheon Press, 2000), 29.

9. One of the world's most overused funnies is the probably apocryphal report of a tourist in New York City stopping a local to ask for directions. "How do I get to Carnegie Hall?" he asks. "Practice, practice, practice," comes the New Yorker's weary response. Still, if the glass slipper fits...

☆

Chapter Four

ACTOR'S GUIDE TO LOS ANGELES

"Oh, typical Hollywood," the wardress sniffed. "White Cadillac, dark glasses, big smile."[1]

☆

The trouble with Hollywood is that too many people who won't leave are ashamed to be there.[2]

☆

The tension here is like a low-grade hum all the time, like static on the radio.[3]

☆

☆

Los Angeles is a megalopolis. When people say L.A. they generally are not referring just to the city of Los Angeles but also to Hollywood, Burbank, Glendale, Venice, Santa Monica, Hermosa Beach, Manhattan Beach, and others. Together these districts and cities make up Los Angeles County, which contains ten million inhabitants and is the most populous in the U.S.

Everything in L.A. is transient; people, fashions, morals and ideas. Especially ideas. This is not a bad thing. It makes Los Angeles what it is, the world's idea lab. It's here, on film and in television, that we look at ourselves and our world. It's here that smart, creative, very powerful people anticipate what we're thinking and feeling and give it back to us to examine. None of this would be possible in a static community. The tradeoff is that there is very little inherent security here. Don't let this freak you out. It gives you a sort of what-happens-in-Vegas-stays-in-Vegas freedom.

> I saw a naked fat lady in Los Angeles one day. She was striding determinedly across an overpass that spans the Hollywood Freeway just north of downtown...The naked fat lady becomes a metaphor for Los Angeles. We are a naked city, vulnerable as hell, striding with great determination toward a destination that remains a mystery not only to most of the rest of the world, but to many of us who live here and attempt to understand the place. If there were a psycho ward for cities, we would be there undergoing intensive treatment for a character disorder, with a 40 percent chance for full recovery.[4]

Now that we've distilled the zeitgeist of our times in Lotus Land, let's consider the most important things to know if you're moving here:

★ Where to Live.

★ How to get around.

★ How to make a living.

★ How to behave.

WHERE TO LIVE

It makes sense to live close to where you'll be going on auditions because, with any luck, that's how you'll be spending most of your time. Be careful with what's called the Studio Zone. It sounds ideally convenient but in fact is a circle whose center lies at the intersection of La Cienega and Beverly Boulevards and whose radius is thirty miles. Thirty Miles! Any Angeleño will tell you that thirty miles here are equivalent to sixty in most other U.S. cities in terms of driving that distance. Los Angeles has been the country's most congested city for a long time. Living farther than ten miles from Hollywood can make you hate acting. And it's going to get worse. The Public Policy Institute of California forecasts that travel time in the state will increase by nearly 50% by 2025. It'll take forever-and-a-half to get anywhere.

1940   Walt Disney's *Fantasia* is released.

1940   MGM debuts Tom & Jerry in *Puss Gets the Boot*. The duo's original name was "Jasper & Jinx."

1941   Orson Welles is nominated for Academy Awards as writer, producer, director and actor. *Citizen Kane* wins only the original screenplay award. Bummer.

The idea, then, is to live as close to casting studios as possible. Of the 400 or so casting directors listed by Casting Networks on their website, 340 are located within a cluster of fifteen cities or neighborhoods that include Hollywood, North Hollywood, Studio City, and Mid-Wilshire.[5]

A good map at www.losangelesalmanac.com/LA/lamap2.htm shows these cities and areas in a clear, color-coded fashion. The following table lists them, the zip codes they encompass, and the number of casting directors that operate there. I cannot stress enough the importance of living close to these casting directors. Also, if you have a day job, it must be one that allows you to make quick audition runs. If you live and work near Hollywood, this is feasible. If you don't, it isn't. If you're starting to think that your whole life will revolve around auditioning, you're absolutely right.

1941   *The Maltese Falcon*, considered the first real film noir, is released. It takes two months to shoot and costs $300,000. It is Humphrey Bogart's first big hit. He plays Sam Spade, among whose best lines is: "You're a good man, sister."

1942   Carole Lombard is killed in a plane crash outside Las Vegas. She's thirty-three.

1942   *Casablanca* premieres in New York. It is one of the most durable films of all time. Less known is Bugs Bunny's 1995 tribute, *Carrotblanca*. Go ahead, look it up.

Casting Directors by Zip Code

Area	Zip Codes	CDs*
Mid-Wilshire	90004, 90036	73
Hollywood	90028, 90038, 90046, 90068	58
Hollywood North	91601, 91602, 91604, 91607	56
Studio City	91604	24
West Fairfax	90035	17
Burbank	91502, 91504, 91506, 91510, 91523	15
Sherman Oaks	91403, 91423	13
West Los Angeles	90025, 90064	13
Universal City	91608	12
West Beverly	90048	12
Culver City	90232	11
Century City	90067	10
Valley Village	91607	10
Hollywood West	90069	9
Encino	91316, 91436	7

* Casting Directors

HOW TO GET AROUND

According to the Los Angeles Convention Bureau website, the portions of the twenty-seven freeways that run through Los Angeles, if placed end to end, would stretch for 615 miles![6] Heck, the 405 Freeway from the 10 to the 105 feels like a thousand miles all on its own.

Los Angeles has a substantial public transportation system and it's possible though not convenient to live here without a car. All you need to know about getting around in L.A. without a personal

> Hollywood may be full of phonies, mediocrities, dictators and good men who have lost their way, but there is something that draws you there that you should not be ashamed of.[7]

vehicle can be found at www.mta.net. However, as an aspiring actor you will need to get to auditions and gigs on time and will often have to carry your own wardrobe. Get a car. It can be costly and this is not environment-friendly advice but without one you will be at a disadvantage.

An invaluable tool for anyone driving in Los Angeles is the *Thomas Guide for Los Angeles & Orange Counties*.[8] This book of street maps has become the standard. So much so that when casting agencies provide directions to auditions, they often also provide *Thomas Guide* coordinates. At about $35 it's not cheap but worth it. These days it even comes on CD-ROM. Yahoo! Maps and MapQuest are fine, but when you're out there in gridlock, late, lost, low on gas and confused, you'll be glad to have a good old-fashioned paper map in the car.

> 1945   The Screen Extras Guild (SEG) is organized.
>
> 1946   The Cannes Film Festival is established. Walt Disney's *Make Mine Music* wins animation award.
>
> 1947   FCC rejects CBS color TV system.
>
> 1947   Elia Kazan, Robert Lewis, and Cheryl Crawford establish The Actors Studio.
>
> 1948   Laurence Olivier wins Best Actor Oscar for his performance in *Hamlet*, a film he produced and directed.

HOW TO MAKE A LIVING

It's a fair presumption that you will not make enough from acting to support yourself during the first year or two of your arrival in Hollywood. Either have sufficient financial reserves to pay your bills or you'll have to get a job. It is not within the scope of this book to offer specific advice on how to make a living. However, these general guidelines may help focus your search for non-acting work:

> You know what they say about Hollywood, everything takes either five minutes or five years, and this baby looks like it's gonna be a five-year pain in the ass.[9]

★ Do as little of it as possible. That way you'll have time to focus on cultivating your acting career.

★ Avoid commuting. Driving to and from work is one of L.A.'s special tortures. It robs you of your time and your spirit. Work close to home. Better yet, work from home.

★ The very best shift is the swing shift, from 4:00 p.m. to midnight or so. This gives you the whole day for acting yet is not as brutal as the graveyard from midnight to 8:00 a.m. Also, most restaurant service jobs are swing shift.

★ Limit your expenses. The less money you spend, the less you have to work. Unless you already have one, do not acquire a pet. I have

> 1948   *Meet the Press* becomes weekly show; Milton Berle's *Texaco Star Theater* debuts on NBC; *Candid Camera* debuts on ABC. The first nightly newscast, *CBS-TV News,* is launched on the CBS network.

it on good authority that it can cost nearly $7,000 to raise a dog to age eleven. Not only that. Someone has to walk the creature, feed it, and take it to the vet. Get a goldfish instead.

★ Consult www.craigslist.com. It is becoming an invaluable resource for local job searches.

How to Behave

Los Angeles is one of those cities that attract metaphors and similes by the yard. It's been compared to heaven and, just as sincerely, to hell. A city with so much character can tell right away whether you get it or not. It's better if you get it. Of course no one can presume to tell you how to behave. However, in the interest of saving you time and pain finding out for yourself, I include here a few distilled pointers that you can take or leave:

> Los Angeles forces you to reassess who you are just about every day; this is the city where sometimes you might only have five minutes to grab what's left of your life and run. Everything that's happening here is going to happen to the rest of the world in ten years. We're the forefront.[10]

★ L.A. is faster than Seattle and slower than New York. Your pace and your expectation of other people's pace should take that into account.

★ Whereas the East Coast tends to be formal, the West Coast, particularly Los Angeles, is casual and relaxed. Except in traffic. Also we have checkout-line rage here. Watch out.

★ Dress here is important. You want to be fashionable. All black all the time works in New York but not in Los Angeles. For one thing, it's too warm. In Portland people dress as though prepared to go camping at a moment's notice. That won't work here either. In L.A. the trick is to be edgy but relaxed; sort of like you just threw on the first thing that fell out of your closet but that somehow, it and you are hot.

★ The same applies to hair. Tousled yet meaningfully so; sharp yet unfussy. Spikes and cones can draw some moans but curls will never hurt you.

★ If you've just arrived from anywhere else, you may feel an overwhelming urge to stare. I have no proof that more people in L.A. are tattooed and pierced and augmented and nipped and tucked than anywhere else, but that certainly seems to be the case. Also, since the weather is so often nice, we wear more revealing clothes more often and therefore more of us is on display. Give it time. After about a year your senses will have adjusted and you'll do a lot less whipping around to catch a pair of plastic DDDs or a man with a propeller through his nose.

★ While driving, do not let your temper or indignation get the better of you. Road rage shootings are rare but, hey, why chance it. I presume here that you won't be shooting anyone either.

1949   The HOLLYWOODLAND sign in the hills overlooking the city has a four-letter amputation and reads HOLLYWOOD for the first time.

1949   TV sales accelerate in the U.S. and are six times higher than in 1948.

1949   Network TV is established in the U.S. by NBC.

1949   Nearly one hundred TV stations operate in the U.S. By 2004 there are 1,500 broadcast and 9,000 cable stations.

The above pointers are very general. Later chapters will provide specific tips on how to behave at auditions and on-set. It may be counterintuitive, but for all of L.A.'s edginess, the tone is conservative on movie and TV sets. Just can't pin this town down.

☆

1. David Niven, *Go Slowly, Come Back Quickly* (Garden City, New York: Doubleday & Company, 1981), 188.

2. Schulberg, *What Makes Sammy Run*, 257.

3. Rawley, *The View From Babylon*, 5.

4. Al Martinez, *A Drive-By Portrait of Los Angeles*, (New York: St. Martin's Press, 1996), 74.

5. http://www.lacasting.com/la_home.asp.

6. LA, Inc., The Convention and Visitors Bureau, http://www.lacvb.com/visitor/jsp/mapsguides.jsp.

7. Schulberg, *What Makes Sammy Run*, 257.

8. Thomas Bros. Maps, a Rand McNally Company, http://www.thomas.com.

9. David Lodge, *Therapy* (London: Penguin Books, 1996), 163.

10. Rawley, *The View From Babylon*, 5.

☆

Chapter Five

PITCH

Even if you're on the right track, you'll get run over if you just sit there.

— Will Rogers

☆

In going through pictures and résumés, it is the picture that first draws you and holds your attention. You see a light in the eyes, something that makes you focus in on that picture. Then you turn it over and look at the back to see what this person has done, what kind of training they have, if they've done any professional work. Very young actors don't usually have a lot on their résumés, and it is their picture that 'sells' them.[1]

☆

☆

O
KAY, NOW we're rolling. If you're still with me it means that you were not intimidated by the chapters on money and crooks, that you have resolved to take a serious shot at Hollywood and that you are already here or planning to move to Los Angeles. The next step in the roadmap is to assemble your marketing tools. You need these to pitch yourself to the people who can employ you or otherwise advance your career. They are talent agents, casting agents and agencies and even production companies. If you don't let them know you're here, they can't hire you. This chapter discusses the tools at your disposal in getting the word out.

HEADSHOTS A TO Z

Absolutely the first step to anything at all in showbiz is having pictures of yourself made. It is not just the first step but possibly the most important. Realize that in most cases people who are looking for actors to hire will not want to see you at all. They will want to see your picture. If they like that, they might invite you in for a reading or an interview. Your headshot is your ambassador to the world of agents and casting directors. It's your own personal Mini Me, to borrow from *Austin Powers: Goldmember*. This photo precedes you into the world; it paves the way; it either gets you invited to interviews or relegated to the many stacks that litter offices all over Hollywood. Make it count.

Getting from photo shoot to ordering the final set of headshots is not as simple as you might hope. The following steps ought to make the process easier for you to manage.

WHAT DO YOU WANT?

Decide whether you want a headshot, zed card, business card, postcard or all of the above. This is an important decision because you'll need to let the photographer know what you're after. She can advise you on what clothes to bring and what to do with makeup. This will also largely dictate what kind of pictures she shoots. My advice is that you at least get headshots, postcards and business cards. There will be lots of opportunities for you to use these marketing pieces—and that's just what they are—to make yourself known in Hollywood. Of course that means more expense up front, but this is one area where you do not want to skimp. Zed cards can be useful but more so if you're modeling. If you can afford it, get them as well.

★ Headshots

The standard headshot is an 8"x10", black-and-white or color photo of you against a neutral background. Since the advent of

electronic submissions, many casting directors insist on close-up head-and-shoulders headshots. That's because the images they see on their monitors are thumbnails and it is difficult to make out the face in a three-quarters shot. Another change from days of yore (like three years ago) is the increased popularity of color headshots. Do you need color? Probably not, but if you can afford it go ahead. Who knows, it might get you that one audition with the grayscale-o-phobic casting director.

Have your name and phone number printed on your headshot. Without this information you could be anybody and, what's worse, you can't be reached! You could have your résumé printed on the back of the photo but it's more sensible to attach it later. That way you can update it more frequently. The best way to decide what you'd want your headshot to look like is to study a number of examples. Luckily, you can do this easily online. See one of the following websites for a wide range of good examples:

www.headshot-photography.com
www.movingheadshots.com
www.vandiveerphotography.com
www.joliuphotography.com
www.wesmcdowell.com
www.studiomark.com

1950   Billy Wilder's *Sunset Boulevard* stars Gloria Swanson.

1950   Zanuck's *All About Eve* wins six Academy Awards

1951   Columbia Pictures establishes TV production company to meet threat of growing television broadcasting.

1951   Stelllaaaaaaa! Brando's Stanley Kowalski storms the screen in *A Streetcar Named Desire*.

★ Zed Card

Another name for this is the composite or comp card. It is used exclusively in modeling but I had some made anyway and attach one to my headshot at auditions. No one has yet refused it. These are 5"x7". On one side they have a headshot. On the other, three or four other

photos in different clothes and poses, as well as measurements. When you include a zed card, especially on commercial auditions, you're showing the casting director several other pictures and helping them see how versatile your look can be. That can't hurt. Note the various looks in the adjacent example. Photo session packages are often quoted on that basis. A basic package may be two looks. By "look" we usually mean a change of wardrobe. A premium package may be five. See the following websites for other examples of zed card layouts:

www.shop.onemodelplace.com
www.joeedelman.com
www.modelcards.com

★ Business Cards

These are nice to have for those times when you are not carrying your headshots. They are especially useful if they have your photo on them. There are many occasions when a business card is a more appropriate handout than a headshot. At parties, for example, or when you run into someone at the grocery store or on a plane. You never know where or when a lucky break will happen.

★ Postcards

Useful as thank you notes and quick reminders and follow-ups whenever you need to correspond with agencies and casting directors. It's hard to estimate how effective these are but the cost is modest and, as traditional wisdom has it, any publicity is good publicity. Sending one to thank a casting director for the opportunity to audition may set you apart from the other faces in the crowd.

FIND A PHOTOGRAPHER

An engineer I once worked with had this sign on his office wall:

And that's how it goes. There are many good photographers in Los Angeles. Some have studios. Others do location shoots. Many do either. In all cases you will have to make a choice that favors two of the above attributes over the third. If you want cheap, fast headshots, you'll probably get inferior work. Not necessarily, though probably.

Finding the right photographer is part diligent research and part voodoo. It's part voodoo because there is something inexplicable in how a photo evokes its subject, something that transcends purely technical aspects. Some photographers have this touch and can capture that certain light in the eyes.

The key to evaluating a photographer's work is finding the one who makes you look your best, not better than that. Also, one photographer's work may be right for some and not for others. A stylized glamour headshot that makes you look sexier or prettier or more rugged than you actually are will not serve you well. That's because you'll show up at an audition and, instead of seeing the person in the headshot, on which basis they had invited you to begin with, casting directors see you in an irrefutably different incarnation. You would be surprised how common a mistake this is. Many times at auditions I catch sight of headshots that look nothing like the people turning them in. On the other hand, if your headshots are of poor quality, you are unlikely to get called in at all. So make sure that your most important calling card, your headshot, is faithful to who you are.

1952   Hollywood introduces 3D to counterattack TV's advance.

1952   Edward Murrow hosts *See It Now*.

1953   ABC and Paramount merge.

1953   NBC televises *The Academy Awards* for the first time.

1954   *On the Waterfront* wins eight Academy Awards, including Brando's Best Actor and Kazan's Best Director.

Another thing to keep in mind is that, nowadays, most submissions are made electronically. Casting directors select actors for auditions based on headshots that are either posted on websites like

> If I were to advise an actor what kind of a picture to select, it would be to have just a plain headshot that captures who you are. Not a glamour shot, not three days' worth of *Miami Vice* beard—just a shot that captures you.[2]

www.lacasting.com, www.showfax.com, and www.backstage.com or are forwarded online by the actor's agent. Make sure that the headshots look good in electronic form as well as in print.

Cost is certainly an important consideration, but not the primary one. No, the primary consideration is quality. That's because your headshot will be the workhorse of your ongoing marketing efforts. Saving fifty bucks and getting mediocre headshots is shortsighted. As the Spanish expression goes: "*Lo barato sale caro*," the cheap ends up expensive. Therefore evaluate several photographers, find those whose work matches your expectations, then compare their prices.

HAVE THE PHOTO SHOOT

A good photographer will prepare you for your photo shoot in a number of ways. She will recommend wardrobe changes. She can help you decide on makeup and hair styling. Do you need them? If you're a man, probably not. If you're a woman, probably so. I'm just saying. She will be easy to get along with, well prepared, and will make the experience a pleasure. If you are booking the session without meeting the photographer in person, and she doesn't ask for one, suggest that you send her a snapshot of yourself. This could make a significant impact on what she suggests as wardrobe and what she uses as background. If you show up in all-white clothes and she has set up a white background, your head will hover in midair and your tanned arms will emerge out of nothingness.

> 1955   Half of America's households own at least one television.
>
> 1955   James Dean, 24, dies in a car crash while on his way to compete in a race in Salinas. He starred in three films: *East of Eden*, *Giant*, and *Rebel Without a Cause*.
>
> 1956   The wireless remote control, Zenith's Space Command, makes its debut in American households. It takes over from the clunky, wired Lazy Bone.

RECEIVE THE PROOFS

Could be electronic or physical. Proofs are sheets on which multiple photos are printed so you can compare them and select the ones you like the most. Often the photos are too small to be properly viewed without a magnifying glass or, as it is called in the business, a loupe.

ANALYZE THE PROOFS AND SELECT YOUR CHOICES

If you have forty-eight shots to select from and many are similar, it can be helpful to ask friends to choose their favorite in each look. Then you can tabulate the results and see which shots are the most popular with your voting public. Don't be timid; ask your photographer for her opinion as well. She has seen many of these and knows what casting directors and agents are looking for. Incidentally, you may be looking for two headshots, one for theatrical and another for commercial submissions.

> 1956   Cecil B. DeMille remakes *The Ten Commandments*, this time with sound.
>
> 1957   The Bridge on the River Kwai wins Oscars for Best Picture, Best Screenplay, Best Director and more. Alec Guinness wins for Best Actor. Twenty years later he is nominated for his supporting role as Jedi Ben Obi-Wan Kenobi on Star Wars.

GET TOUCH-UPS

Once you've made your choice for a headshot or headshots, you may need to return these to your photographer for touching up, borders and captions, including your name and phone number. The lab could also do this. The purpose here is not to airbrush you to ravishing sublimity, but to remove artifacts and blemishes.

GET THE NEGATIVES OR RETOUCHED HEADSHOTS TO THE LAB

It is possible—preferable, actually—to work only with a photographer and printer without having to deal with a lab. This depends on whether the photographer shoots in film or digital formats. Digital is overtaking the market and making lab processing unnecessary. Some photographers, however, particularly those who do serious creative work, still shoot film and collaborate with handpicked labs. Others will rely on a printer who has an in-house lab.

> 1957   The Space Age roars in with the launch of Sputnik by the USSR.
>
> 1958   *The Blob* and *The Fly* are made.

FIND A PRINTER AND ORDER REPRODUCTIONS

There is a fine line between ordering too many reproductions and too few. Generally speaking it costs less and less to order in larger quantities. For example, if 250 headshots cost $80 or 32¢ each, then 500 might cost $100, or just 20¢ each. Err on the side of having too many rather than too few. Appendix E lists a few of the many printers in

> 1959   *Ben-Hur* wins eleven Academy Awards, breaking *Gigi* record of nine.
>
> 1959   Aroma-Rama, a technology that pipes odors into theaters to enhance the movie, is introduced. It stinks, bombs.

Los Angeles. Work closely with your printer. They can advise you on many aspects of preparing your marketing materials. The ones listed in the appendix specialize in working with actors and models.

THE FUTURE OF HEADSHOTS

Some people believe that all printed matter is circling the drain of obsolescence. It's not hard to imagine how packing a stack of headshots can become a thing of the past. This is important because an actor must deal in whatever medium the casting community deals in.

For example, a new type of headshot is available that takes full advantage of today's high-resolution digital photography and the Internet. The Los Angeles trailblazers in this innovation are Joan Lauren and David Knell, founders of MovingHeadshots. If Joan's name sounds familiar it's because she did my own headshots. MovingHeadshots offers two breakthrough products: MovingHeadshots and CastingClips. The first is a thirty-second program that combines stills with video and voice-over. The second is specifically designed for dancers, musicians and models and is all video with music soundtrack.

Ordinarily, casting directors select talent from online pages of thumbnail photo stills. It's that half-second view of your headshot

> I'm looking for the unexpected. I'm looking for things I've never seen before.
>
> — Robert Mapplethorpe

that either gets you an audition or doesn't. With these new products, when a casting director clicks on your image, it comes to life, showing you in motion and with sound. It's a mini-movie showcase of your talents. Call 323-651-4070 or visit their website at www.movingheadshots.com for prices and information.

HEADSHOT COSTS

Budgets for Sample Headshot Packages

Item	Minimum	Average	Premium
Photographer	$250	$500	$1000
Makeup	$100	$150	$300
Hair Stylist	$100	$150	$300
Retouching	$25	$75	$250
Reproductions	$200	$350	$500
Shipping	$10	$20	$50
Total	$685	$1,245	$2,400

DEMO REELS

Another item in your self-marketing toolbox is the demo reel. These are usually one- to five-minute productions that slice together examples of your work. If you are just starting out and have no work to show off, you can still put one together in which you demonstrate your acting skill in a monologue or an amateur play.

As you get gigs, you will have the opportunity to compile your performances into a demo reel. Hollywood Demo Reels charges $100 to $200 to produce one of these things if you supply the footage. They will also shoot and edit original video for $100 per edited minute. These rates are about average. Visit the following providers for additional information.

www.planet-video.com
www.hollywooddemoreels.com
www.quicknickel.com

RÉSUMÉS

I'm guessing this will not be the first time you've had to put together a résumé and so will dispense with the basic mechanics. An actor's résumé is a one-page listing of facts that are relevant to agents and casting directors. It is normally attached to and submitted with a headshot.

See appendix G, "Sample Résumé." The following tips should help you differentiate yours without getting in trouble.

★ Be concise. Casting directors don't have time for literary epics.

★ Do not exaggerate, fabricate or equivocate your experience.

★ Keep your résumé up to date.

★ Neatness counts.

CYBERSPACE

The Internet is the most powerful enabler of commerce in our time. You can buy and sell just about anything online. It is vast. Sophisticated search engines that

> An artist is a dreamer consenting to dream of the actual world.
>
> — George Santayana

were designed to help us navigate it are now themselves massive businesses. There are search engines for search engines. In chapter 7, "Auditions," I discuss how you can submit yourself for parts online. That's probably the single most valuable application for you.

Email can also be a useful tool for keeping casting directors and agencies informed. As you build your network in the industry, make a habit of compiling a contacts database that includes email addresses. When you are appearing onstage or onscreen, send out an announcement to your list of contacts. These emails should be brief and occasional, or you could spam yourself into everybody's blocked addresses list.

Having your own website can also be suitable for self-promotion, but rarely when you are just starting out. Even when you are established, casting directors know that they can review your credits and filmography on the Internet Movie Database (IMDB). They are more likely to use a subscription website like IMDB than to go hunting for yours.

---

1. Brouwer, *Working in Hollywood*, 123.

2. Ibid., 124.

☆

Chapter Six

AGENTS

While you were in space, I created a way for us to make huge sums of legitimate money, and still maintain the ethics and the business practices of an evil organization. I have turned us into a talent agency; the Hollywood Talent Agency.

— Number Two (Robert Wagner) *Austin Powers: Goldmember* (2002)

☆

People will tell you, "Oh I hate my agent" but you have to make people work for you. Don't hate him, keep him working in your direction. That is the way to go.[1]

☆

☆

Thomas (dropcap T) HEY SAY that the two stiffest obstacles to launching a Hollywood career are finding an agent and qualifying to join the Screen Actors Guild (SAG). Chapter 10 is dedicated entirely to SAG and other performers unions. For now, this chapter deals with what you need to know about agents, how to find one, how to work with one and, if it comes to that, how to cut one loose.

You must know this: in the vast majority of cases, your career will go nowhere without a good agent.

> Talent agencies, like any other form of brokerage, are essentially in the information business.[2]

Your challenge is to figure out who that is and to convince him to take you on. Some pundits will tell you that you employ an agent. Others tell you that an agent employs you. The truth is that the very best relationship with an agent is a partnership. Your mutual success is entirely dependent on each of you delivering your end of the bargain.

WHAT IS AN AGENT?

Agents are individuals who will help you secure employment in showbiz and in return receive some percentage of your earnings. Here's how the Division of Labor Standards Enforcement (DLSE) defines it:

> "Talent Agency" means a person or corporation who

> 1960   First televised presidential debates between Nixon and JFK. Nixon sweats, Kennedy wins.
>
> 1960   Alfred Hitchcock makes *Psycho*. Twenty-three years later Richard Franklin makes *Psycho II*. Anthony Perkins returns as Norman Bates, having spent the hiatus in jail.
>
> 1960   90% of U.S. homes have TVs.
>
> 1961   Sophia Loren wins Best Actress Academy Award for *Two Women*.

engages in the occupation of procuring, offering, promising, or attempting to procure employments or engagements for an artist or artists. Talent agencies may, in addition, counsel or direct artists in the development of their professional careers.[3]

Do we care what the DLSE says? Yes, because a talent agent may not operate in California without a license issued by the DLSE.

How difficult is it to get into the talent agency business? Not too terribly. The process is straightforward. An interested individual must:

★ Submit an application and pay a filing fee.

★ Post a surety bond. Since 1986 this has been $10,000. Governor Schwarzenegger has signed legislation, however, that ups it to $50,000.

★ Undergo an investigation of their character and responsibility.

★ Undergo an investigation of their place of business.

★ Pay an annual license fee.

★ Behave and follow the DLSE's rules.

1962   Broadband communications, including trans-global live TV feeds are made possible by satellite technology when AT&T launches Telstar I. By 2005, nearly one thousand satellites orbit Earth. Telstar I's still up.

1962   *Dr. No*, first of the James Bond series of films, is released.

1962   Studios divest their talent agencies to comply with new federal regulations.

1962   Marilyn Monroe is found dead from a drug overdose in Brentwood.

1962   Johnny Carson takes over from Jack Paar on *The Tonight Show*. He stays behind that desk for thirty years.

Do all of the above and, bingo, you too can be a Hollywood talent agent. Now, just because someone is licensed by the State of California does not mean that they know what they're doing, are scrupulous, or are willing to dedicate enough time and energy to your success. There's more on how to find a good agent later in this chapter. For now, here is a summary of the rules that a talent agent must follow, taken from the California Labor Code:[4]

★ An agent may not collect a registration fee from an artist.

★ An agent may not refer you to a third party, like a photographer or a school, if he has a financial interest in it. This is the no-kickback rule and is in place to protect you and discourage your agent from upgrading his wardrobe at your expense.

★ An agent may not send you to a place where your health or safety is in jeopardy like, say, a nuclear test site.

★ An agent may not allow "persons of bad character,"—a euphemism for hookers, drunks, pushers and psychos—to hang out at his place of business. If you're any of these things please don't take offense; I just report the law, I don't write it. This clause is also intended to inhibit pimps from pandering under the cover of a talent agency.

★ An agent may not send you to a gig where a strike is ongoing before first alerting you to that fact. You can be a scab if you want to be, but not inadvertently.

These are the headlines. There is a long list of compliance issues, including what the contract you sign with your agent must include and how much information he must keep on record about you.

If you're interested in additional detail or are having trouble sleeping, you can read the California Labor Code online at www.dir.ca.gov or contact the DLSE at the following address and request their brochure titled *Laws Relating to Talent Agencies*.

Department of Industrial Relations

Division of Labor Standards Enforcement

PO Box 420603

San Francisco, CA 94142

There is a special breed of agency, called Advance-Fee Talent Service, that is also sanctioned and licensed by the DLSE. So, an agency asking you for money up front is no reason for you to run screaming from the room. First ask what the agency proposes to provide to you in exchange for that fee. All agencies are forbidden by the DLSE from collecting a registration fee, but not an advance fee for which they will provide a particular service apart from representing you. If they fail to provide this promised service or product, you are entitled to a full refund within forty-eight hours of your request for it. This is how the DLSE defines the fee:

"Advance Fee" means any fee due from or paid by an artist prior to the artist obtaining actual employment as an artist or prior to the artist receiving actual earnings as an artist or that exceeds actual earning received by the artist as an artist.[5]

1963   The JFK assassination is televised. Two days later Harvey Lee Oswald stops Jack Ruby's bullets on live TV.

1964   Sony launches home video recorder. It weighs forty-six lbs. Ungh.

1964   The Beatles appear on *Ed Sullivan*. American teenyboppers freak.

1966   The Hays Code is revised, easing film decency standards. Still no frontal.

1966   First TV in-color Academy Awards. *The Sound of Music* nabs Best Picture. Julie Christie and Lee Marvin win top thespian honor for *Darling* and *Cat Ballou* respectively.

It is possible that your agent will advise you to take classes or purchase head shots or do something else that costs money but that will benefit your career. It is also possible that you agree to give him the money to pass along to the school or photographer they have recommended. As long as the agency receives no financial benefit of any sort from this, they are not breaking any rules of state licensing. An advance-fee agent must file a separate application and bond with the DLSE.

SAG-FRANCHISED AGENTS

SAG used to require its members to be represented by agents who were franchised by the guild. No more. Now you can have any agent represent you as long as they are licensed by the State. Requiring agents to be SAG-franchised was the guild's way of ensuring protection for artists beyond what DLSE licensing provides. In order to be franchised by the guild, an agent agreed to conform to Rule 16(g): SAG Agency Regulations. The heart of these regulations is the standard SAG representation contract, which incorporates clauses that are not present in most general service agreements (GSAs) offered by non-franchised agents.[6] The following table summarizes the differences between the two contracts:

SAG	NON-SAG
★ General Service Agreement Initial contract term is limited to one year.	★ Initial contract term limited to no more than seven years by California State law.
★ Agent maximum commission is 10%.	★ In California may be as high as 25%.
★ Several limitations on how much of a performer's income is commissionable. Residuals on certain productions are exempt from commission.	★ All of a performer's income can be commissionable.
★ Limits commissions on employment that occurs after expiration of contract.	★ May allow agent to claim commission on extensions, additions and supplements even if they are negotiated after the term of the contract.
★ Offers SAG arbitration in dispute resolution.	★ Can leave performer to litigate disputes and deal with State laws.
★ Can be terminated if you have not worked more than 10 in the last 91 days.	★ In some cases may not be terminated as long as you're offered one day of work within the past 160 days.

Now that you know the difference between the two most general categories of agents, which should you hunt?

The answer is that it matters very little what your agent charges you in commission if he can't find you work. You may be represented by one of the most prestigious

> I take this business very personally. I'm not selling Cadillacs. I'm selling human beings. I'm selling artists' souls.
>
> — Scott Manners: Stone Manners Agency

agencies in the business. It may be SAG-franchised and occupy palatial offices in Beverly Hills. Still, what if you never get work? Or you may be represented by a one-man agency that is a member of no associations and is not franchised by any union but gets you out on many auditions and those sometimes result in work. Where are you better off?

All this to reemphasize that your agent could be the most influential person in your budding career and that his value is measured by how much work he finds for you. If it turns out, for whatever reason, that you are not going on auditions, then there is a number of things you can do, including changing agents. More on this in chapter 8, "Work."

TYPES OF AGENTS

Aside from the two general SAG and non-SAG categories, agents fall into several other classifications. The Association of Talent Agents provides the following long list of types of agents:[7]

★ Actors	★ Dancers	★ Stunts
★ Commercials	★ Print	★ Commercial Celebrity
★ Broadcasters	★ Singers	
★ Choreographers	★ Youth	★ Interactive Multimedia
★ Voice-over	★ Directors	
★ Writers	★ Athletes	★ Performers w/Disabilities
★ Theater or Legit	★ Hosts	
★ Below-the-line	★ Puppeteers	

Think of these as specialties. Agents who represent singers, for example, are plugged into casting directors and producers who hire singers. Many agents represent a wide range of talent. Notwithstanding the long list, the two broadest categories are theatrical and commercial agents.

Theatrical agents primarily represent actors for roles in film and TV. Commercial agents represent actors for roles in, yup, commercials, typically for TV but often for print and nowadays increasingly for the Internet. Some agents claim to work across-the-board. That is, they will represent their clients on all sorts of gigs. This is possible but unlikely. The bottom line is that agents will submit their talent pool for roles that meet the following two golden criteria:

★ Have the highest potential compensation.

★ Correspond to that actor's look and skills.

MANAGERS VS. AGENTS

The following are essential differences between agents and managers:

AGENTS

★ To operate as a talent agent in California requires a license that is issued by the Division of Labor Standards Enforcement, which is part of the California Department of Industrial Relations.

★ Someone who is licensed to be an agent can also be a personal manager.

★ A talent agent is allowed to find work for their clients and to negotiate the client's compensation for that work.

★ An agent can have a very large number of clients, in the hundreds.

★ An agent's primary job is to search the database of available roles at any time and submit their clients for those roles that match their look and skills.

★ Agents have a national association: The Association of Talent Agents (ATA). It is not a requirement for an agent to be a member of this or any other association.

MANAGERS

★ A personal manager does not require a license issued by the DLSE. They merely need a license to do business in California, which is the minimum regulatory hurdle to conducting commerce in the State.

★ A manager is not allowed to operate as an agent unless he is licensed to do so by the DLSE.

★ A manager may not submit their clients to casting directors and may not negotiate their compensation.

★ A manager will typically represent a small number of individuals since he must dedicate more time and effort to each.

★ A manager's job can be much broader than an agent's. A manager may be involved in publicizing their client, handling scheduling and appearances, directing their careers and even helping to manage their finances.

★ Managers have their own association, the National Conference of Personal Managers (NCOPM). It is not a requirement for a manager to be a member of this or any other association.

Do you need a personal manager? Yes. Two heads are still better than one. Having someone else worry about your career and be constantly doing what they can to

| 1968 | *2001: Space Odyssey, Planet of the Apes* and *Night of the Living Dead* redefine the Sci-Fi film genre. |
| 1968 | Gov. Ronald Reagan eases tax burden on films to curb runaway productions. |

further it is a good thing. As usual, there are a couple of hairs in this otherwise tasty bouillabaisse:

★ You have to pay for a manager's services. Their fee is typically 15% of your earnings. The downside can be limited if you negotiate a deal where your manager only gets paid when you get paid, just like an agent. None for you, none for him. It's fair.

★ Your relationship with your manager will be contractual. Unforeseen differences might lead to litigation. That's America.

★ A manager could spend a whole lot of time and effort guiding your career. He may even be well intentioned and honest. Still, he could be incompetent or have bad judgment and as a result drive your career in a direction that is not the best possible.

So, if you decide to go ahead and hire a manager, maximize your chances of landing a good one by following these guidelines:

★ Check with the local Better Business Bureau to make sure that they do not have a long list of complaints against them.[8]

★ Contact the National Conference of Personal Managers. This organization holds its membership to a code of conduct, offering you additional assurance that you will be dealing with a scrupulous and capable professional. The trouble is that

1969	700 million world-wide watch Neil Armstrong's lunar walk on TV. Cosmic.
1969	Woodstock is so far-out it's way in.
1969	Sony demos videocassette recorder.
1969	*Sesame Street* goes on the air.
1969	*Midnight Cowboy*, at the time rated X, wins Oscar for Best Movie. Later rated R.

their website, www.ncopm.com, lists only a handful of California personal managers whereas, depending on the source you check, hundreds are known to operate in the area.

★ Casting Networks at www.lacasting.com lists 132 management firms on its website. This is probably the best place to start your research. The list is available free of charge.

★ Contact Talent Managers Association (TMA), 3518 Cahuenga Blvd. W., # 202, Los Angeles, CA 90068, 818-563-1814, www.talentmanagers.org. TMA's website offers helpful information and a free list of its members. Here's an encouraging excerpt from its home page:

> The Association exists for the benefit of its members, the talent represented by the members and the profession of Talent Management.

★ Have an attorney review any contract that you are asked to sign. This is standard operating procedure. If your prospective manager is reluctant to agree to this or appears unhappy about it, make for the nearest exit.

★ Do not make an up-front payment of any kind to your manager.

★ Check all available resources to verify a manager's credentials, experience and track record. Ask them for the names of three other clients with whom you can talk prior to signing on.

★ Get a clear statement of responsibilities. What will this manager do for you in exchange for the 15% or 20% you will be paying them out of your paycheck?

★ Last but not least, do a gut check. If you have a bad feeling about the individual who wants to manage you, there's probably a reason. Trust your instincts. It's critical that your relationship with your manager be collaborative and not tripped up by bad chemistry or, who knows, biology.

Most actors do not have managers and there's a good reason for it: they're not yet bankable. Why would anyone invest their time and effort in your career if you have not demonstrated that you can be successful and, by extension, make them successful too? So, answering yes to whether or not you should have a manager is academic until you are an appealing enough investment to attract one. In the meantime, be careful and refer to the "Wolf in Sheep's Clothing Scam" in chapter 2, "Crooks."

SIGNING WITH AN AGENT

So, now that you know what an agent is and isn't, you need to find one and sign an agreement with them to represent you and submit you for roles so you can start getting some auditions.

The first step is to get them to invite you in for an interview. How you go about that is not important, as long as you do. Industry experts recommend going through friends—casting directors, actors, directors—who can refer you to a reputable and capable agent. There are other methods. You could get a list of agents and their phone numbers and start calling around. You'll almost certainly annoy half the people you talk to because unsolicited phone calls are a pain in the neck even on a good day. Still, you might get lucky, particularly if you have a distinctive phone voice. Another, less obnoxious approach, is to write a nice cover letter and send out a focused or general mailing that also contains your headshots. Will you get a response? Maybe. However, If you don't have a friend or industry insider who can recommend you, there is little you can do but market yourself directly to agents in whom you're interested.

There is a number of good sources for agent lists, addresses, and classifications. If you're looking for commercial agents, you can download a list and labels, free of charge, at www.lacasting.com. You can get a member list on the Association of Talent Agents website.[9] Alternatively, you can go online or to your favorite local bookstore and buy a copy of the *Hollywood Agents and Managers Directory* by Hollywood Creative Directory Staff. It includes 4,600 names of agents and managers as well as addresses and phone numbers.

Many, particularly folks who have been in the business for a while, will warn you against jumping into a relationship with an agent. I find that the doomsday scenarios these people predict are overblown. The reality is that if you don't have a résumé and you don't have a friend in the business, you will probably wind up taking the first agent who takes you,

> Once, when watching a play, the actor Walter Hudd found himself sitting next to a man whose face he thought he knew. All through the first act he cast sidelong glances, he could not concentrate on the play, he was certain they had met, but where? Who was he? In the interval he went to the bar and there next to him was the same man... "Forgive me, but don't I know you?" "Yes," said the man, "I'm your agent."[10]

unless he works out of a psych ward. If you sign with an agent and find that he is not getting you auditions or that you are not compatible, it is likely that he or she will be just as glad to see the back of you as you are anxious to dump him. Then you can start your agent hunt all over again.

A successful relationship between you and your agent happens at the intersection of your interests: you get lots of auditions and jobs while he makes commissions. For this to occur the agent must have access to casting directors and you must have a desirable look. One without the other will not work.

Nevertheless, do the same due diligence before you sign up with an agent as I suggested you do with a manager. Some of what follows is the same as in the previous section, but it bears repeating:

★ Check with the local Better Business Bureau.

★ Ask the agent for their license number and verify their status with the State Labor Commissioner's Licensing Unit (SLCLU) online at www.dir.ca.gov/databases/dlselr/talag.html. This site also provides some interesting reading on disputes between actors and agents. Check out case #63-93, Pamela Denise Anderson vs. Robert D'Avola, unlicensed, "significant" procurement, "hip-pocket" agent.

★ Have an attorney review any contract that you are asked to sign.

★ Do not agree to making up-front payments of any kind.

★ Check all available resources to verify an agent's credentials, experience and track record. Ask him for the names of three other clients with whom you can talk prior to signing on. If you can, check with casting directors who know the agent.

★ Get a clear statement of responsibilities. What will this agent do in exchange for the 10% or 15% you will be paying them out of your paycheck? If an agent asks for more than 10%, the SAG commission ceiling, you should expect that they operate somewhat like a manager and be available to you when you want to talk about how your career is going.

★ Last but not least, trust your instincts. If you have a bad feeling in your gut and you haven't recently lunched on shellfish, it could be that there's something not quite right about this agent.

Something else you should know: in some states it is okay to have more than one agent representing you at the same time. Not in California. Not unless they are representing you in different areas of work. For example, you could have a commercial agent and a different theatrical agent but you cannot have two commercial agents.

1969   A man went looking for America and couldn't find it anywhere.
Easy Rider promotional slogan.

Regardless of the rules, that would be untenable and expensive. Once you've found an agent to represent you, be clear on his area of specialty and on whether or not you need to look for a different agent for other areas.

BREAKING WITH YOUR AGENT

We are creatures of habit. It really upsets us to have to change something we've become accustomed to. Just think of an item of clothing that you've had for years and that you cannot bring yourself to part with, even if you haven't been able to get into it since *Mork and Mindy*. It's no wonder then that the prospect of dumping your agent will cause you a significant bit of grief.

Why would you break with your agent? The number one reason is that he is not keeping you busy. The best and most reliable measure of an agent's performance is the number of auditions you get. In the next chapter, "Auditions," I discuss the various reasons that could be behind a lack of audition opportunities. You'll see that it is entirely possible, in fact probable, that your agent is not at fault. However, let's say you've looked at the situation and decided to leave your agent; here are some guidelines to make the divorce as amicable as possible:

★ Hard as it may be, particularly if you dread confrontation, you must notify your existing agent of your desire to jump ship. He'll probably be as happy to see you go as you are to leave. Pay him a

> 1969   Sharon Tate, Roman Polanski's actress wife, is one of the victims of the Manson murders. The year prior she had been nominated for the Most Promising Newcomer Golden Globe award for her turn as Jennifer North in *Valley of the Dolls*.

visit. Take him to lunch. Explain your problem and your thinking; thank him for his help so far and tell him that you are moving on. In most cases the separation will be uneventful and your agent will wish you well. You'll have to pay for the lunch.

★ If a personal meeting is not possible, write a nice letter and offer to discuss the matter on the phone.

★ Do not engage or sign on with another agent before you have terminated your relationship with your existing agent. This would cause consternation all around and, what's worse, could obligate you to pay two agencies in the event you get a gig from either. At a minimum you will be in the eye of an awkward fuss.

★ Try not to burn bridges with your existing agent. After all, you may discover that the real cause for your limited success in getting auditions was not his fault but rather poor headshots or some other thing. You may regret your departure and want to come back.

★ If you have a particularly good relationship with your agent, talk the situation over with him. It may turn out that what you need is a different commercial agent while your existing agent continues to represent you on theatrical work. Get him on your side and ask for his advice.

IT'S WHO HE KNOWS

Does it matter that your agent be well-connected in the industry? Of course it does. But why? Well, maybe the best way to see this is from the perspective of the director who is looking for talent to act in his project. Tim Armstrong, a Los Angeles director, points out that he uses the same casting agencies all the time.[11] It makes sense that an agent who has a good relationship with casting agents will therefore have better access to directors and projects. Perhaps the best indicator of the reach of an agent's network is the length of time he has been in the business. This is another consideration when selecting an agent and further proof that, in Hollywood as in elsewhere, it's not necessarily what you know, but who you know.

☆

1. Estelle Parsons, from an interview with Wickham Boyle, *Downtown Express* 17, no. 15, (September 3, 2004).

2. Ed Wood Jr., *Hollywood Rat Race* (New York: Four Walls Eight Windows, 1998), 8.

3. State of California, "California Labor Code," http://www.leginfo.ca.gov/cgi-bin/displaycode?section=lab&group=01001-02000&file=1700-1700.43.

4. Ibid.

5. Ibid.

6. SAG, "What Every Member Needs to Know...," June 29, 2004, http://www.sag.org/sagWebApp/Content/Public/agencyposting.htm.

7. Association of Talent Agents (ATA), "Membership Directory," 2005, http://www.agentassociation.com/frontdoor/membership_directory.cfm.

8. http://www.bbb.org.

9. http://www.agentassociation.com.

10. http://www.anecdotage.com/index.php?aid=3958.

11. Tim is the Armstrong behind Armstrong Moving Pictures. In addition to his work as director, he has produced a video version of that old standby, *The Wheels on the Bus*. The clincher: Roger Daltry of The Who sings the voice of Argon the Dragon. http://www.thewheelsonthebusvideo.com.

☆

Chapter Seven

AUDITIONS

What an experience!
It was like going to the chair.
Auditions are hell. I honestly
don't know how anyone even
gets a job based on them—they
show an actor at his worst, in
the glare of a naked spotlight,
surrounded by strangers, laying
his life on the line.

— Lauren Bacall[1]

☆

Use what talent you possess:
the woods would be very silent
if no birds sang except those
that sang best.

— Henry Van Dyke

☆

☆

YOUR CHANCES of getting auditions and hopefully work are not arbitrary. SAG's *2004 Annual Casting Report* makes clear what the business is going through. Some of it is not great news.[2] The following table shows the overall decline in TV and theatrical member roles:

Annual Decline in Roles

Year	2001	2002	2003	2004
Decline	9.3%	6.5%	1.6%	7.8%

The report also identifies gender and age as possible barriers to opportunity in showbiz. Women received just 38% of roles cast, even though they account for over 50% of the population. Women over forty were given just 27% of total roles cast for women. Men over forty did better and were cast in 39% of total roles for men. If you're over forty and you have a choice, be a man.

In terms of racial classification, only Asian/Pacific actors had a gain in total roles cast in 2004. Every other category lost roles, but African Americans bore the brunt of it, down nearly 30% from 2003.

The principal culprits for the decline in the number of roles across the board are:

★ Non-union roles and productions.

★ Runaways, a Hollywood term for productions that do not occur here but especially those that "run away" to Canada or Mexico or somewhere else where it costs less to produce shows.

★ Reality shows, which have made a serious dent in the business and show no sign of slowing down.

According to the report, SAG members were cast in a grand total of 40,826 roles, down 3,456 from 2003. This translated into 236,696 days worked, down from 252,809 in the prior year. SAG estimates that the guild has about 120,000 members. The data indicate that only one role was available for each three members of SAG for the whole of 2004. Even more depressing, there were just under two days of work available for each SAG member to compete for all year long!

This is just SAG. There are many non-union productions out there but even then, there is no reason to assume that the percentages are any better. Non-union actors would have to work twice or three times as often as SAG actors to make the same money.

Bottom line? There aren't that many roles for which to compete, there won't be that many auditions and your chances of landing a role are slim. These are not glad tidings but better that you know what you're up against before you're up against it. Fooling ourselves is pointless. The more you know and the better you prepare, the more likely you are to be in the minority that does get the auditions and the parts. Also, and this is what really matters, the more likely you are to plan your Hollywood campaign intelligently and with a realistic estimate of how long before your career can support you.

1970   IMAX format demonstrated at Expo '70 in Osaka, Japan. The first IMAX film is Donald Britain's *Tiger Child*.

1970   *Love Story*, starring Ali McGraw and Ryan O'Neal, is a six-hanky sob-fest.

1971   *All In The Family* debuts on CBS.
   Edith (Jean Stapleton): Are your neighbors all poor?
   Gloria (Sally Struthers): No, why?
   Edith: Because they're all sitting in a circle sharing the same cigarette.

1971   George Lucas releases his first feature film, *THX 1138*.

HOW AUDITIONS HAPPEN

In my first meeting with Victor Kruglov, he becomes my agent. Victor is not the world's warmest fellow, at least not until you get to know him. So our first chat is curt. It's also inherently funny. From a distance our meeting would have looked like a tête-à-tête between Saddam Hussein and Leonid Brezhnev. I don't mention this to Victor, who seems preoccupied, clicking the mouse and peering intently into the computer screen. "From now on," he says as he half looks at me, "your *job* is to go on auditions. If you go enough you will get jobs and you will make money." There it is. Showbiz in a Ukrainian nutshell.

"So, Leonid...er...Victor," I say as I admire the Hollywood Hills through his office window, "How do I get these auditions?"

"Well," says Victor, "I check breakdowns and submit you to casting directors and if they like your look, [Victor is a realist: he understands that it's the look that gets people invited to auditions] then they will call me and I will call you and you will go."

"Okay, sounds like a plan. Er...what's a breakdown?"

Indeed, what the heck is a "breakdown"? In the casting business, a breakdown is a list of roles in a particular film or TV show. It identifies the parts that need to be cast and provides a description of each. Here's an example:

Project: *The Great Banadoora Heist*

Producer: Monadim Maysa

Director: Rakan "The Hun" da Cruz

[Amin Chorbachi] Middle-Eastern male, early 20s, computer nerd, handsome, athletic, loud. Tattoos a plus. Lead.

[Alexandra Lamirande] Female, early 20s, pretty girl-next-door but martial arts expert. Ruthless yet demure. Lead.

[Adriana Lamirande] Female, mid-20s, Alexandra's sister and undercover ex-KGB operative. Must be able to do Russian accent. Lead.

[Karim Kubeisy] Male, Middle Eastern, 40s or 50s, serious and severe as well as thuggish. Facial scars a plus. Supporting.

You get the idea.

Like any good agent, Victor is a valuable source of information about anything and everything in the business. He's been at it for eighteen years, most of those as a SAG-franchised agent. However, there are more ways to get auditions than through your agent, including services that provide the individual actor with access to casting directors.

Thanks to the Internet, the flow of information between actors, agents, casting directors and production teams is becoming more efficient. Technology is taking the middle man out of the middle and allowing actors to connect directly with casting directors and producers. The following sections discuss alternative methods of getting auditions.

AGENT SUBMISSIONS

Once an agent has taken you on, he or she will begin to submit your headshots to casting directors whose projects call for someone with your look or skills. Back in the old days, the process relied heavily on courier services, which shuttled headshots and résumés from agent to casting director. If the latter found your headshot interesting, he would notify the agent who would in turn notify you and set up the audition. Nowadays the process is fundamentally the same, except that it happens electronically. In theater, submissions are still almost entirely hard copy. In commercials they're all electronic. In TV and film there is a mix of hard copy and electronic submissions.[4] Thanks to the Internet, agents have access to database platforms that are provided and maintained by companies like Casting Networks, Backstage.com, and Actors Access. Here's how it works:

> Especially during auditions, please, please, please, please get the words right.
>
> — Director Jane Anderson[3]

★ Casting agency is hired by the director of a theatrical production or the ad agency responsible for a commercial production or some other entity seeking to cast a production.

★ Casting director or coordinator logs on to a website like www.breakdownservices.com, www.lacasting.com, www.playersdirectory.com or www.nowcasting.com and posts the specifics of a project and the breakdown of roles involved.

★ Talent agent accesses website and reviews the lists of parts.

★ If a role matches your profile, your agent submits a hard copy or electronic version of your headshot to the corresponding casting director. He can do this because your profile, including your pictures and résumé, are already in a database to which agents and casting directors have access.

★ The casting director scans your submission and notifies the agent, via email or phone, that they want you to audition.

★ The talent agent calls and gives you the specifics of the audition.

★ You attend your audition. If it's for a commercial production, a tape of your performance is sent to the ad agency and another is sent to the director. The agency and the director agree on their top choices and invite them back for callbacks. In a theatrical production the casting director almost always decides who is called back.

★ You attend the callback. This time the director and producer—or several producers—and the casting director could all be present.

Your agent will be more likely to think of you and submit you often if you are getting called out by casting directors. If his first few submissions do not bear fruit, and you are not selected, then he will eventually lose interest. This process is, by its nature, subjective. If casting directors are not calling for you, it's not always obvious what the problem is. It could be any of the following:

> 1972   HBO delivers first cable programs in Wilkes-Barre, PA.
>
> 1972   Coppola releases *The Godfather*. Brando turns down Oscar. George C. Scott had beaten him to the stunt by refusing to accept the Oscar for *Patton* (1970).

★ Your headshot is not working for you.

★ Your agent is submitting you for the wrong projects.

★ Your look is good but others have bigger résumés.

★ Your headshot is fine, but your look is not in demand. This does not mean that something is wrong with it. It could be that not enough is wrong with it. Maybe it's not sufficiently unusual!

★ Your agent does not have confidence in your look and has not really been submitting you, despite what he says.

★ Casting agencies do not know or trust your agent and therefore do not favor his submissions.

SELF SUBMISSIONS

Several of the auditions and gigs I got came as a result of submissions I made, not my agent. This is thanks to a number of services that list current projects and their corresponding breakdowns online. By becoming a subscriber to these services, anyone with headshots can submit themselves electronically for projects whose casting directors agree to list on the site. Not all casting directors use these services and those that do withhold certain projects from individual submissions. They reserve these for agents because they want someone else to vet submissions beforehand. Here's where an agent comes in handy.

> 1973   The Watergate hearings in the U.S. Senate are broadcast live on PBS, ABC, CBS and NBC.
>
> 1973   There are six thousand fewer cinemas in the U.S. than in 1943.
>
> 1973   Bruce Lee kicks Han derriere in *Enter the Dragon*.

Casting Networks at www.lacasting.com is a very popular site that provides breakdowns and allows actors to self-submit. Craig's List at www.craigslist.com features a surprisingly large database of acting jobs.

1973   George Lucas releases *Star Wars* with Twentieth Century Fox.
1973   Warner Brothers releases *The Exorcist*.

And it's free of charge. SAG also intends to launch a casting service that will allow casting directors to search for talent and will allow actors to self-submit. Academy Players Directory at www.playersdirectory.com charges a $75 annual fee for which you are included in their online directory for one year. Actors Access at www.actorsaccess.com charges a modest annual membership fee for which you get online access to a large number of project breakdowns. Some of these services offer an automatic notification service that sends you an email when a breakdown matches your profile. Following is an example of the emails I receive from Actors Access when that happens:

From: "actors access(SM)" <notifications@actorsaccess.com>

To: "RIF HAFFAR"

Subject: Projects match your profile - 12/8 - 11:30 AM Pacific

Date: Thu, 8 Dec 11:32:16 -0800

Hi RIF,

Our exclusive Advance Roles Notification feature at actors access, has just posted the following role(s) in the following project(s) that fit your profile. Click the link under the project name to view the project so you can submit immediately if interested. You may need to log in to actors access before you are able to submit yourself.

UNTITLED RELIGIOUS FILM/Open Call

JOSEPH

Jesus' father, in his 50s, Middle-Eastern...

3-MINUTE DEMO FOR NEW TV COMEDY

MARVIN

Age 30-40. An "actor's actor" is how he introduce...[5]

If one of the above roles is a good fit for me, I can submit myself online and attach to my submission one of several electronic headshots. A casting director reviews these submissions. If they like mine they'll invite me via email to come in for an audition.

Having this sort of access to casting directors calls for discipline on the part of the actor. If you are careless in your submissions, you are likely to shoot your career in its foot, or both feet. For example, if

1974	Richard Nixon resigns on TV.
1974	*Chinatown*, with Faye Dunaway and Jack Nicholson, is directed by Roman Polanski.

you are 6'2", weigh 250 lbs., have white skin and fair hair, do not submit yourself for the part of an Indonesian jockey. I know this is an extreme example and that no one playing with a full deck would do that. It illustrates the point, however, that casting directors want to maximize their effort in the time they have set aside for screening submissions. If you're not serious and professional in submitting yourself, you will be passed over. A corollary to this advice is: do not audition for something that you know you will not be available for. Should you get a callback or even get the part, you will have put yourself and the casting director and your agent in a jam.

CASTING DIRECTORS

One of the best things that can develop as you begin to audition is for casting directors to take a liking to you. This happens when you

Talent shmalent!

— Anonymous casting director

read for a particular part and impress them with your look, your talent, or even just your pleasant disposition.[6] Maybe even a combination of all of the above. Whatever it is that touched them, these casting directors will now invite you to audition for any role that might fit you. After all, it is their top priority to show producers and directors a good range of talent from which to select the actors for their show. If you're on time, if you're presentable and professional, if you listen during the audition and follow instructions, if you're pleasant and friendly and give your best every time, you'll find that casting directors will ask for you.

As in all things, a little marketing does not hurt. Just as you sent a headshot around to a list of agents and got representation that way, also do a mailing to a list of casting directors. Do not expect any calls in response. This mailing serves to create some familiarity with your face among casting directors and to raise the odds of their calling for you the next time they see your headshot.

Lists of casting directors are available from many sources, including www.lacasting.com. Or you could order a copy of the *Los Angeles CD* [Casting Director] *Directory*. Here's what they have to say about it at www.breakdownservices.com/store/directories.html:

> The Los Angeles CD Directory is an alphabetical listing of all feature film and television casting directors in Los Angeles. The CD Directory is published quarterly and updated every two weeks. Because casting directors' locations change frequently, the update becomes an invaluable feature of the CD Directory, providing you with the most accurate information available for casting directors' phone numbers and addresses. Purchase a single issue or subscribe to the CD Directory for one year. All subscribers receive free updates every two weeks as well as three directories.[7]

And here's a tip: when you join Showfax, (Actors Access' sister), you have access to www.breakdownservices.com. On this site you will find an annual listing of casting agencies that have been assigned to most major productions, including TV and film. This list is free if your annual subscription to Showfax is paid up. With it you can target outfits that are casting shows on which you would like to work. Send headshots directly to these casting agencies. Call and ask to come in and read. Ask if they hold open auditions. This kind of focused, thoughtful marketing will yield better results than the shot-gun approach of mailing headshots to all the casting directors in town.

1975   *One Flew Over the Cuckoo's Nest* wins Oscars for Best Picture, Best Director, Best Actor, Best Actress, and Best Screenplay.

1975   *Jaws* scares us out of the water and grosses more than $100 million doing it.

1975   *The Jeffersons* airs on CBS.

1975   Kathleen Nolan is first female SAG National President.

1976   VHS format is introduced by JVC.

An excellent resource for casting director and other showbiz directories is Samuel French Bookstore at 7623 Sunset Boulevard, Los Angeles, CA 90046, 213-876-0570. This should become one of your habitual stops. I visit every couple of months and browse their shelves. They stock a comprehensive selection of works for people in showbiz, including how-to books, histories, scripts, and more.

And then there's the Casting Society of America (CSA) at 606 N Larchmont Boulevard, Suite 4B, Los Angeles, CA 90004-1309. The society's website is at www.castingsociety.com and provides a searchable list of its membership. More than 360 members are listed nationwide, with 239 in California. It is also possible, through the website, to invite members of the CSA to an actor's performance. Call the CSA at 323-463-1925.

AUDITION GUIDELINES

Mr. Nicholson's advice applies not just during shooting, but also in auditions. Casting director Michael Donovan, who cast *The Jersey* and *Closing the Deal*, corroborates this when he advises actors to make a choice in how to play a particular audition and then be committed to it. As he says, "If you're going to fall, fall hard!"[9]

> If you get an impulse in a scene, no matter how wrong it seems, follow the impulse. It might be something and if it ain't—take two!
>
> — Jack Nicholson

My agent says, "Auditioning is your *job*!" It makes sense, therefore, to prepare for it. Many excellent actors work far less than they otherwise might because they don't audition well. That's not surprising; the audition is a cruel institution, unique to the acting profession. Imagine if a firefighter had to pass a fitness test every morning before work or if a politician had to be reelected each day. That's essentially how it works for actors. They only work if they pass a test, the audition. They only work again if they pass another audition and so on. There are exceptions: actors whose work is so bankable that they are sought after and will never again need to audition. The rest of us, however, must fight and claw our way to the gigs.

It is difficult to quantify one's odds of landing a part from an audition. On any given day, a casting studio can see between 75 and 100 people. Therefore, if you know that a production is holding two days of auditions for the role you're after, then you can guess you're competing with between

> It's a funny business, casting. It's a gift, like fortune telling or water divining, but you also need a trained memory. Amy has a mind like a Rolodex: when you ask her advice about casting a part she goes into a kind of a trance, her eyes turn up to the ceiling, and you can almost hear the flick-flick-flick inside her head as she spools through the mental card-index where the essence of every actor and actress she has ever seen is inscribed.[8]

150 and 200 people for it. One casting director recently received 4,700 submissions for an auto commercial. The ad agency was looking for sixteen people. That's 300 submissions per role.

Your challenge is to improve the odds in your favor. How? By approaching auditions in a professional and deliberate manner; by preparing for them and staying focused on the techniques that lead to successful auditions. One of the best ways to do this is to take a workshop and be advised by experienced casting directors. I recommend Jan and Jon Commercial Workshop at Lien Cowan Casting. Jon Smet and Jan Bina are experienced actors and casting directors with an impressive list of credits. They conduct the workshop in an actual casting studio, share their insider knowledge and provide you many opportunities to perform on camera and receive constructive evaluations.

Jon and Jan advise actors to prepare as follows:

> Before you go to any audition, before you look at the script or storyboard, say to yourself, "This is a story about me." Instead of trying to make the auditors like you, think of what you can do to help them bring the material to life. Until you arrive for the first call, the commercial is just a concept. It's your interpretation of the material that brings the spot to life. Make choices that are specific to you. Please yourself rather than trying to second-guess what they are looking for. Thoroughly imagine the environment and see it in your imagination. Commercials today are rarely about a sell; they are more about entertaining the viewer. What is different about acting in commercials is the compression of time. Often you will only have five seconds on camera and yet that five seconds still must be emotionally truthful. The notion that acting in commercials must always be upbeat and positive simply isn't true. Directors are looking for good acting. Be flexible.

As for the mechanical aspects of auditioning, Jan and Jon provide the following list of dos and don'ts:[10]

★ Do listen. Just calm down and listen. You'll avoid a multitude of sins and improve your auditions 100%.

★ Do read the instructions. Stop and read the instructions! Nothing is more irritating than to have an actor come in to audition and say, "Oh, I didn't know I had to have that filled out."

★ Do bring a pen or pencil. Sounds silly but if there aren't any around and you have to pester the session director—well, you get the picture.

★ Don't make us go looking for you. It's great to run into friends at auditions, but please schmooze on your own time.

★ Do have your picture and paperwork ready. It's maddening to stand there with the clock ticking while an actor rummages around looking for their picture, size sheet and name strip. Have everything ready.

★ Don't say, "Which picture should I use?" as you spread four or five headshots out on the desk. Use common sense. Make the decision.

★ Don't ask the session director why you haven't been in to audition for a while. Often they don't know and if they do, they're not about to tell you. It just creates discomfort.

★ Don't ask to have your Polaroid taken over again (unless your eyes are closed in the shot). There is nothing at stake in the quality of the Polaroid other than bruised vanity. They are for ID purposes only!

★ Do come in with ideas. More often than not you get two takes, so come up with different approaches for both takes. Come in to the room ready to work creatively.

A word here about audition appointments: even though these are typically specific to the minute, you can arrive anytime after they start and will probably be seen early. Showing up late is not the same. In fact, if there is one universal law in Hollywood, it's: *never be late!* At auditions it's a red flag for the casting director and they will surmise that you are unreliable. God help you if you get a job and are late to the set. You'll be holding up a lot of people at a lot of expense. It's not an effective way to build a good reputation. Hollywood has a long memory.

On the other hand, if you are there promptly and are kept waiting one hour or more past your appointment time, you may be entitled to compensation. This applies to SAG members auditioning for a principal performer part on a commercial. For details contact your local SAG office.

Finally, avoid the temptation to treat auditions as your personal trials. They are that, of course, as long as you don't submit yourself for roles that don't suit you just so you can have the practice. Hoping to use auditions as a place to learn how to perform is like hoping to learn how to kiss at a CPR class: damn near impossible and likely to tick people off.

AUDITIONS TROUBLESHOOTER

What do you do when you're going on lots of auditions but not landing any parts? There are many possible explanations for this and here are a few:

★ You're an excellent actor but you audition poorly.

★ You're a terrible actor.

★ You're nervous and it shows.

★ Your look is not desirable. It's true that the casting director asked you to audition after they saw your headshot, but maybe you no longer resemble it.

★ You're going on the wrong auditions. There is lots of room for human error. If your agent misses a breakdown, you have no way of knowing that.

★ You're unlucky.

So what can you do? Review the dos and don'ts of auditioning from earlier in this chapter. Take acting lessons. Work on your confidence. Get new headshots. Maybe even change agents. You'll know, as you tweak all these elements, what works and what doesn't. But persevere. Above all, persevere. The ability to stick to it and outlast others seems to be the one bit of advice that all veterans agree to. On the other hand, wasn't it W. C. Fields who said, "If at first you don't succeed, try, try, again. Then quit, no use being a damn fool about things"?

You'll know when that is.

> 1979   300 million households in the U.S. own at least one television.
>
> 1979   *The China Syndrome* is released less than two weeks before nuclear accident at Three Mile Island.
>
> 1979   Johnny Carson emcees the Academy Awards—"Two hours of sparkling entertainment spread over a four-hour show." *The Deer Hunter* is Best Picture.

THE MONOLOGUE

You may occasionally be asked to perform a monologue. This is simply a prepared speech of your choosing. It's not a bad idea to have a couple of these ready, just in case. Actors can get all tangled up in finding just the right monologue. In fact it's what you do with the text that matters. Pick a piece that is between two and five minutes in length. If

you're up to it, study two: one
comedic and one dramatic. Make
sure this is material that you are

> Leap and the net shall appear.
>
> — Julia Cameron[11]

comfortable with. Even if you are never asked to perform it, rehearsing
a monologue is great preparation and its own reward.

☆

1. Lauren Bacall, *Lauren Bacall By Myself*, (New York: Ballantine Books, 1978), 41.

2. SAG, "TV Performers Again Take Hit From Reality Programming, 2004 Casting Data Shows," October 5, 2005, http://www.sag.org/sagWebApp/index.jsp.

3. Asher, *The Actors at Work Series*.

4. At a SAG Commercial Industry Guest Panel Discussion, April 11, 2005.

5. http://www.actorsaccess.com.

6. "Read" is another term for "audition."

7. http://www.breakdownservices.com.

8. Lodge, *Therapy*, 29.

9. At a SAG Commercial Industry Guest Panel Discussion, April 11, 2005.

10. Jan and Jon Commercial Workshop at Lien Cowan Casting, 7461 Beverly Boulevard, Suite 203, Los Angeles, CA 90036. 818-997-7792.

11. Julia Cameron is a prolific writer among whose notable books is *The Artist's Way*.

☆

Chapter Eight

WORK

DON'T TRY TO BREAK INTO MOVIES IN HOLLYWOOD

Out of 100,000 Persons Who Started at the Bottom of the Screen's Ladder of Fame

ONLY FIVE REACHED THE TOP

—1921 Ad run by the Hollywood Chamber of Commerce[1]

☆

"Mr. Greenfield, what kind of work do you do?"

"Oh, I don't work for a living, honey; I'm an actor."

"An actor? Isn't that a very insecure profession?"

"Only financially."

— Toni (Goldie Hawn) talking to Harvey (Jack Weston) in *Cactus Flower*, (1969).

☆

☆

MARK TWAIN called work "a necessary evil to be avoided." Very few of us would disagree with Mr. Twain on this score. Sadly, even if you are contemplating a career in showbiz, you'll still have to work for a living. The trick is to do more acting and less of whatever else you have to do to keep body and soul from parting ways.

You may have a particular medium in which you intend to build your acting career. Maybe you want to work in TV. Maybe you're especially interested in sitcoms. Or maybe nothing short of a starring role in a feature film will satisfy you. Eventually you can achieve whatever you set your mind to achieving. On the way there, however, it's good strategy to get as much work as possible, in as many disciplines as possible, as long as you don't compromise your moral and ethical standards, such as they are.

Work for actors is hard to come by and extremely competitive. The Bureau of Labor Statistics (BLS) reports:

1980   Ronald Reagan, actor and once-president of SAG, is elected president, his toughest role yet.

1980   United Artists is nearly bankrupted by *Heaven's Gate*, a massive flop. *The New York Times* calls it an "unqualified disaster." UA is eventually sold to MGM.

1980   Interactive TV is demoed in Ohio. We've come a long way since Marvin Middlemark invented the rabbit ears in 1950. Less useful—certainly less momentous—is his water-powered potato peeler.

Steve believes that there are lots of nice actors in the Hollywood unemployment line. The bastards live in the wooded estates of Beverly Hills and Bel-Air. And, for the most part, he's right.[2]

> In 2002, actors, producers, and directors held about 139,000 jobs, primarily in motion picture and video, performing arts, and broadcast industries. Because many others were between jobs, the total number of actors, producers, and directors available for work was higher.[3]

There is a broad variety of gigs for which your agent can submit you or you can submit yourself. The following is a nearly comprehensive list, culled from such casting websites as www.lacasting.com, www.actorsaccess.com and others:

Types of Acting Assignments

Advertisement	Miniseries	Short Film
Commercial	Movie for Television	Special
Director's Reel	Music Video	Staged Reading
Documentary	Open Call	Still Photo Shoot
Episodic	Photo Shoot Pilot	Stock Photo
Feature Film	Print	Student Film
Industrial	Promo	Theater
Infomercial	PSA	Trailer
Interactive Project	Radio	Video
Interstitials	Reality TV	Voice-over
Live Project	Shockumentary	

Some of the above projects could run on multiple media. Commercials, for example, could be shown on television, the Internet, and in movie theaters. There are subtle and not-so-subtle differences in what's expected of a performer in each of the above projects. Doing voice-over work, for example, requires that you have a familiarity with sound recording booths. Acting in half-hour sitcoms calls for a different style of performance than acting in one-hour dramas. And so on.

Whatever type of gig you land, preparation is key to accomplishing it well. How to prepare for an acting job is on the one hand very simple and on the other incredibly complex. How can that be? Well, it's simple because everyone agrees that good acting is merely being. In other words, a good actor does not act— in the sense of emote. He or she inhabits and becomes that character so that an audience cannot imagine them otherwise. This is certainly the message in *No Acting Please* and the many other books on acting that hope to help you veil the boundaries between yourself, your actions and the role you are playing.[4]

1981   MGM acquires United Artists, regains picture-making business.

1981   Dan Rather takes over from Walter Cronkite as *CBS Evening News* anchor.

On the other hand, acting is incredibly complex because it requires of you a level of discipline and concentration and fearlessness that are rarely demanded in other professions.

Imagine that you've auditioned for and won the part of the wife in a romantic comedy. You are happy about that but your life is otherwise an unrelenting mess. Money is tight and you're behind on two credit card bills. You had a dust-up with your husband over some stupid thing and now he's sulking. This morning the baby was inconsolable and the sitter half an hour late. On top of all that you're bloated and feel a cold coming on. Now you're on-set and the scene calls for you to be delighted with news that you've won the lottery. The director shouts "Action!" Can you, in a split second, on command, acquire the personality and behavior of this character you're playing and leave your real life behind? Can you lose yourself in the part and become it? Can you understand what the director wants and deliver a performance that satisfies him? Can you do multiple takes of the same scene without going flat? Can you control your natural nervousness and use it to your advantage? Can you remember your lines? Can you appear overjoyed even though you're sick, you're tired, and you have pandemonium at home to look forward to?

> I just couldn't understand how these actors could behave like me, invent a world of make-believe, and call it work! And I turned to my father at the first intermission, and they probably heard me all over the theatre I was so excited, as I said, "Papa, Papa, that's what I'm going to do."[5]
>
> Eleven-year-old Ingrid Bergman, recalling attending a performance of *Patrasket* (The Rabble) by Hjalmar Bergman.

Not so simple after all, is it?

Fortunately, many great minds and talents have applied their efforts to the paradox of good acting, and many have published books on the topic. You'll find a few in the bibliography as well as a discussion of the most important schools of thought on acting technique in chapter 9, "Training."

A DAY IN THE LIFE OF AN ACTOR

It is said that you act for free but you get paid to wait. As you read the following sequence of events in an actor's day, you will realize that a lot goes on that has nothing at all to do with actual acting.

Armed with information provided by the casting agency or production office, you begin your day by driving to the specified location. In Los Angeles, driving anywhere demands courage and patience. If you live in Hollywood, you're probably closer to most studios than if you live elsewhere. I'm in the South Bay, so the commute to the set is a major chunk of the day. Sometimes call time, which is when you are required to report to work, is at the crack of dawn, ahead of the real traffic snarls.

> 1982   Vanna White joins *Wheel of Fortune*, replacing Susan Stafford. "Vannamania" grips the nation.
>
> 1982   Spielberg makes *ET: The Extra Terrestrial*.
>
> 1982   Vic Morrow is killed in a helicopter crash during the filming of *Twilight Zone: The Movie* (1983).

Other times there's no avoiding gridlock. Once you arrive at the studio or location shoot, your day will take a predictable course, with occasional variations. It goes something like this:

★ **Park**: This is not a trivial matter. If you were a principal or one of the big fish on the set, you would park adjacent to your trailer, or in a lot close to the set. If you're an extra, you will probably be instructed to park on the street or in a remote lot from which you will trek or be shuttled to the set. This is supremely annoying if you're hauling a garment bag and a shoulder tote and the newspaper and a folding chair.

★ **Get Shuttled**: You clatter onto the shuttle van with all your stuff and are taken to the set. Often you have to wait for the shuttle to arrive and sometimes you sit on the bus and wait for others to show up. Relax.

★ **Check In and Receive Voucher**: Your first mission on arrival is to find the individual, normally a 2nd AD, who is checking in the actors. If you're lucky enough to be there as a principal, you will be shown to your trailer. Don't imagine a fancy, sleek, silver thing. You are assigned a tiny space on a trailer with multiple rooms one of which is yours. Sometimes you have to

> 1983   *M*A*S*H* signs off. Finale is seen by 125 million Americans.
>
> 1983   Tom Brokaw becomes sole anchor of the *NBC Nightly News*.
>
> 1983   THX, an advanced sound system for movie theaters, is introduced.

share this with one or several other actors. There is often a difference between the treatment SAG members and non-members get. Non-union productions are not obliged to provide the same amenities as union ones. So they don't. If you're there as an extra, there's usually a sign that points the way to Holding and there or near there you will see a person carrying a stack of vouchers. That's your man. Or woman. The 2nd AD will hand you your pay voucher. This is white for union members and blue for non-union. If you're there in a principal role, you will receive a more substantial contract to sign. Whether you're on-set as a principal or extra, as a union or non-union actor, your day will start with a document that lists at least the following: name, social security number, time of call, date, production name and number, marital status, contact information, work hours, set dismissal and meal periods. Make sure you have one of these because it is the document that triggers your paycheck.

> As the camera got to the end, the actor said, "And that's all I have to say." He sat down and actually died. Realizing what had happened, an assistant said, "Yes, he's dead. Better get him out of here." They started to remove the body, when [director] Woody Van Dyke yelled, "Hold it! Hold it!" He took out his viewfinder and got down in back of the actor's body, looking for an over-the-shoulder shot. "All right," Van Dyke finally said, "take him out, but leave the coat." And he kept on working.[6]

★ **Wardrobe**: The 2nd AD will now send you to Wardrobe. This department often operates out of a truck or a trailer. If you've brought your own stuff and are properly attired for the scene you're in, they send you back to your trailer or to Holding. If you're not they will select something for you from their inventory and take your voucher as collateral. At the end of the day, when you report back to Wardrobe and give them their clothes back, they release your voucher.

★ **Hair and Makeup**: In most cases, for extras, this is a perfunctory stop on the way to Holding. Once in a while, though, you'll be groomed or made up, particularly if you're a woman. On a couple of occasions I've been asked to remove certain facial hair. As a principal, you will receive more attention from Makeup before and during the shoot.

★ **Props**: Another stop you will make en route to the set is at Props, where you will be assigned whatever things your character needs to carry. These could include a stethoscope, a pen, a writing pad, a gun—depends on the part. Extras leave one copy of their voucher here to secure the props. The voucher has multiple copies and so it's possible for Wardrobe and Props to each have a piece of it.

★ **Holding:** Extras Holding is the area where extras do what they do most: wait. It can be a bench on the loading dock, a comfortable lounge or a dingy room with old crappy furniture. The latter is more likely.

★ **Wait:** I haven't actually made an empirical study of this but estimate that 50% of an actor's day is spent waiting to be called to the set. I sat for a whole day in Holding once without being called to the set at all! As I mentioned above, Holding is more likely to be spartan than cushy, and it is not unheard of for it to be cold and uncomfortable. You can ease life for yourself by carrying with you all that it takes to deal with the physical discomfort and the boredom. These things make up the Actor's Survival Kit and are listed later in this chapter.

★ **Find the Honey Wagon:** I wish they would just call it the WC, or toilet, or men's, or whatever. But on the set it's known as the honey wagon and that's how it's known. Principals get to powder en suite.

★ **Report to Set:** "Background, five minutes! Five minutes, background!" Often that is how the 2nd AD will call the extras to the set. The work begins. If you're not an extra, your call to the set will be somewhat more personal than that; the 2nd AD might even come to your little trailer micropod and summon you with a polite knock on the door.

★ **Lunch:** Good food is one of the perks of acting. There are labor regulations that require production companies to provide water, food, breaks and restrooms. Lunch generally consists of a buffet and lasts one hour. On some sets there is a difference between the food that is provided to extras and to non-extras. Sometimes lunch is what's called a walk-away. In this case you get an hour or a half-hour to go away and kill your own lunch.

★ **Back to Trailer or Holding:** And from here further calls to the set.

★ **Wrap:** When the day's schedule has been completed, the director wraps everybody. Some people are wrapped before others. In order to control costs, actors are released when they've finished their scenes for the day. This is the responsibility of the 2nd AD. Incidentally, it is customary, when a guest star is wrapped at the end of a production, for the cast and crew to applaud as that actor leaves the set. It's one of many such kindnesses of protocol that apply in the business.

1984   U.S. Supreme Court rules that home video recording is legal.

1984   *The Cosby Show* premieres on NBC. It runs for eight seasons.

1985   Blockbuster Video opens first store in Dallas. Twenty years later there are 5,500.

★ **Return Props and Wardrobe:** As mentioned earlier, you need to retrieve your voucher before you can leave. Without a voucher to give the 2nd AD, you won't get paid.

★ **Checkout:** After you return your wardrobe and props and receive your voucher in return, you can find the 2nd AD and check out. They retain all the copies of

> Moviemaking is a pragmatic art, and Hollywood is the kind of place where this phrase is not an oxymoron. Being a genius involves more than talent here; it involves a shrewd working knowledge of the mechanics and logistics of "the system."[7]

your voucher but one, yours. Keep this and file it in a safe place; it is the only record you have of the day's work and the production company's financial obligation to you.

WHO'S WHO AND WHAT'S WHAT

Showbiz is big biz. The scale of media companies that own production studios is astonishing. Let's say you've landed a bit part on *Crossing Jordan*. You're instructed to follow the 101 Freeway to the Universal Studios Blvd., exit right and follow the signs to the studios. Enter through Gate 3, park in the adjacent garage, and walk to Stage 44, where you will look for the 2nd AD and check in.

As you join the forty or fifty people who are involved in shooting this episode, consider that you are, for the duration, part of a huge machine called NBC Universal, which itself is a holding of GE, one of the world's largest and most diversified conglomerates. GE's annual revenues are a staggering $165 billion.[8] NBC Universal accounts for about $15 billion of that and owns the following operations:[9]

Broadcast Networks	Cable Channels	Theme Parks
NBC	CNBC	Universal City
Telemundo	MSNBC Bravo	Orlando, FL
	Mun 2	Osaka, Japan
Television Stations	Sci Fi	Barcelona, Spain
14 NBC stations	USA Network	
15 Telemundo stations	Trio	**Studios**
		Universal Pictures
		NBC Studios

Each of the above entities has a complete management hierarchy consisting of dozens, maybe hundreds of people. And there, at Studio 44, is a small production unit that eventually contributes to the company's bottom line. All this to say that understanding who is who in showbiz can be difficult. That is why, for our purposes, this discussion is limited to the individuals who are directly involved in making TV and film productions. I purposely exclude the suits who are not unique to showbiz.

Living in Oblivion is a funny and poignant 1995 film, written and directed by Tom DiCillo and starring the inimitable Steve Buscemi as Nick Reve, movie director. This satirical look at independent filmmaking captures the dynamics and chemistry of life on a production set. IMDB provides the following taglines:

> Nick is about to discover the first rule of filmmaking: if at first you don't succeed...PANIC!

> He only needs three things to get through the day...an espresso, an aspirin, and a miracle.[10]

Spend a day on the set of any movie or TV show and you will agree: it's nothing short of miraculous that anything at all gets done. There are so many people performing so many specialized tasks, in such tight synchronization, that the slightest miscue can have the whole gang starting over. There's something exciting in being a part of this sort of team effort where, even if you have the smallest part, you still contribute to the final product.

1986   Ted Turner buys MGM's library of nearly 3,700 titles and creates controversy in colorizing some classics.

1986   *Top Gun* and *Crocodile Dundee* are top-grossing films for the year.

And what a product! In the eighteen months during which I worked on Hollywood productions, I rarely witnessed a shot successfully completed in less than three takes. *Guinness World Records* gives the record for most number of takes (a stupefying 342!), to a scene in *City Lights*, Charlie Chaplin's 1931 classic.[11] Okay, that's a bit much but as a rule most scenes will require from four to a dozen takes before everything works as it should. There is so much complexity in making movies and TV shows that it couldn't be done, certainly not on a commercial scale, with anything less than a tightly coordinated group of specialists whose roles and reporting relationships are clear.

As a beginning actor, you can be more professional and certainly more effective if you understand what happens on the set and who the production players are. The next section outlines the major roles and their reporting relationships. The section after that describes the process of making movies and TV shows. I will emphasize what happens on the set in the hope that, after reading this, you can feel quite at home there.

WHO'S WHO?

Understanding who's who in showbiz is no simple task because the organizational structures of the various companies involved is not just complex but also fluid. Linda Buzzell, in her excellent book on showbiz, categorizes power players in Hollywood according to the following original taxonomy:

The Bullies and Abusers

The Yellers and Screamers

The Smiling Cobras

The Casting Couch Lotharios

The Ruthless Climbers

The Tricky Thieves and the "Sue Me" Sharks

The Good Guys[12]

> The word "element" is often used in the business to characterize either an actor, a script, a producer, a director, or any and all of the above.[13]

You'll know them when you meet them.

The dynamics vary. On some sets everybody mingles. On others there is strict separation between the principals, the big shots, and the rest of us. This can also apply to all collateral services, like catering. On the set of the short-lived futuristic courthouse drama *Century City*, a marvelous spread was put out for everyone working on the show. It included various barbequed meats, chicken, fish, salads and desserts. On the set of *Crossing Jordan* at Universal Studios, the story was quite different. There we had an anemic fruit plate and sundry packaged snacks plus a sad cake with a mystery filling. Whether you're savoring fresh-caught grilled Alaskan salmon shoulder-to-shoulder with Clooney or forcing down a soggy BLT with Voluptua the Ventriloquist, you'll soon see that showbiz is very much a caste system. Crew hang with crew; above-the-line talent and creative executives hang with each other; extras hang with extras and that's the way it is. In *Hollywood Anecdotes*, Paul Boller calls

Hollywood not one community, but several. "Totally Unauthorized" is a popular blog at www.filmhacks.blogspot.com, written by production crew member Peggy Archer [her nom-de-keyboard]. It includes an interesting account of her relationship with an actor and reveals the sort of invisible divisions that exist on the set and in the business.

Every production brings together different specialists for the purpose of completing a specific project. They may or may not work together again. For example, I worked on three episodes of *JAG*. There was a different director each time and the production crew included people I'd seen before and others that I hadn't. The talent, naturally, always includes guest stars and new extras.

There are multiple complex relationships between individuals and organizations in film and TV production. That's because these relationships exist on the following four different planes which, as though not intricate enough, often overlap.

BUSINESS HIERARCHY

Who reports to whom and who hires whom? This is typically how things work in the corporate world. Everyone knows that a senior vice president is senior to a plain vice president and that a chief executive officer is senior to a chief operating officer. It's not quite that simple in showbiz because some titles have a range of meaning and relative influence. A producer could be someone whose contribution was integral and without whom the movie would never have happened or, occasionally, a friend who helped get the screenplay optioned.

CREATIVE HIERARCHY

This dimension of the business is also somewhat hierarchical but based on completely different criteria. The director, for example, may very well be lower in the business hierarchy than an executive producer, but there is no question that the latter usually takes a back seat to the director's artistic and creative influence. In some cases the director is the supreme being on a production.

ABOVE- AND BELOW-THE-LINE

Production budgets have two general categories of costs: creative and line. The folks in the first group are those who create, design, finance and plan a production. In the second group are those who carry out these plans, the troops. A line separates these categories in the budget, hence the above-the-line and below-the-line classifications. This view of the business is arcane and of limited usefulness but, when in Rome...

CHRONOLOGICAL

Film and TV projects follow a clear, chronological process. In the broadest sense every project goes through four stages:

★ Development

A writer pens a script and finds someone to produce it. That someone then finds someone to finance it.

★ Production

The producer hires a director, the cast and production crew. The show is filmed or taped.

★ Postproduction

Editors are brought on to assemble footage, audio and effects.

★ Distribution

Publicists get busy and the show enters the distribution network.

The chart that follows combines the first three of the four perspectives listed above: business hierarchy, creative hierarchy and above- and below-the-line. The chronological perspective is discussed in the section that follows, What's What?

The chart has three main branches: Finance, Creative, and Logistics. Within each branch are the positions whose primary function fits best into its functional specialty. Many positions have scopes that cross over from Creative to Logistical, and certainly from Logistical to Financial.

The chart also shows the general hierarchy and reporting relationships, though here again there is overlap and matrix reporting.

Finally, the boxes with the gray background are below-the-line positions whereas the white ones are above-the-line.

Hollywood Organization Chart[14]

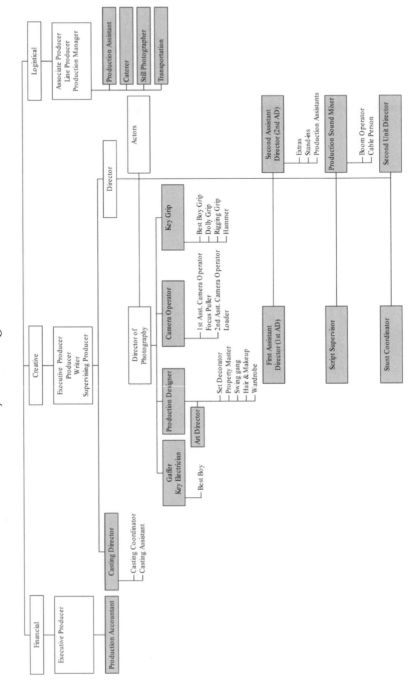

WHAT'S WHAT?

Making a movie or a television show is a complex project. It requires the participation of experts in many disciplines working at the same moment in a coordinated effort, something like a rocket-launch. In show business, every take is a rocket-launch. A general chronological order of events does exist, however, and it is as follows:

★ Someone gets an idea and writes a treatment or script or concept outline. How often does this happen? Thousands of times each year. Following is a scene from the *The Player* (1992), with Tim Robbins as the stereotypical opportunistic Hollywood studio producer who accidentally kills one of the writers he had previously given the brush to and winds up marrying the man's widow. In the scene, Grif (Robbins) is talking to June (Greta Scacchi), the girlfriend of the defunct screenwriter. They're having a romantic evening at a resort in the desert. Even if the numbers Grif throws up are half true, they would be startling.[15]

June: Tell me about the movies you make.

Grif: Why?

June: Because I want to know what you do.

Grif: I listen to stories and decide if they'll make good movies or not. I get 125 phone calls a day and if I let that slip to 100 then I know I'm not doing my job. Everyone who calls wants to know one thing. They want me to say yes to them and make their movie. If I say yes they think that come New Year's, it will be just them and Jack Nicholson on the slopes at Aspen. That's what they think. I can only say yes...the studio can only say yes twelve times a year and collectively we hear about 50,000 stories a year. So it's hard.

★ If the project is picked up, it goes into development and, sometimes, development hell. Watch James Brooks' *I'll Do Anything!* (1994) starring Nick Nolte, for a tragicomic look at development and the hell it can be when a project gets stuck in it. How long can a project be stuck in development? *The Doctor and the Devils* took 32 years to get from script to screen![16]

★ This creative concept is adopted by a person or organization with the money to bankroll it and the connections to broadcast or distribute it.

★ All required contracts and paperwork are completed.

★ A director and the main stars are hired.

★ A production team is assembled, including the roles identified in the organization chart above.

★ Locations for shoots are found and reserved.

★ Auditions commence to cast the parts in the script.

★ Logistics are arranged, including transportation, on-set accommodations, catering, technical services and payroll.

★ The sets are built. This is ongoing throughout shooting.

★ Now that all is ready, shooting begins and, for every scene:

• Lights are set.

• Stand-ins play through the scene and their positions are blocked.

• The first team is called in and rehearses the scene. Meanwhile, the camera and sound teams are also planning their own moves for the shot.

• The director is satisfied all is ready and says, "Let's shoot it."

• The 1st AD asks everybody to settle down by calling out, sometimes with a great deal of passion, "Quiet on the set!"

• The cameras roll and the 1st AD calls, "Rolling."

• The camera team takes its first position and says, "Set."

• The sound engineer checks audiotape and says, "Sound speed."

• The director calls "Action," sometimes after "Background action."

• The actors go through the scene.

• The director, script supervisor, producers and writers monitor the action and call for additional takes to correct and fine-tune various elements of the scene such as actor performance, lighting, etc.

• If the director likes the take he will instruct that it be printed.

• The director could be satisfied with a take but still ask that it be reshot. He will call, "Let's go again," or, "Back to one." "One" is shorthand for "position one," at which everyone began the scene.

★ Eventually, when all is just right, including the acting and the camera work and the sound, the magic words, "Cut, print, check the gate" will come.

★ When a substantial amount of shooting has been done, post-production can begin. Footage is viewed, edited, enhanced, overlaid with sound and special effects, and the whole shebang is assembled into the final product, a film or TV show.

When it works, this collaboration can be a beautiful experience that bonds people for life and results in an outstanding product. When it doesn't work, it can lead to lawsuits and feuds and wrecked careers and flops. Even those are remarkable in their complexity. Consider *Water World*. Here's a movie on which critics and the public heaped scorn. But step back a bit and consider the sheer scale of the project, the courage it took to back it, the determination and resources to make it and, even though you might think it's a lousy movie, you would have to admit that it is a phenomenal accomplishment.

1987   Earliest HDTV over-the-air tests.
1987   10,000 computers are connected to the Internet. In 2005, 44 million are.
1987   Michael Douglas wins Best Actor Oscar for *Wall Street*. Cher wins Best Actress for *Moonstruck*.
1987   The Federal Communications Commission (FCC) rescinds the Fairness Doctrine, which had required broadcasters to show both sides of controversial, public issues. Hence today's blatantly skewed news reporting.
1987   *The Cosby Show* tops the ratings.

BACKGROUND WORK

One of the quickest ways to infiltrate Hollywood is as an extra. It's also a pretty good way to gain some exposure and learn a few things about the business while you pursue your acting career. This, though, is not universally agreed. Some will say that working as an extra will hurt your odds of getting real parts. My take is that nobody really cares and that you will not adversely impact your chances of stardom by doing background work early in your career.

The typical day for an extra closely follows that of a typical movie or TV actor but without the money, fame, or prestige.[17]

WHAT IS AN EXTRA?

Tune in to any TV program or watch any movie and you will see a vast number of people who are on-screen but who say nothing. These are background actors. They play pedestrians, nurses, doctors, lawyers, juries, audiences and policemen. These folks outnumber the stars and principals. Without them there would be no show. They are the extras, the salt of the earth, the masses, the humans that complete the illusion. Everyone else on the set gets a credit for the final product. The actors, the crew, the director and his assistants, the producers and the writers and the special effects people; all of them get a credit. Not the extras. In the Hollywood caste system, extras are at the very bottom of the heap. That's just the way it is. These long-suffering, ignored individuals are given various sobriquets:

★ Extra: the traditional moniker, now mildly non-PC.

★ Background: the standard, considered polite.

★ Nondescript: okay but somewhat dehumanizing.

★ Atmosphere: better than nondescript but not by much.

★ Props with Appetites: technically correct but too candid.

WHY BE AN EXTRA?

There are few occupations in this world that have the glamorous attraction of working in Hollywood. Being in movies is right up there, on the sexiest occupation list, with being an astronaut. One of the main reasons for being an extra is to be in showbiz when you can't immediately be a star, which is always.

There are good and bad reasons for becoming an extra:

★ **As a means of breaking into show business.** "Breaking into" may be a bit heroic; "edging in" is more the case. This was not lost on Ayn Rand who in 1926 made her way to Hollywood and landed a job as an extra on Cecil B. DeMille's *The King of Kings*. She was actually interested in becoming a screenwriter and of course eventually became one of the most influential writers and philosophers of our time.[18] Hey, if Ayn Rand wasn't above doing background work to further her career, who are we to kick? Many now-famous and successful actors at one time were background players. These include such luminaries as Sylvester Stallone, John Travolta, Julia Roberts and Whoopi Goldberg. Morgan Freeman describes one of his earliest experiences as follows: "I got work as a movie extra. If you look really hard, you can see me in [1965's] *The Pawnbroker*, walking down the street during one of Rod Steiger's flashbacks. When I saw that, I took it as a sign. I thought, I must be on the right track."[19] Well, he wasn't wrong, as his 2005 Oscar for Best Supporting Actor proved once and for all. There are many more. So it can be done, but not easily.

★ **As a means of making some quick cash.** In the constellation of no-skills-or-experience-required jobs, few offer the same potential pot at the end of the rainbow as being an extra. It is believable to say "I'm an actor getting valuable experience doing background work while I wait for my big break." You can't really say that as convincingly if you're shearing sheep.

★ **As a way to stay active and meet people.** It's tough to beat doing extra work as a social activity. You are cooped up with a dozen or more characters all day. Most of these folks are agreeable and quite willing to have a conversation. Some are fascinating, though these are also more likely to be as nutty as a pecan grove.

★ **As a reliable means of meeting and talking to famous actors.** This is not a good reason to do extra work because it is considered gauche to ambush the principals and stars on the set. These people have lines to learn. Some are so deep in character that they are unapproachable. However, it is sometimes possible to rub elbows and have little chats during breaks or at the craft services table.

★ **As a way to study the business close up.** Whether you're pursuing a career in production, directing, or acting, it is hard to imagine a more fertile environment in which to learn the trade. As an extra you spend your days watching pros doing precisely what you yourself hope to be doing in the future. It's the ideal classroom.

How Can I Become An Extra?

You can set yourself up as an extra in no time at all. The general requirements follow, and of these only the first two are essential:

★ Get Headshots

It helps if you walk into an extras casting agency with headshots, but even snapshots will do. The agency will take your picture anyway.

★ Register With a Casting Agency

Extras casting agencies provide production companies with actors to populate the TV and feature productions that happen in L.A. every day.

They're essentially staffing firms. Production companies hire them because they vet applicants and perform the hairy exercise of paying all these extras. Even if an extra works just one day, a check must be cut. Casting agencies relieve the production house of the paper nightmare this can be. There is a number of reliable extras casting agencies in L.A. See appendix B, "Casting Agencies" for a representative few.

> Three hundred thousand. That's how many extras were used on Attenborough's *Gandhi* (1982). Only a third of these were actually paid. The rest volunteered. Not much difference since the pay was fifty cents each.

★ Get Booked

Once you have registered with a casting agency, there are two ways in which you can get work:

• Call In

This is tedious and time-consuming. You call a specially equipped number and listen to recorded listings of available gigs. Select the ones you like and speak to that casting agent. If they agree that you are suited for that part, they book you.

• Hire a Calling Service

Let someone else's fingers do the walking. The trouble with this approach is that you can control your schedule only by giving the calling service your exceptions ahead of time. Otherwise it is their job to book you as often as possible.

★ Be Available

Extra work usually consists of twelve-hour days on-set. If you have a part-time job that takes you out of circulation for several hours a day, you will not be able to do it.

★ Have a Wardrobe

When you are hired as an extra, you are almost always expected to show up with a change of clothes. A good wardrobe is one of the signs of the serious professional extra.

THE ALMIGHTY UNION VOUCHER

A union voucher merits its own section because it is central to the life of a professional extra. "Union voucher" or "SAG voucher" are among the first words you'll hear when you kick off your career as an actor, and for good reason. The advantages of working on a union voucher are:

★ Higher pay

★ Eventual union membership

★ Prestige

Belonging to the Screen Actors Guild (SAG) is not merely a question of prestige. It's a matter of more money. A non-union extra earns $54 for an eight-hour day. SAG extras make twice that. The following table shows the daily rate structure for union and non-union extras.

SAG vs. Non-SAG Table of Hourly Wages

	SAG	Non-Union
First 8 Hours	$15.25	$6.75
Hours 9 & 10	$22.88	$10.13
Hours 11 & 12	$22.88	$13.50
Hours 13, 14, 15	$30.50	$13.50
Hours 16 and beyond	$122.00	$13.50

To illustrate how all this plays out, let's say that you are non-union and your friend Rich is SAG. You're working the same show as extras and each put in sixteen hours. The following table works out the math:

SAG vs. Non-SAG Table of Daily Earnings

	Rich's Hourly Rates	Rich's Wages	Your Hourly Rates	Your Wages
First 8 Hours	$15.25	$122.00	$6.75	$54.00
Hours 9 & 10	$22.88	$45.75	$10.13	$20.25
Hours 11 & 12	$22.88	$45.75	$13.50	$27.00
Hours 13, 14, 15	$30.50	$91.50	$13.50	$40.50
Hour 16	$122.00	$122.00	$13.50	$13.50
Total		$427.00		$155.25

In the above scenario, Rich makes $271.75 more than you do for the same hours worked. It is not a typical example because that 16th hour, known in the trade as "golden time," rarely happens. Without that, Rich would have made $305.00 and you would have made $141.75. Now the difference is $163.25.

The above workout should make it clear why getting into SAG is such an important step. How do you do that? According to SAG's website, the following are the legitimate ways:

★ Three days of working as a SAG extra.

★ A speaking role in a SAG production.

★ Membership in another affiliated union.[20]

However, the system is full of holes and therefore abuse and some commerce of the voucher system exists. One woman I met got four vouchers within the first month of starting to work as an extra. She said she knew somebody. On the other hand, many people work for years without achieving that vaunted status. SAG is aware of the problem and in 2004 joined the Los Angeles City Attorney in launching the first-ever, criminal suit against someone using vouchers fraudulently. Furthermore, it is expected that the voucher system will be retired sometime in 2006.

While it may seem like a no-brainer, getting union status may not be all that great. Many background actors report that they work less after joining the union. This is because production companies prefer to pay the lower wages of non-union actors, and are only required to hire a certain number of union people before completing the cast with non-union people. The quotas are as follows:

★ TV: first twenty background actors, including one stand-in, have to be union and the rest can be non-union.

★ Film: first fifty background actors have to be union and the rest can be non-union.[21]

1988   The Writers Guild of America (WGA) strikes for nearly six months, delaying the fall TV season.

1988   Pixar wins Oscar for Tin Toy. First Academy Award for computer-animated film.

1988   The American Experience debuts on PBS with a film about the devastating 1906 San Francisco earthquake.

1988   60% of households that own a TV also own a VCR. In 1982 only 4% did.

1988   Who Framed Roger Rabbit is released, showcasing cutting edge integration of live actors with character animation.

THE DOS AND DON'TS

Now that you have a pretty good idea what a typical day in the life of an actor is like, pay close attention to the following lists. There is nuance and tact and protocol to observe. How well you play the game will have a lot to do with if and when you're invited back.

Do:

★ **Be Cordial to Everyone.** In Hollywood, just as in the corporate world, there are those who are obsequious to their superiors but at best dismissive and at worst offensive to everyone else. They manage up. These scallywags will come to no good end because the people they pass on the way up are also the people they will pass on the way down and because, in the words of Thomas Jones, "Friends may come and go, but enemies accumulate." So be at least cordial to everyone and, if it's in you, be nice.

★ **Stay Out of the Way.** There is a small paradox to being a successful actor. You get better on-set reviews by being invisible. If the crew is stumbling over you on the set, or your needs keep PAs and ADs running, you may wind up doing yourself more harm than good. You could be seen as a nuisance, or worse, a distraction. So, to the extent that you can, stay in one spot and avoid getting in anybody's way. At the same time, cultivate relationships with the crew, but do it unobtrusively.

★ **Follow Directions.** When the 1st or 2nd AD or even occasionally the director himself says something, pay attention. It could be you they're talking to. They hate having to repeat themselves.

★ **Silence Your Phone.** Turn off your cell phone, pager and all other devices that can beep or buzz or whir or any other noise that can embarrass the hell out of you in the middle of a scene. The microphones that are used on-set are extremely sensitive and will pick up almost any sound. On the set of *Century City* I learned this first-hand when my cell phone, which was set on "vibrate," did just that. I could hear it and so could the two people next to me, but none of the other people on the set. The audio man, however, picked up the buzz on the boom microphone and started looking around for a bee or fly or whatever else was producing the annoying hum. Luckily he did not stop the take and I was not exposed. From that time on I turn my cell phone off while on-set. This also eliminates sitting on the thing and making a butt call.

★ **Fill Out Your Voucher.** Unless you're a principal, It annoys the corpuscles out of 2nd ADs to have to do it for you.

DON'T:

★ **Leave the Set Without Permission.** It is perhaps the greatest frustration in a 2nd AD's life to have to go looking for an actor when that actor is needed immediately on-set. If you must leave, even just to take a leak, let the 2nd AD know.

★ **Talk While on the Set.** Everybody talks on-set: principals, extras, crew, everybody. That's why the word you will hear most often in the course of a day of shooting is "Ssshhhhhhhh!" It's human nature. You can't spend the whole day with the same people at close quarters and not talk. But if you must, remember that, just because the cameras are not at the moment rolling and the director has not called "Action" does not necessarily mean that there isn't work going on. Actors could be rehearsing, crew could be setting up for the next shot, and the director and the DP could be conferring.

1989   The Berlin Wall is taken down.

1989   Pay-per-view reaches 20% of cable households.

1989   TV broadcast networks reach just 55% of total audience, a new low.

1989   *The Simpsons* debuts on Fox. Doh.

1989   Warner Communications and Time Inc. merge to form the world's largest media company.

1989   Jessica Tandy wins Oscar for *Driving Miss Daisy*. Morgan Freeman is nominated for Best Actor and loses to Daniel Day-Lewis in *My Left Foot*.

★ **Hit on Anyone.** There is no quicker way to alienate a fellow actor than to hit on them. There is no faster way—with the exception of burning down the set—to become unemployed, than hitting on a big star. This is not to say that these productions do not spawn friendships and affairs and even the occasional nooner. It is rather to say: tread lightly and use good judgment.

★ **Talk to the Stars of the Show.** There are exceptions to this rule. It's a matter of discretion. If you find yourself shoulder to shoulder with a star during a break, by all means say hi and take the conversation where it wants to go. Never, on the other hand, approach an actor while they are in character on the set. Never ask for an autograph. Never hand anyone a script on the set.

★ **Hand Out Your Business Card.** Unless someone asks for it or you feel that you have spoken long enough that an exchange of contact info is a natural progression. Otherwise you will seem too needy and that, as you know, is the universal turn-off.

ACTOR'S SURVIVAL KIT

Experienced actors are prepared for any contingency. They carry with them all the things they might need in the course of the very long days they spend on-set. With a few exceptions, the list of items in an actor's survival kit is the same as that of a business traveler.

★ **Chair.** Okay, most business travelers don't, but you can tell the experienced extras by the chairs they carry. There is a whole range of folding, portable chairs in all sorts of configurations and colors available on the market. These things roll up to a compact tubular package that you can sling over your shoulder. They unfurl to provide a reasonably comfortable reclining bed.

★ **Beverage.** Although there is almost always a big supply of water on the set—it is after all the law to provide it—you'd do well to have a small bottle of your favorite brand in your bag.

★ **Drugs.** The essentials are good to have on hand, including something for pain, heartburn and diarrhea.

★ **Reading Material.** The things an actor does most are sit and wait. Therefore it is essential to have something to read. If you don't like to read bring a portable DVD player but always use a headset.

> Making it, especially in Hollywood, is all about a commitment to perpetual forward motion. Aspiration. Upwardness. It's all about traction and trajectory...It's about striving, reaching, grabbing, moving, shaking—not sitting with your back to the wall, waiting for the party to come to you. To survive and prosper, you have to go with the flow, even if you have to create the flow yourself.[22]

★ **Music.** Apple iPods are all the rage now and make for a lightweight and long-playing music source.

★ **Ear Plugs.** One of the greatest inventions ever made. These little miracles can block out the noise of aircraft engines, screaming babies, and loud people of every stripe. They can be lifesavers when you're surrounded by stentorian talkers.

★ **Eye Shades.** I have never had the guts to use these in a crowd but have seen people do so.

★ **Wet Wipes.** You're munching on a nice sesame bagel with strawberry cream cheese when some of the schmear squirts out the side and onto the lapel of the navy blue jacket that Wardrobe gave you. Nightmare scenario: you have already been in several scenes, with the famously temperamental star, in that jacket. Clearly, unless you can remove all traces of the cheese, you will be distressing a whole bunch of people when you appear on-set wearing your smudge.

★ **Cell Phone.** It is best to keep your cell phone off unless you are actually making a call. A production set is no place to take calls.

★ **Computer.** I've tried many times to do some writing while working on a show. Half the time it just doesn't work because I get called to the set and have to leave my laptop behind. Odds are nothing will happen to it but why take the chance? If, on the other hand, you are working on a show that provides comfortable and secure facilities, then by all means take your computer along and make the most of your time. Turn the speaker volume off or wear headphones.

> It's just a funny thing about this racket—the bigger you are, the jumpier you get.[23]

★ **Appropriate Clothing.** Sound stages as a rule are not terribly well air-conditioned. In winter you can freeze your wits off and in summer it can be sweltering in there under the lights. Holding is quite often cold. Be prepared to layer on or layer off.

★ **Towel.** As Douglas Adams writes in *The Hitchhiker's Guide to the Galaxy*, "A towel is about the most ·massively useful thing an interstellar hitchhiker can have." Also applies to actors.

Armed with the information from this chapter you should be confident as you approach your work opportunities. Remember, this is a multi-round contest. Pace yourself and be patient; it's your stamina and perseverance that will get you there.

INDUSTRY FORECAST

You will be happy to know that the Bureau of Labor Statistics (BLS) forecasts healthy growth in showbiz for the coming few years. Here's what they have to say:

> Employment of actors, producers, and directors is expected to grow about as fast as the average for all occupations through 2012. Although a growing number of people will enter these professions, many will leave the field early because the work—when it is available—is hard, the hours are long, and the pay is low. Competition for jobs will be stiff, in part because the large number of highly trained and talented actors auditioning for roles generally exceeds the number of parts that become available. Only performers with the most stamina and talent will find regular employment.[24]

You've come across the idea many times in this book, that one of your most valuable assets as you take on Hollywood is stamina. Here you have independent confirmation from the BLS.

☆

1. Bruce Torrence, *Hollywood; The First Hundred Years*, (New York: Zoetrope, 1982), 88.

2. James Bacon, *Hollywood is a Four Letter Word* (Chicago: Henry Regnery Company, 1976), 232.

3. Bureau of Labor Statistics, U.S. Department of Labor, "Occupational Outlook Handbook, 2004-05 Edition, Actors, Producers, and Directors," http://www.bls.gov/oco/ocos093.htm.

4. Morris, Eric; Joan Hotchkis and Jack Nicholson. *No Acting Please* (Los Angeles: Ermor Enterprises, 1995).

5. Donald Spoto, *Notorious, The Life of Ingrid Bergman* (London: Harper Collins Publishers, London, 1997), 17.

6. Boller, *Hollywood Anecdotes*, 97.

7. Lynda Obst, *Hello, He Lied and Other Truths from the Hollywood Trenches* (New York: Little, Brown and Company, 1996), 73.

8. Yahoo Finance, Quotes and Info, http://www.finance.yahoo.com/q/ks?s=GE.

9. Richard Verrier and Elizabeth Jensen, "New Day Dawns for NBC Universal," *Newsday*, 2004, http://www.medialit.med.sc.edu/nbcu.htm.

10. IMDB.com, http://www.imdb.com/title/tt0113677.

11. http://www.guinnessworldrecords.com.

12. Linda Buzzell, *How To Make It In Hollywood*, Second Edition (New York: Harper Collins, 1996), 19.

13. Brouwer, *Working in Hollywood*, 5.

14. George Brook, "Surviving the Roller Coaster: Worst and Best Practices in Project Management within the Television Production Industry," International Institute for Learning, 2004, http://www.allpm.com/modules.php?op=modload&name=News&file=article&sid=922.

15. *The Player*, dir. by Robert Altman, 124 min., Avenue Pictures Productions, 1992, videocassette.

16. http://www.guinnessworldrecords.com

17. Larry Garrison and Wallace Wang, *Breaking Into Acting for Dummies* (New York: Wiley Publishing, Inc., 2002), 208.

18. The Ayn Rand Institute, "A Brief Biography of Ayn Rand," 1995, http://www.aynrand.org/site/PageServer?pagename=about_ayn_rand_ayn-rand_biography.

19. David Hochman, "Before I Was Famous," *Life*, 18 February, (2005): 8.

20. http://www.sag.com.

21. American Federation of Television and Radio Artists, "Actors Secure $200 Million TV/Theatrical Contract," January 21, 2005,

http://www.aftra.org/press/pr_2005_0120_20millcontract.html.

22. David Rensin, *The Mailroom: Hollywood History From the Bottom Up*, (New York: The Ballantine Publishing Group, 2003), xxiii.

23. Schulberg, *What Makes Sammy Run*, 162.

24. Bureau of Labor Statistics, "Occupational Outlook Handbook, Actors, Producers, and Directors," U.S. Department of Labor, 2004-2005, http://www.bls.gov/oco/ocos093.htm.

☆

Chapter Nine

TRAINING

Education is an admirable thing,
but it is well to remember from
time to time that nothing that is
worth knowing can be taught.

— Oscar Wilde

☆

Genius without education is
like silver in the mine.

— Benjamin Franklin

☆

...the actor's most important
quality—or better, his primary
duty—is comprehensive study.

— Sarah Bernhardt

☆

☆

How you train for your acting career may reflect Wilde's, Franklin's, or Bernhardt's philosophy but will more likely be a mix of all three. Unlike most other occupations, acting does not follow a prescribed timetable or curriculum. If you want to be a certified financial planner you have to complete educational and work requirements which eventually lead to certification. The majority of professions adhere to a similar pattern. Not acting. To be an actor you merely have to decide that you want to be an actor, start calling yourself an actor and begin your hunt for auditions and work. No one can dispute that you're an actor. You may be a lousy one. You may be a prodigy. You may even be an out-of-work actor. Some of the best often are. The fact remains, there is no university degree, no board oversight, and no license of any sort upon which your decision or prerogative to act depends.

Why is this chapter so far back in the book? Shouldn't training come first? It depends on whom you ask. Traditionalists insist that you must prepare rigorously before you try your hand at acting. Others insist that, particularly in TV and film, training is not an essential first step. They hold up as proof stars who are reputed never to

> 1990   The Children's Television Act requires additional educational content from broadcasters. Barney the purple TV dinosaur is three years old and going strong.
>
> 1990   Kevin Costner's *Dances With Wolves* is first Western to win Best Picture Oscar since *Cimarron* in 1930.
>
> 1990   First dial-up commercial Internet provider, The World, is launched.

have studied seriously. "Are you kidding me? Look at Russell Crowe. The dude's a genius. He won an Oscar and he's had no formal training at all, not a bit of it!" Well, maybe. Less far-fetched are cases of individuals who work regularly not because they are talented but because they have a look that is in demand. A man I met at an audition said that his mullet has earned him nearly fifty thousand dollars since 1999. Everyone agrees, however, that it is necessary to receive training of some sort, at some point in your ascent, if you are to sustain a career in showbiz.

This stands to reason. In a business that is fiercely competitive, any advantage you can grab is worth grabbing. If you're serious about a career in acting, then you must seize any educational opportunity you can. You will learn something or meet someone that will benefit you in some way. Of course it's a gamble every time you sign up for a class and some training can be worse than none at all. But, as Anna Freud said, "Creative minds have always been known to survive any kind of bad training."[1] There's also the important benefit of listing your education on your résumé. That can help tip the scales in your favor when you are competing for a role with other actors who have not had it.

> Jack Lemmon recalled his early days under director George Cukor: "Every time I'd deliver my lines, he'd say, 'Less.' After several times of hearing him say 'Less' after I'd finished, I said, 'Mr. Cukor, if you keep it up, I won't be acting at all.' And Cukor said, 'You're beginning to get it, my boy'."[2]

Educational opportunities can take various forms, from the highly formal, like a bachelor's or master's degree, to the shorter, less structured offerings like improvisation workshops. Whether you realize it or not, you've been training all your life. From the moment you smiled as a child or threw your first tantrum, you were on your way to becoming an actor. If you have the slightest doubt about this, observe any kid between the ages of two and five. Note how masterfully they slip in and out of the many roles in their repertoire. One moment they can be content and quiet; the next they can wail like a mad monkey. Tears can pour heavy down their bereaved faces until you succumb to their petulance. Now the falls of grief suddenly run dry as glee washes over the little ruffians.

This uninhibited state, this childlike carte blanche to immediately shift to the forefront whatever emotion and behavior suits the moment; that is the Holy Grail of acting. If you could magically peel away the many layers of psychological armor and social conditioning that your years have cast you in, you would be an electrifying actor. Without exception, this is what all acting schools of thought are after. They go about it in vastly differing ways but are all designed to help you let go, shed inhibitions, become a child again, short of pooping your pants. Unless, of course, you feel a pressing need to actualize your character in that way.

> Attempt the impossible in order to improve your work.
>
> — Bette Davis

MAJOR ACTING THEORIES

Whatever others may tell you, there are only four fundamental theories on acting, and they're all related. You could spend months studying the history and theory of

> It is intimacy and the total revealment of self that makes for a good screen actor.
>
> — Gregory Peck[3]

acting, and maybe you should. For now, let me summarize the four theories using my own grossly simplified terminology.

THE MONKEY SEE MONKEY DO APPROACH

We are all disciples of this theory, whether we know it or not. It is everybody's and nobody's school. It has no structure and no guidelines. It is utterly free of method or system or premeditation. It is the theory upon which you can hang your hat as a beginner but not for long. At some point you'll realize that you're under-equipped and that a random-walk approach to this profession is inadequate. It is

> 1991   The World-Wide Web is born.
>
> 1991   *Beauty and the Beast* from Disney is first animated film nominated for Best Picture Oscar, wins two for Original Song and Original Score.
>
> 1991   The Soviet Union is nyet. Reagan credited with toppling the "Evil Empire."
>
> 1992   75% of U.S. households have VCRs. Spending on buying or renting video tapes more than doubles movie box office.

based on that coarsest of social behaviors, mimicry. You have an idea how to act sad or happy or concerned or whatever because you have seen others do it. The limitation of this acting philosophy is that it is at best mechanical and at worst feeble. Actually, it is at worst utterly absent. By that I mean that just knowing how you ought to act devastated does not mean you'll be able to conjure up the illusion when you need it. Achieving that kind of readiness comes with training, practice and lots of both.

THE OUTSIDE-IN APPROACH

When playwrights and actors realized that Monkey See Monkey Do had limitations, they set about developing a more scientific approach. The poster child of this school is François Delsarte (1811-1871). This inventive Frenchman devised a presentational system—he called it a language—of acting. It focused on associating specific expressions, gestures and body positions with corresponding representations. He was building on the germ of an idea, earlier discussed by playwright Denis Diderot, that an actor faces a paradox: the only way for him to portray reality is through artificiality.[4] In other words, you are faking what you're doing so well that it appears real.

Delsarte's is a mechanical approach. If you want your audience to see that your character is sad, you must hunch your shoulders, cock your head slightly, look down, and perhaps place your right hand on your left breast. Or something like that. If you want them to hear sadness in your voice, you must speak in subdued tones, slowly, and once in a while choke back an imaginary lump in your throat. Whatever the desired emotion: terror, remorse, expectation, hope, determination, scorn or contempt—Delsarte codified over a thousand gestures, body positions and expressions. If you would like to see a great example of the Delsarte approach, rent any silent movie. A particularly impressive though exhausting specimen is Griffith's *Birth of a Nation*.

> 1993   Brandon Lee is shot dead with a prop gun during filming of *The Crow*.
>
> 1993   *Cheers* airs final episode.
>
> 1994   Steven Spielberg, David Geffen and Jeffrey Katzenberg form DreamWorks SKG.
>
> 1994   The Northridge quake rattles L.A., killing seventy-two. It is the costliest natural disaster in U.S. history to that time.
>
> 1994   Tom Hanks wins his second Best Actor Oscar in a row for *Forrest Gump*. In 1993 he had won it for *Philadelphia*.

THE INSIDE-OUT APPROACH

Be a tree.

Now be a sad tree.

There is very little question that the theories and work of Constantin Stanislavski (1863-1938) represented a major shift in the craft of acting. Stanislavski, who was director at the Moscow Art Theater, developed what has come to be known as "The Method." At its heart is the notion that, above all, an actor's performance must be real. It must come from an actor's own emotional experience, rather than a contrived set of emotions and actions that are thought to be appropriate for the role. It's a simple and compelling idea. Getting there, sadly, is very difficult indeed. Many have taken

> The Method, which seems even more confused than politics, is merely the sum total of the experience of the great actors throughout all ages and countries.
>
> — Lee Strasberg[5]

Stanislavski's basic concept and worked to interpret and refine it. Among them are the late Stella Adler and Lee Strasberg of The Actors Studio.

Adopting The Method as your approach to acting demands a level of commitment, dedication and focus that eventually weeds out the irresolute. A truly capable actor, a Method actor, has you believing that he or she *is* the character. Examples include Marlon Brando in *On the Waterfront* (1954), Jack Nicholson in *One Flew Over the Cuckoo's Nest* (1975), Al Pacino in *Scarface* (1983) and Susan Sarandon in *Dead Man Walking* (1995).

> 1995   A standard is defined for the new DVD format.
>
> 1995   The fifty-two games of the World Cup of soccer are viewed by a cumulative 33 billion people around the world.
>
> 1996   Communications Decency Act prohibits dissemination of indecent material on the Internet. It is ruled unconstitutional in 1997. Seemed the decent thing to do.
>
> 1996   18″ digital satellite dishes hit the market. A bazillion channels now offered.
>
> 1996   Four of five nominees for Best Picture Academy Awards are by independent studios. *The English Patient* wins.

THE HYBRID APPROACH

If you watch the late Uta Hagen on video teaching an acting class, you'll see that she used a combination of all the previously mentioned approaches. She insisted that, whereas it's important to prepare emotionally—from the inside out—there is no acting without the body. In her workshops she developed a series of exercises that focused the actor on specific actions in specific situations. In summing up one such session, she said: "All the exercises should, ideally, set up an automatic rehearsal process, so that you'll rehearse all day long." No matter what an actor happens to be doing, she encouraged him to constantly practice "self observation." This awareness of oneself acting naturally becomes the foundation, the reflexive inventory on which the actor draws when in similar situations on-set.

> Laurence Olivier always focused on the onstage illusion of acting, as opposed to the Stanislavski technique of "becoming" the character offstage. When Dustin Hoffman, his co-star in *Marathon Man* (1976), showed up on the set looking properly haggard for the part he was playing after deliberately avoiding sleep for two nights, Olivier couldn't help teasing him. "Dear boy, you look absolutely awful," he cried. "Why don't you try acting? It's so much easier!"[6]

YOUR OWN APPROACH

In practice, an effective and evocative performance is alchemy. It takes emotional and physical elements and transforms them into indisputable reality. If the performance is too mechanical and systematic and relies on a Delsartian approach, it will surely seem wooden, just as the silents seem to us today. On the other hand, if the performance totally disregards convention, it will confound the audience.

> 1997   *Titanic* dominates the year and the Oscars, receiving a record 14 nominations and 11 wins. Neither Leonardo DiCaprio nor Kate Winslet receive Oscars. The top acting awards go to Jack Nicholson and Helen Hunt for *As Good As It Gets*.
>
> 1997   The Mini DV digital video cassette is introduced. This new digital recording format allows copies without loss of quality.

With time, each actor develops his own system and his own preparation rituals. As a rule, however, actors go through certain obligatory phases in delivering a good performance. You might want to consider these for your own groundwork:

★ Analyze the part and establish the character's motivation. What does this character want? How does the character interact with the other characters in the script? What is the character's contribution to the story? Why is he behaving in this particular way? Where is he? Remember: Who, What, How, Why and Where?

★ Prepare yourself emotionally for the role. Especially if you are a Method actor, this means looking inward and finding the situations in your own life that elicit the emotional memory that will energize your performance.

★ Prepare yourself physically for the role. How does this character walk, sit, stand, turn his head or move his mouth. Does he have particular physical quirks that help the audience understand him? An extreme example of this would be the role of Felix Unger in *The Odd Couple*, or Detective Monk on the TV series *Monk*, starring Tony Shalhoub. In both cases, the characters are obsessive and their physical quirks are pronounced. Generally you needn't go to such lengths but should give your character their very own physicality.

> I did a lot of plays, a lot of failures...My theory was that the only way to learn was to keep working. Maybe other people could learn from books and classes, but I had to get up there to do it.
>
> — Carl Malden[7]

★ You must also prepare vocally. This is part of an actor's ongoing training but takes special immediacy when preparing for a role. It's obvious when an accent or dialect is called for, as in Frances McDormand's riveting work on *Fargo* (1996). But it can be subtle, as in Will Smith's *Ali* (2001).

★ Learn you lines. Strong though you may be at improvisation, a script is there for a reason: to provide the words that you are expected to use. Directors tire very quickly of actors who fail at this most fundamental of actor preparations.

TYPES OF SCHOOLS AND PROGRAMS

LIFE

Lessons acquired in the school of hard knocks are probably the most memorable. Ordinary situations are full of instructive moments. Everyone is our teacher in the school of Life. For an actor, people-watching is a tool of the trade. This is partly what Uta Hagens taught. Just as self-observation can be a form of continual rehearsal, so people-watching can be a form of inspiration.

> 1998   Bob Barker's *The Price is Right* airs its 5,000th episode on CBS.
>
> 1998   The American Academy of Pediatrics says that by the time he's eighteen, the average American teenager will have watched 25,000 hours of TV, more than time spent learning in the classroom.

INSTITUTIONS OF HIGHER LEARNING

The gold standard is the Master of Fine Arts (MFA) with an emphasis on performance or acting. This is typically a two-year, sixty-credit program that follows a Bachelor of Fine Arts (BFA) degree.

> To get started as an actor it takes a lot of luck. You've got to keep at it, keep working. Little parts, big parts—keep working. Keep knocking on doors and one day, one of those doors will open and you'd better be good, 'cause it's not gonna open again.
>
> — Director Arthur Hiller[8]

Many universities in the U.S., including the following in the Los Angeles area, offer BFA and MFA degrees: California State University (CSU), University of Southern California (USC), and the University of California in Los Angeles (UCLA).

TWO-YEAR COLLEGES

If a BFA or MFA is not in the cards, there is always the option of a two-year Associate of Arts (AA) degree at one of the many community colleges that offer programs in theater arts or drama. A few also offer programs in TV and film production. The latter programs, though not specifically focused on performance, are excellent all-round training for the aspiring actor because they familiarize you with all the elements of the work. An actor who understands what goes on behind the camera is likely to be better than one who doesn't.

Los Angeles City College offers a two-year Actor Training Certificate. Long Beach City College has an AA degree program in theater with emphasis on acting.

WORKSHOPS & SEMINARS

This category includes all organizations that offer acting and related instruction but are not two- or four-year schools and therefore are not subject to the same accreditation bodies. Los Angeles is full of schools offering acting workshops. Visit www.google.com, click on "Local," and search for "acting workshops" in Los Angeles. You'll get scads of hits!

The Acting Corps Actors' Boot Camp is a good example of the type of program you might expect to encounter. This is a daily, four-week course that immerses students in Method technique, scene study, cold reading, on-camera and voice and speech training.[9]

Another school that has become something of an institution in the Los Angeles area is Milton Katsela's Beverly Hills Playhouse.[10]

And of course there is The Actors Studio in West Hollywood, in which life membership is free as long as the actor passes two auditions in front of members of the organization. The Actors Studio is not a school in the traditional sense of the word and it is not for beginners. It is rather a workshop in which professional actors gather to work with each other and to test and refine their craft. Anyone over eighteen and with the requisite training may apply for membership. But beware; this is the big

> I had ten years of dramatic lessons, diction, dancing...then the studio made a test. Well, they didn't like my nose—slanted this way a little. So I went to a doctor and had it fixed. They made more tests and were crazy about my nose. Only they didn't like my acting.
>
> — Betty Schaefer (Nancy Olson)
> in Sunset Boulevard (1950)

leagues. It took Al Pacino three tries to get in. Information is available from The Actors Studio, Inc., 8341 DeLongpre Avenue, West Hollywood, CA 90060-2601, Phone: 323-654-7125.

Online

"You Must Act!"

Apart from that driving urge that you feel if you have read this far into the book, "You Must Act!" is also the title of an acting course that is offered via online download or on CD by Bob Fraser.[11]

Entire books are offered online. *The Actor's Roadmap of Essential Actions* is a lucid discussion of acting technique. The book can be read online at www.home.earthlink.net/%7Eactorsroadmap.

Nowadays, there is a treasure of resources online for any field of interest. If you do not have online access, get it. If you have it, use it often as a tool to learn more about your craft. It is available free at most libraries. Websites exist that allow you to submit yourself for auditions, that provide advice and tips for actors, that connect you with people who are in the same boat and with whom you can commiserate and share information. Any organization in the world that is worth knowing about has a website. Appendix C, "Online Resources" contains a list of some of the most useful sites for the beginning actor.

Books

It will eventually be possible, though not desirable in my view, to do without books. Almost all relevant human knowledge will be accessible online. Google has launched a project to scan the world's greatest works of literature. E-books are already widely available.

1999	The Y2K scare comes and fizzles.
1999	TiVO debuts.
1999	*Blair Witch Project* costs $25,000 to produce, grosses $240 million. It takes eight days to shoot. That's 960,000% return on investment (ROI).
1999	*Star Wars, Episode I – The Phantom Menace* grosses over $430 million. Costs $115 million. That's 370% ROI.

Until that happens, and even then, you'll find a wealth of information and inspiration in books. If you paid for this one, you know what it's like to own a book and mark it up as you please and return to it as you might to a favorite place or person. If you're reading it at the library or have borrowed or stolen it, please go buy one. Or two.

Among the best books on acting technique are the following:

Respect for Acting by Uta Hagen

The Art of Acting by Stella Adler

An Actor Prepares by Constantin Stanislavski

Being and Doing: A Workbook for Actors by Eric Morris

To The Actor by Michael Chekhov

Between them, these books will expose you to more acting theory than you'll know what to do with.

PERIODICALS & MAGAZINES

An actor's education includes current events. You must know who's producing what, where, and when. There are numerous periodicals and tabloids that deal with showbiz. The advantage that these have over books and even online resources is that they are new every time and the information within them is up-to-the-moment. The granddaddy of showbiz trade papers is *Variety*. It has daily, weekly and online editions. Many more publications exist. See appendix F, "Publications."

> I play John Wayne in every part regardless of the character, and I've been doing okay, haven't I?
>
> — John Wayne

COST

How much will training set you back? There is a wide range of fees. Group workshops can run from $100 to $500 a day. Individual sessions from $75 to $500 an hour! Tuition costs range from $3,000 per year at a two-year community college to $25,000 per year at a private four-year school.

> Eli: You did that very well.
>
> Cameron: Hey, I just listened.
>
> Eli: There are a few actors only in the entire world who have mastered that art.
>
> — Director Eli Cross (Peter O'toole) to unwitting stuntman Cameron (Steve Railsback) in Richard Rush's *The Stuntman* (1979).

Don't acquire big debts to finance your acting career, even if you must compromise and go to a less prestigious school. As you saw in chapter 1, "Money Matters," it will be difficult to make a living in acting. Starting with a deficit could make it just about impossible.

1. Anna Freud is not merely the daughter of Sigmund, but also the mother of child psychoanalysis. She knows a thing or two about education.

2. Boller, *Hollywood Anecdotes*, 137.

3. Ibid., 127.

4. Denis Diderot, *The Paradox of the Actor* 1773 (New York: Hill and Wang, 1963).

5. Cindy Adams, *Lee Strasberg: The Imperfect Genius of the Actors Studio*, (Garden City, NY: Doubleday & Company, 1980), 7.

6. Boller, *Hollywood Anecdotes*, 170.

7. Paul Zollo, *Hollywood Remembered: An Oral History of Its Golden Age*, (New York: Cooper Square Press, 2002), 77.

8. Asher, *The Actors at Work Series*.

9. http://www.theactingcorps.com.

10. http://www.katselas.com, 245 S. Robertson Blvd., Beverly Hills CA 90212. 310-855-1556.

11. http://www.youmustact.com.

☆

Chapter Ten

PERFORMERS
UNIONS

This is a pivotal, challenging
time of change in our country
and within the American labor
movement. The road ahead
won't be easy...But nothing
worth accomplishing ever
comes easy.

— Alan Rosenberg

SAG President

☆

I just think that the unions realize they have to be more flexi-
ble. The people that live here
want to work here,
but if it's cost-prohibitive,
people go elsewhere.

— Spike Lee

☆

☆

Why JOIN a performers union? Easy: at some point in your career, you will be obligated to. This is the result of hard-fought agreements between employers and the major performers unions. It is best illustrated by example. Suppose you are the producer of a TV drama that employs a number of principals and extras. Your contract with the Screen Actors Guild (SAG), the union under whose jurisdiction your show operates, states that all your principals and the first twenty extras you hire will be members of SAG. It's that simple: if an actor wants to make a career on TV or in feature films that are produced by the major studios, he or she will eventually have to join the American Federation of Television & Radio Artists (AFTRA) or SAG. Of course it is possible to never join a performers union if you plan on working only in non-union projects. That strategy's trade-offs are discussed later in this chapter under "The Paradox of Membership."

There are numerous unions and guilds that represent performers and other professionals in showbiz. Here's a partial list:[1]

Actors' Equity Association (AEA)

Alliance of Canadian Cinema, Television & Radio Artists (ACTRA)

Alliance of Motion Picture & Television Producers (AMPTP)

American Guild of Musical Artists (AGMA)

American Guild of Variety Artists (AGVA)

American Federation of Musicians (AFM)

American Federation of Television & Radio Artists (AFTRA)

Directors Guild of America (DGA)

Producers Guild of America (PGA)

Screen Actors Guild (SAG)

Writers Guild of America (WGA)

THE BIGGIES: SAG, AFTRA AND AEA

SAG and AFTRA are the two most important unions if you're trying to make it in Hollywood because they have agreements with producers of film and TV and because they represent performers who work on union productions. I include Actors' Equity Association (AEA) because a significant minority of TV and film actors also does theater.

SAG

SAG's website provides the following description of the organization:[2]

> Screen Actors Guild is the nation's premiere labor union representing actors. Established in 1933, SAG has a rich history in the American labor movement, from standing up to studios to break long-term engagement contracts in the 1940s to fighting for artists' rights amid the digital revolution of the 21st century. With 20 branches nationwide, SAG represents nearly 120,000 actors in film, television, industrials, commercials and music videos. The Guild exists to enhance actors' working conditions, compensation and benefits and to be a powerful, unified voice on behalf of artists' rights. SAG is a proud affiliate of the AFL-CIO.[3]

To join SAG you must satisfy one of the following three conditions:

★ Work for one day as principal performer on a SAG project. We have the Taft-Hartley Act to thank for this. See glossary.

★ Work as a background performer on a SAG project under a SAG voucher for at least three days.

★ Be a member in good standing for at least one year in an affiliated union and work as a principal performer during that year. This includes AFTRA, AGMA, ACTRA and AGVA. To navigate this alphabet soup, please refer to the list earlier in this chapter.

SAG offers a wide range of benefits and services to its members. For questions and to request more information you can reach them at:

2000   Time Warner and AOL merge.
2001   *Gladiator* wins Best Picture and Russell Crowe wins Best Actor Oscars.
2001   *Harry Potter and the Sorcerer's Stone* grosses nearly $320 million.

Hollywood National Contact
5757 Wilshire Boulevard
Los Angeles, CA 90036-3600
323-954-1600 Main Switchboard
www.sag.org

AFTRA

AFTRA's website describes the union as follows:

The American Federation of Television and Radio Artists (AFTRA) is a national labor union representing nearly 80,000 performers, journalists and other artists working in the entertainment and news media. AFTRA's scope of representation covers broadcast, public and cable television (news, sports and weather; drama and comedy, soaps, talk and variety shows, documentaries, children's programming, reality and game shows); radio (news, commercials, hosted programs); sound recordings (CDs, singles, Broadway cast albums, audio books); "non-broadcast" and industrial material as well as Internet and digital programming.[4]

To join AFTRA you must meet only one condition: have the money. The union's website states that you must have performed or intend to perform in one of the

| 2000 | HDTV technology is used for the first time in a Hollywood feature film, Clint Eastwood's *Space Cowboys*. |
| 2000 | DVD movies rival VHS tape. |

union's jurisdictions. That's the same as saying you just have to have the money. The initiation fee in 2005 is $1,300. Annual dues are calculated on a sliding scale that is pegged to earnings. If you earn $2,000 or less in one year, your annual dues will be $127.80. As you earn more your dues will increase to an annual maximum of $2,025.00.[5]

AFTRA, like SAG, is affiliated with the AFL-CIO. In fact, AFTRA and SAG collaborate on a number of joint projects and initiatives and often negotiate in tandem.

AFTRA's Hollywood offices are at the following location:

5757 Wilshire Boulevard, 9th Floor
Los Angeles, CA 90036
323-634-8100
www.aftra.org

AEA

AEA's website states the following:

Actors' Equity Association is the labor union representing over 45,000 American actors and stage managers working in the professional theater. For 90 years, Equity has negotiated minimum wages and working conditions, administered contracts, and enforced the provisions of our various agreements with theatrical employers across the country.[6]

The criteria for joining Equity are similar to SAG's:

★ Employment under an Equity contract.

★ A minimum of one year's membership in a sister union.

★ Participation in AEA's Membership Candidate Program.

Actors' Equity Association western regional offices are located at:

Museum Square
5757 Wilshire Boulevard, Suite One
Los Angeles, CA 90036
323-634-1750
www.actorsequity.org

It's nice when things are convenient. SAG, AFTRA and AEA have all thoughtfully situated their offices at 5757 Wilshire Boulevard. A trip to this building and you can, in one swell foop, gather up all the information you want on these three stalwart pillars of organized showbiz.

THE PARADOX OF MEMBERSHIP

The paradox of membership is that, like everything else in life, you have to give up something to get something else. When you join a union you give up the prerogative of working on non-union projects. On the other hand, you become eligible for union work and the higher wages that it entails. Where's the rub? It's in the numbers. If, for argument's sake, there are more non-union parts up for grabs than union parts, and your odds of getting non-union work are significantly higher, then it may make more sense for you to stay non-union. I've talked to many actors who have found that SAG membership caused their career to slow. Is that because there are fewer SAG jobs than non-union jobs? Is it because the caliber of SAG talent is higher and therefore non-union actors find themselves out of their league? Could it be because their agents are not SAG-franchised and so do not get the same attention from casting directors who are working on union shows? Could be any or all of these things.

2001   The world is shocked by the World Trade Center and Pentagon attacks. Live TV airs the carnage. *The West Wing* postpones its season premiere, quickly produces a new script and shoots the episode in two weeks. It is titled "Isaac and Ishmael" and airs on October 3rd.

The membership paradox is almost intractable because there's no perfect data on what proportion of projects is union. An analysis of three months of casting data on Casting Networks reveals this much:

Analysis of Projects by Union Affiliation

	Number of Projects	Percentage of Total
ACTRA	1	0.10%
AEA	5	0.65%
AFTRA	23	3.00%
AGVA	2	0.25%
SAG	133	20.00%
Union Subtotal	**164**	**24.00%**
Non-Union Subtotal	**517**	**76.00%**
Grand Total	**681**	**100.00%**

In other words, for every union project, three non-union projects are available for self-submission.

In background work there is a compelling reason to think that gaining union status is not necessarily a good thing. Producers have agreed to minimum levels of union background players on TV shows and film. Union TV shows must hire a minimum of twenty union extras before they can begin to hire non-union actors. In feature films that number is fifty. Actors who derive a good chunk of their income from background work may find that they work less if they join a union. On the other hand, they earn double what they otherwise would. For a detailed discussion of this issue, please refer to "The Almighty Union Voucher" section in chapter 5, "Work."

2002   *General Hospital* airs 10,000th. episode. Its debut was in 1963.

2002   *The George Lopez Show* premieres on ABC.

2002   *Spider-Man* is released and grosses over $400 million.

2003   First camcorder is released that allows direct-to-DVD recording.

Another element to consider in your decision to pursue or avoid union membership is benefits eligibility. If you stick to non-union work, you will not receive any benefits. That much is certain. Joining a union does not guarantee you benefits eligibility either, but at least you have a shot at it. SAG offers medical insurance and retirement benefits with a catch. In order to qualify for these benefits you have to earn a minimum of $13,000 or have seventy days of employment in one year on SAG projects. If you refer to chapter 1, "Money Matters," you'll immediately realize that this is more than most SAG members will earn or work. It follows that most SAG members therefore never qualify for benefits.

2003   Arnold Schwarzenegger is sworn in as governor of California.

2004   *The Lord of the Rings: The Return of the King* wins the Best Picture Oscar.

2004   *Shrek 2* earns more in gross receipts than any previous animated film.

Well then, what do you do? Do you join or not? There is no answer that applies all the time to everyone and, what's more, either decision is risky. Here are the two courses of action and how to assess them.

Join the union if:

★ You have no choice. In other words, you have already worked the maximum number of union jobs without having to join and you have just been offered a union role that you cannot pass up.

★ You are serious about a career in broadcast TV and features.

★ You have the initiation fee. It is approximately $1,500.

Do not join the union if:

★ You don't have to and can still work union parts at union rates. Remember, you can work two union jobs before you are obliged to join. It's that third one that pushes you up against it.

★ Intend to focus on areas of work that are typically non-union, like industrials and independent films and print.

★ You think that you can work three times more, as a non-union actor, than if you joined the union. You'll earn as much, even if it's three times as hard to do it.

These guidelines will sharpen your thinking on the subject. But your decision depends on personal circumstances and your unique perspective. If you have an agent, ask him for advice.

There is another aspect to the paradox of membership. As a member of the union, you might have to strike. If you strike, you don't work. The 2005 SAG election gave the union's leadership to groups who have promised a tougher stand in negotiations with producers. There is a chance that, when it's time to renegotiate the guild's contract, disagreement may lead to a strike. Hopefully it won't. Keep an eye on this situation when you become eligible for SAG membership.

FINANCIAL CORE

If you think there may be a way to have your cake and eat it too, you'll want to explore something called Financial Core status. This is a thorny issue that gets every SAG official's dander up. It is essentially a way for you to do both union and non-union work. How can that be? Well, it's the law. Specifically, it is the consequence of a 1983 U.S. Supreme Court decision against compulsory unionism. Here's how it works:

> 2005   Passengers on a JetBlue airliner watch live on-board as news channels report on their plane's crippled nose gear. Has reality TV gone too far?
>
> 2005   Alan Rosenberg defeats Morgan Fairchild and Robert Conrad to become president of the Screen Actors Guild.

★ Join SAG when you have to.

★ Continue to audition for non-union roles.

★ If you land a good non-union part, send SAG a letter resigning as a full member and opting instead for Financial Core status.

You can now work on non-union projects without fear of suspension from SAG. But there are other consequences. Most serious is the possibility that you won't be readmitted to full membership when your career takes off and your earnings qualify you for the health and retirement benefits that the union offers. Also you can't vote. Of course you will still be paying dues. Then there's the stigma that comes with Financial Core. Union actors, whatever the law says, are not going to be delighted to see you if they know that you are doing non-union work.

There is no easy answer to the Financial Core question. Keep the option in your back pocket. If you

> "Well," he said, "it's taken me forty years of doing it for a living to learn the secret. I don't know that I want to give it away." Urged, he relented. "Okay," he said, "I'll tell you. The art of acting is—learn your lines."
>
> — Garson Kanin from an interview with Spencer Tracy[7]

find, after you've joined SAG, that you are working far less and having to pass on many non-union projects, Financial Core may be a useful course of action. Discuss it with SAG, with

> Financial Core is an individual liberty issue protected by the U.S. Supreme Court.
>
> — Charlton Heston

your agent, and with people whose opinion you value. It is not a trivial decision.

If you wish to explore Financial Core further, you may want to purchase Mark McIntire's *Financial Core Handbook*. The 2004 edition costs $22.95. More information is available at www.markmcintire.com.

☆

1. http://www.agentassociation.com/frontdoor/links.cfm.

2. SAG, About SAG, http://www.sag.org/sagWebApp/application?origin=hnav_bar.jsp&event=bea.portal.framework.internal.refresh&pageid=Inside+SAG.

3. SAG & AFTRA concluded negotiations in 2005 of a new three-year contract with the studios and networks. This contract goes into effect on July 1, 2005 and expires on June 30, 2008.

4. AFTRA, http://www.aftra.org/aftra/whatis.htm.

5. AFTRA, http://www.aftra.org/member/dues_calculation.htm.

6. AEA, http://www.actorsequity.org/AboutEquity/index.html.

7. Garson Kanin, *Tracy and Hepburn: An Intimate Memoir*, (New York: Bantam Books, 1970), 7.

☆

Chapter Eleven

DIARY

I cannot talk, I cannot sing,
Nor screech nor moan nor anything.
Possessing all these fatal strictures,
What chance have I in motion pictures?

— 1929 *Photoplay Magazine*

☆

The best laid plans of mice and men
often go awry.

— Robert Burns

☆

☆

So far in this book I have laid out specific steps that you can take in pursuit of your goal to be a working actor. The roadmap to stardom looks good on paper. In life, however, things rarely go exactly as planned. So, to complete the picture, this diary chronicles my own attempt to follow the roadmap. The entries are in chronological order. Each heading shows the actual date and the nature of the event.

Please approach this section of the book as an exploration. Look through it as you would a curio box. It is full of facts, like names of casting directors and production companies and studio addresses and such. But its best value is in giving you a real sense of time and sequence of events, as well as how I felt as I went through various steps of the roadmap. You may relate to and gain some consolation from knowing, for example, that you are not alone if you feel nervous at an audition. Or that sometimes the phone doesn't ring for what seems like forever. On the other hand you will see that there is a lot of pleasure and reward in working in Hollywood, sometimes in the most unexpected places and at the most unexpected times. Also, as you read this diary, you will react as you do when you read anything: it will give you ideas. It will get you thinking about approaches that you had not considered or, just as likely, how you might do things more effectively than I did.

☆

TUESDAY, JUNE 2, PHOTO SHOOT

I'm surprised that Joan Lauren wants to do the photo shoot outdoors. I sort of expected to be in a studio with lights and makeup and all the rest of it. Nevertheless, she comes very highly recommended and her website is impressive.[1] A few days ago I sent her a snapshot of myself via email. Sure enough, she called and suggested a couple of wardrobe options. Seeing my picture helped her figure out what would look better on me. So here I am in this parking lot at Marina del Rey when she drives up. It's a weekday morning; a little foggy so the light is diffuse. Should make for good pictures. Not many people around. Just as well; I'm not sure I'd feel comfortable doing this in front of a crowd. Joan has used this lot before. She quickly hangs a backdrop against the wall of a storage shed and sets up her camera. We shoot for about two hours. That works out to a little more than $200 an hour. It may seem like a lot, particularly since some photographers or studios will charge that much for an entire session, but I'm going on my good friend Sibel's recommendation. Sibel Galindez (neé Ergener) knows her way around Hollywood. She lived here for years and had considerable success as an actress, including a number of appearances on *JAG*. When I first got the idea to have a go at acting, she was extremely helpful and generous with advice and contacts. I figure a recommendation from her is solid.

Joan shoots four rolls of film in the time we spend together. She is easy to work with. We do a few shots of me in my car and others of me walking on the beach. The rest are three-quarters or head-and-shoulders shots against the backdrop. I do three looks, including suit, jeans, and shorts with short-sleeve Polo. Meantime I'm thinking, hell, if I never even act in anything, at least I'll own some good photos of myself while I still had my looks, such as they are.

☆

TUESDAY, AUGUST 26, ORDERED FINAL HEADSHOTS

I don't know why it's taken me so long to get to the point of ordering my headshot. I guess part of that is that I've also wanted to order a zed card. My strategy here is to hedge my bets and be prepared for acting or modeling jobs, whatever comes first, assuming something does.

To model, it turns out, you need a zed card, which is two-sided and has a number of different shots as well as measurements. So I've taken a whole lot of time researching printers and finally settling on Imagestarter in Hollywood. All in all I wound up spending $150 at the lab and $350 at Imagestarter.[2] The $350 included three hundred 5"x7" zed cards and one hundred 8"x10" headshots as well as some additional prints of shots that I liked in the proofs and wanted to keep for when I no longer have hair.

I'm very happy with the way the pictures have turned out but the proof of the pudding is in the eating and we'll just see if I get any calls when I send them out.

☆

THURSDAY, OCTOBER 30, MAILED HEADSHOTS TO AGENT LIST

I'm having trouble getting this thing started. Even though I had the photo shoot with Joan nearly four months ago and have had the prints ready for nearly three months, it's just now that I'm getting to the first real step in the roadmap, trying to get an agent. Part of the problem has been where to get a reliable list. I was also traveling during September. Then there's that procrastination thing. Anyway, finally downloaded a list of agencies from Casting Networks' website and have prepared a simple cover letter stating that I am looking for representation. Now I'm sending that out to about 110 commercial and theatrical agents and hoping to get a couple of hits. I'm putting a cover letter, headshot and zed card in each manila envelope and keeping my fingers crossed. Each package costs about $2 tops for the envelope, the postage, the cover letter paper and printing. So the whole mailing is setting me back nearly $220. Including the photo session and printing, all in all I'm $1,000 or so into this. I could've bought a round-trip ticket to Tibet.

☆

MONDAY, NOVEMBER 2,
ALESE MARSHALL STUDIOS, TORRANCE
ORIENTATION MEETING

That was fast. Got a call from Alese Marshall inviting me in for an orientation meeting. Alese is a hospitable and pleasant woman who says that she has been involved in modeling and acting for many years. She introduces me to Ken James, her lead acting instructor. The Alese Marshall Talent Agency is also a school.[3] Alese points out that there is a lot of work for people in my age group—late forties to early fifties—and she recommends the TV Commercial Class. However, although Alese's organization appears legitimate and her credentials and those of Ken James substantial, this is not a talent agency that is licensed by the State of California. It cannot act as my agent.

FRIDAY, NOVEMBER 7, KELLOGG COLD READ AUDITION
CASTING AGENT: DANIEL HOFF
1800 HIGHLAND, SUITE 300
LOS ANGELES, 90028
ROLE: EXTREMELY ZEALOUS KELLOGG EATER

I was happy to get a call from Daniel Hoff Agency saying that they had received my headshot submission and inviting me to come in for a cold read. So far this is the third response out of the hundred agencies that I mailed headshots to.

Now here I am at my first-ever audition. I'm standing in a narrow hallway. Fifty others are standing around or sitting on the floor or pacing. There's a faint but pervasive body odor. All are preparing for their moment in front of the camera. It's tense in here. A "cold read" or a "cold reading" is where you show up at an audition, are handed something to read and get very little, if any, time to rehearse. Most of the people waiting in this hallway are in their twenties. I walk inside the office and am directed to add my name to the sign-up sheet. There are two long pages of names ahead of mine. The nice young woman at the desk says, "Help yourself to sides." I have no idea what she's talking about. My vacant expression betrays me so she reaches across the desk and hands me the dialogue I'm expected to read. So "sides," it turns out, is the actor's portion of a script or dialogue. Go figure.

I take my sides back into the hall and find a corner into which I face and begin to prepare for my reading. I'm nervous as hell and a little self-conscious but am heartened by many others doing the same thing, some with abandon. Maybe too much abandon. One guy, about twenty years old, short and hyper, may as well be on his own planet. He is reading his lines over and over again at normal volume, utterly oblivious to the rest of us. A number of others in his immediate vicinity keep giving him dirty looks but he is either too focused or too thoughtless to care. He'll probably be the one to make it; the next Brad Pitt.

The dialogue is asinine. It has something to do with really, really wanting and needing in the worst way the Kellogg cereal in question. I just can't get into it. I have trouble doing irrational exuberance.

A spindly, Chinese young woman with long black hair down to her tush invades my space, takes off her shoes and begins to repeat the dialogue into the wall while rocking on her heels. I flash on a visit I once made to the Wailing Wall. Then, bam, she turns to me and says:

"What's your name?"

I tell her.

"Hm," she says, "funny name."

"Heh, yup, it's actually an abbreviation. My real na..."

She smiles—actually she grimaces but I know that she means to smile—and interrupts: "I'm Sue." She gives me her hand. "Where're you from?"

"Lebanon," I say.

"Huh?"

"You know, Beirut? Over there on the Mediterranean."

"Oh, yah, my geography is soooo bad."

"Don't be too hard on yourself."

"You been acting long?"

"Nope, just starting out."

"Cool. Can I have your phone number?"

I hand her my business card, return to my sides and dig deep for the emotional memory I need to joyfully declare, "Gotta have my Kell..."

The audition itself is quick, like an inoculation. My name is called. Julie comes to the door and leads me to a back room where a small video camera is set up on a tripod. She tells me to stand at the spot marked— that's why they call it a mark—with tape on the floor. I do. Now Julie says, "I'm just going to slate you." I must look adrift because she goes on, "Face the camera and say your name, then turn to show profiles." I do all this and am happy that, apart from not knowing what sides and slate are, I have not done anything else dreadfully humiliating.

"Now," she says, "go ahead and read your lines into the camera, and have fun with it!"

Ahem—Okay. I wonder if she can hear my knees knocking.

Trouble is I know and she knows that I can't summon up the requisite enthusiasm. I'm about as miscast selling cereal to an American audience as, say, Joe Pesci narrating *A History of Britain* to the House of Lords. Still, I give it my all. Julie says: "Good job!" Bless her heart.

I had waited forty-five minutes in the hall but the audition itself is over in two minutes and she escorts me out graciously, gathering another hopeful actor in the front office and taking him back with her. It must be tedious work, having to be kind all day long to people like me.

On the way home the 405 is jammed and my car is acting up again. It has the famous self-leveling suspension that must have looked really slick on paper when Jaguar engineered it into these 1988 XJ6s. Trouble is the thing goes spastic on a regular basis and begins to arbitrarily raise and lower the rear end. Here in L.A. where you're only as hot as your car, nothing entertains the beautiful people in their Mercedeses and BMWs and Hummers and Porsches more than an old, convulsive Jag.

My mobile phone warbles. It's Sue. She's calling to ask me out. I apologize and stutter a bit as I prepare to politely inform her that I am in a relationship. She hangs up before I finish my sentence. That's Show Business! Or, as the late Julia Phillips calls it in her tell-all *You'll Never Eat Lunch in This Town Again*, the "Business of Show." I guess there was nothing more to discuss.

☆

FRIDAY, NOVEMBER 7, SIGNED WITH AN AGENT

My second meeting today is with Victor Kruglov. He called when he received my headshots. Victor is a man of few words. He calls himself Russian but is technically Ukrainian and speaks with a distinct though not unintelligible accent. We meet at his office on Beverly Boulevard. A long bank of windows reveals a panoramic view of the Hollywood Hills. The walls are covered with autographed photos of celebrities and stars. Everywhere there are stacks of headshots. Victor is a one-man show and the process of signing up is painless. He used to be a SAG-franchised agent but no longer is. I'd be concerned about that but I have no idea what I'm doing. The agreement he asks me to sign requires that I pay him 15% off the top for any work I receive directly or indirectly through him. It's a single piece of paper. Time kills deals so I sign before he has a chance to change his mind. What the hell! We'll see how it goes. It's not like I have a lot to lose. For all I know, he may be the only real agent to call. And anyway, even though he's a bit laconic, I like him.

☆

MONDAY, NOVEMBER 17, *NEXIUM IV COMMERCIAL* AUDITION
CASTING DIRECTOR: DANIELLE ESKINAZI
LOCATION: CASTING UNDERGROUND
1641 NORTH IVAR, HOLLYWOOD 90028
ROLE: GOLFER

Victor, my brand new talent agent from yesterday, calls. Because of his accent it takes me a minute to realize he is saying "audition" and not "admission." Also he calls me "Roof." He has been in this business for nearly twenty years and knows that the only real money for opportunists like me—as opposed to passionate actors who are doing it for art's sake— is in commercials. His plan is to submit me for as many of these as he can and hope that I have the right look for one of them. For this one he says I must dress like a golfer and show up with an actual club. I go to Big 5 Sports and buy a five-iron for $19.95. The audition is at the Casting Underground on North Ivar. Parking is always a problem in L.A. but I find an abandoned lot up the street that has a booth and signs but no attendant. I take a chance and leave my car there. Most car thieves are above boosting this old heap. Five-iron in hand I make my way back down the street. A thirty-something fellow all in red golf attire is leaving the building as I get to it. He's carrying a driver and has a bounce in his step. As he passes me he touches the tip of his cap and nods. Top o' the afternoon to ya, Paddy, I think to my distracted self. The Casting Underground, not unexpectedly, is in the basement.

I sign in and fill out a size sheet. I now know what sides are and fear-lessly ask for them. Several other men ranging in age from the mid-thir-ties to the mid-fifties are here and most are carrying golf clubs. This is much more my demographic than the cereal people. I feel less jumpy than I did at the Kellogg read. We are sorted into groups of four. When my foursome is invited into the studio, we are asked to set our drivers and irons aside. Turns out the scene is in the clubhouse and we are hav-ing a drink after our round. *Note to self: Don't take Victor's instructions literally.*

As we walk in the casting director looks us over and asks me if I have an accent. Damn, I know the answer to that one but does he want me to have one or not? I say I do so he assigns me the role of Man #4, who has no lines. I don't mind. I sense that he's looking for white and black middle-aged guys. Probably not a Latino and certainly not a Middle Easterner, both beige. Those last two are my looks.

The scene is simple. We're sitting around a table. Man #1, #2 and #3 read the few lines of dialogue from cue cards on an easel. I nod and react meaningfully. The whole thing is over in five minutes.

Already it's obvious to me that getting work as an actor will not be an easy thing. First I was most concerned about being too anxious or inept to win a part. Now I see that the single biggest hurdle is the sheer number of competitors. This is a buyer's market. A whole lot of other guys in my age group are out there hustling as well. Most look to me like they know what they're doing. I leave the audition not at all hopeful that I'll be called back.

Postscript: Never heard back but I did see the commercial on the air and, indeed, there were no beige golfers involved.

☆

MONDAY, NOVEMBER 17, *MISS MATCH* AUDITION
NETWORK: NBC
CASTING AGENT: ZANE PILLSBURY
LOCATION: 1800 STUART
SANTA MONICA, 90404
ROLE: MR. BEDI

I'm early. The casting director isn't here yet. There's a script lying on a table by the audition room door so I pick it up. I hope I don't get busted. I already downloaded the sides at www.lacasting.com, but peruse the rest of the script, searching for the essence of my character, the backstory. Sheesh. Any minute now someone's going to call out, "Impostor!"

Actors start to arrive. One woman is in a sari and looks like she just stepped out of a taxi in Bombay. I tell her this. She's delighted, particularly since she's Armenian. Nothing in Hollywood is what it seems to be. Or you could say that everything in Hollywood is something else. The cameraman and the casting director arrive. My name is first on the sign-in sheet and I get called first. I immediately torpedo any chance of getting this part by plopping down on the couch next to the casting director. I may as well be wearing a big sign that reads: Fifty-Year-Old ROOKIE. She nevertheless directs me politely to the chair facing the camera. I hand her my headshot. I have no résumé, of course, and they diplomatically overlook that.

I begin to read but soon stumble. One of Mr. Bedi's lines is marked "Mrs. Bedi" on my copy of the sides—could have been a printer smudge—so I gaze meaningfully at the young man reading Mrs. Bedi, hoping that he will go ahead and utter the blasted line.

"Um, Rif...your line."

"My line?"

"Uhuh."

"It says...ahem...Mrs. Bedi."

"Does it? Hm."

"That was very good, thank you," says the casting director, breaking the impasse. She's being courteous as heck but I can see the pity in her eyes. No surprise. I expect to run into embarrassing situations in which my ignorance and lack of training are exposed, but I am determined to shrug them off. My immediate goal is to not be the very worst on any given audition. Second-worst is fine. Just so I know that someone else is wasting the casting director's time even more shamelessly. Not the case today. The only way someone could be worse today is if they threw up on-camera, *on* the camera.

Hollywood people are polite. You might not have expected this if you've read some of the horror stories in the folklore. In fact they go out of their way to be kind and gentle, particularly at auditions. Nobody wants to hurt your feelings or demean you. That's because they understand the fear that comes from trying to do this for a living. Also because as careers come and go, it's truer than ever in Hollywood: you pass the same people on your way down as you do on your way up.

Back at the apartment I run into my neighbor Catherine in the elevator. She's an actress. I tell her that at the rate things are going, getting actual work for actual pay is going to be tough. She asks if I've considered doing extra work. "Um...no, I haven't," I say, trying hard to seem cavalier about that option, like I've known about it all the time but have been too busy managing my wide-ranging assets to bother. In truth I am utterly surprised to hear of such a possibility and I can tell that Catherine suspects as much. She suggests that I go see Central Casting in Burbank and register with them. That's how she pays her bills, doing extra work between speaking roles. Her eyes say: "Dude's clueless."

☆

SATURDAY, NOVEMBER 29, CENTRAL CASTING
LOCATION: 220 SOUTH FLOWER STREET
BURBANK, 91502
818-562-2755

I've taken Catherine's advice and driven up to Burbank to register with Central Casting. As usual in L.A., parking is a pain in the butt. I'm a couple of blocks away and notice several other people hunting for spots. I'm sure they're on their way to Central Casting as well. It's amazing how many people want to get into acting!

The process is surprisingly simple and, inside of an hour, they've taken my picture and my $25 registration fee, I'm in their database and can now begin to prospect for extra gigs. Central hands me a brochure for Extras! Management, which is a calling service that's located across the street, so I go over and sign up.[4] A calling service, I learn, is a company that does the legwork for background actors by calling and securing gigs through Central Casting and other extras casting agencies.[5] If you don't hire someone to do this, you yourself have to call daily and listen to recorded announcements of available roles, then speak to a casting director and try to get them to book you. Sounds like an awful lot of work to me. Chris at Extras! Management takes my picture in three different changes of clothes—I'm changing, not him—then goes over the rules with me. The most important is that once I'm booked, *I'm booked*. If I don't want to work on a particular day, I must call ahead of time and let them know I'm unavailable. But heaven help me should I get booked then call to say I'm unavailable.

I leave, dubious that I'll get called at all but prepared to write off the $68 I paid Extras! Management for this coming month's service. Not two hours later—about as long as it takes for me to drive back to Hermosa Beach—they call to say that I am booked on *JAG* the following Monday! My first gig as an extra! I have no idea what to expect but am more excited than a Pug at a dog social.

☆

MONDAY, DECEMBER 1, *JAG* EXTRA GIG
NETWORK: CBS
EPISODE: GIRL'S BEST FRIEND, # 194
START AT 9:00
WHERE: JAG STAGES, 28343 CROCKER AVE, VALENCIA
ROLE: CIVILIAN STREET ATMOSPHERE
SCENE: EAST COAST WINTER
PAY: $59

My first, paid showbiz job. I'm here along with about twenty other people, young, old, male, female, we make quite an assortment. Some look like they know just exactly what they're doing. I am completely at a loss and follow people around ears wide open.

JAG stages are in Valencia, thirty miles north of where I live, so I set out very early and arrive an hour ahead of call time. The very first person I meet in this new career is Ann-Marie Elia, a friendly and engaging young stuntwoman. She has been in L.A. for a few months. Her plan is to do background work, take classes and train while she works on getting stunt work. As we chat, other extras arrive and join us in the dingy room they call Holding.

"So, how long've you been doing this?" Says Ann-Marie.

"One day."

"You're kidding."

"Nope."

"Hm."

I'm sure people must wonder why someone storming fifty would be messing around with this kind of thing. But I see a lot of older people doing background work and auditioning. Of course most roles call for young people—Hollywood didn't get sexy doing geezer flicks—but there are also many, many more younger people competing for those roles.

Alan, the 2nd AD, shows up and invites us to follow him. We trail along goose-file to another part of the studio where we line up again, this time to be inspected by Wardrobe. Then we fall in behind Alan again and return to Holding. An hour later, just as I'm starting to nod off, we get called to the set.

My thespian exertion for the day consists of a walk past Petty Officer Second Class Jennifer Coates (Zoe McLellan) and Mattie Grace (Hallee Hirsh) who are having a chat in the street. I am paired with Betsy who, thankfully, has been acting for a while and knows just what to do. On the 1st AD's command, we walk into the scene, past the principals, off camera, then back again. We do several takes and then all the extras are wrapped for the day. It isn't even noon. This is my kind of workday!

Postscript: When the episode aired a few weeks later I saw myself on television. It was exciting but very brief. I was satisfied to see that I looked, as I was supposed to look, cold.

☆

THURSDAY, DECEMBER 4, *DAWN COMMERCIAL* EXTRA GIG
SHOW TITLE: DAWN CHALLENGE
LOCATION: IRWINDALE SPEEDWAY, IRWINDALE 91706
STARRING: ROBBIE KNEIVEL
CASTING DIRECTOR: DEBE WAISMAN
ROLE: BLEACHERS SPECTATOR
PAY: $50

This morning I'm en route to the Irwindale Speedway. This is a cattle call, Hollywoodese for an event at which hundreds of would-be actors or models are called up to audition for a role or, in the case of extras, to populate a set that requires a big crowd. I arrive and discover that the front parking lot is already full. A uniformed attendant directs me to the back lot. Holy cheap labor! Can there be this many people here? From that lot it's a half-mile walk to the area where the casting agency has set up a couple of kiosks to check in the one thousand extras called for this event. The lines are long and it's a cold morning.

We're shooting a commercial for Dawn, the dish detergent. Robbie Knievel, a renowned stuntman like his dad Evel, will jump his motorcycle over a hurdle built from ten thousand dishes that have been washed with just one bottle of Dawn. Only in America! I'm wondering why anyone would choose this line of work. I'm also wondering why anyone would call their kid Evel.

Extras arrive in shifts, starting at 6:00 a.m. After getting checked in we proceed to an outdoor dining area where we are served a simple breakfast of scrambled eggs with a little salsa and a tortilla. The plates are then washed by a platoon of extras hired expressly for that purpose. A couple of cameramen are milling about recording all this activity. After breakfast we all shuffle along to a grandstand and sit and wait and wait and wait while the plates are stacked in preparation for the big jump.

Even though this is just my second day as an extra, I run into people I met on the *JAG* set last week. Ann-Marie the stuntwoman is here. This is right up her alley. So is Ehécatl, the Mexican who is named for the Aztec God of Wind and Weather. He looks like a Native American action hero and has a master's degree in drama. Ehécatl is bound to do well. We are joined by others and in no time have formed a small clot of conversation. The producers of the event have provided a pudgy emcee and a DJ spinning everything from hip-hop to oldies. Somehow five hours pass, the plates are all stacked—final count is about thirteen thousand—and Bobbie Knievel makes the jump. Then he rolls up to where we're sitting and exclaims, "I'm gettin' too old for this!"

We figure that's our cue and set off a dignified stampede toward the checkout area. There is a lot of queuing in the life of an extra. You line up to check in, you line up for Wardrobe, you line up for meals, and you line up for checkout. Sometimes this lining up happens outdoors. Often you're shivering or sweating, depending on the day's weather. We've done both today.

Again the lines are long but I'm close to the head of one of them. This is a good thing because, unexpectedly, my agent calls to say that I have an audition in L.A. "Roof," Victor says, "I khave awdition for you in Khollywood. Eet is for Toyota Toondra. The casting agent is Anissa Williams. You must dress like feesherman. Aaddress ees 8899 Bayverly Boulayvard." I love this guy. Luckily I'm in jeans, a denim shirt, and a sleeveless black fleece jacket; close enough to what a fisherman might wear. I can drive straight to there and make my audition. This time it works out but I can see how I might have trouble balancing extra work with auditioning. If Victor calls and I'm unable to go to an audition because I'm working background, he is sure to wonder why the hell I'm wasting his time. Going to have to deal with this before it comes up.

☆

THURSDAY, DECEMBER 4, *TOYOTA TUNDRA COMMERCIAL* AUDITION
CASTING AGENT: ANISSA WILLIAMS
LOCATION: CASTAWAY STUDIOS, 8899 BEVERLY BLVD.
LOS ANGELES, 90048
ROLE: FISHERMAN

I arrive at Castaway and see a horde of men in jeans, button-down denim or plaid shirts, and fishing jackets. There are several studios here auditioning different groups of actors for various projects. An array of tall, slinky, young women adorns part of the foyer. They're here for a Guess audition. The fishermen are happy.

I approach the sign-in table and am greeted by Anissa's assistant, a young man with spiked blond hair. He collects my headshot and snaps a Polaroid of me. He can tell I'm curious and explains that these are just for ID purposes since headshots are designed to make their subjects look just as good as possible. Sometimes they become "glamour" shots that bear little resemblance to the actual human whom they depict.

I hang out in the lobby. People are pacing and reading lines and otherwise keeping themselves occupied but there's very little idle chat. That's because, beneath our placid exteriors, most of us contain a rich mix of fear, anticipation, adrenaline, and hope, to say nothing of the ongoing fantasy that Fame is behind the audition studio door. Soon I'm called in with three other guys. Half a dozen creative types occupy couches in the back of the room, behind the camera. I know enough by now to guess that this is not the first round of auditions. Those are usually not attended by the production folks. Across from this gallery of judges four chairs are arranged in two rows of two to simulate the interior of a Toyota Tundra. The four of us auditioners are asked to slate. It's a good old-fashioned lineup. We each state our name and height. The two guys to my left both say they're six feet tall. This is awkward because I'm 5'10" but it's clear for all to see that I'm just as tall as one and taller than the other. I'm tempted to also overstate my height but opt for truth and say 5'10", to which half the room smirks and at least one of the people on the couch raises a quizzical, plucked eyebrow.

In any case, we are asked to enact a scene in which the four of us are getting back into the truck after a day of fishing. There's no dialogue. Thank God. I'm in the back seat. We open the imaginary doors and climb into the imaginary truck—I feel that my door-opening is really lame and glance enviously at the guy playing the driver; his is much more compelling. I figure if I were really just getting into the truck following a full day of fishing, I'd be tired, drunk, or both. Well into my character now, I close my eyes, yawn and stretch luxuriously, accidentally kicking the chair of the driver. It's a minor thing but missed by no one in the room. They're thinking: the man can't stretch his legs without ruining a scene. We're thanked politely by the couch-people and leave. The driver gives me a parting look that's part disdain and part amusement.

I don't yet know enough about this business but it sure looks like these auditions are a numbers game, especially in commercials where it seems that look is almost always more important than acting ability. For all I know the other guys in the room have résumés as long as my arm and all kinds of training. How much difference can that make when the audition consists of pantomiming getting into a car?

Now absent-minded in my real car on the way back to Hermosa Beach I realize that I'm tailgating a Toyota Tundra. This is a good omen, a sign from Genesius, the patron saint of actors. This unfortunate sap was an actor who received the divine spirit while on stage making fun of Christianity. Well, he converted right there on the spot. Bad move. The Romans took his head off. Talk about lousy timing!

Postscript: Genesius must be busy. I never hear back.

☆

FRIDAY, DECEMBER 5, *WITCHES OF THE CARIBBEAN* AUDITION
TYPE OF PROJECT: FEATURE FILM
CASTING AGENT: VALORIE MASSALAS
LOCATION: 10990 WILSHIRE BLVD.
LOS ANGELES, 90024
ROLE: MAGISTRATE

A few days ago I subscribed to Showfax and Actors Access. Now I can view breakdowns and submit myself. This is my first self-submission and I got an email yesterday requesting my presence for a 2:00 p.m. audition. I show up noonish, hoping that I can be seen early. The lobby is full of young women here to read for the part of Bethany. It's tough enough dealing with rejection when you're my age and swarthy. Must be really hard when you're young and beautiful. Paul, the casting coordinator, agrees to let me read but is not happy about my premature arrival.

Nevertheless, he's civil and leads me into the studio where an inscrutable woman is sitting on the couch. Another, younger man, probably a casting assistant, reads the other parts.

I feel good about this one, better than the *Miss Match* audition. Here I make it through with no stumbles. Still, I really don't know what I'm doing nor what the casting folks are looking for. I'm going to have to take an auditions workshop; this is trickier than I thought.

Postscript: No callback. This is getting old in a hurry.

☆

Friday, December 5, *U101* Audition
Type of Project: Industrial Non-Union
Production Company: Pilgrim Films
Casting Agent: Extras Casting Guild
Location: 4730 Woodman Avenue
Sherman Oaks, 91423
Role: Hamoud

Carla Lewis from Extras Casting Guild calls.[6] She saw my submission on Actors Access for the role of Hamoud or Abou Fahd in an industrial production titled, simply, *U101*. Pilgrim Films is making it. They have a lot of work to their credit, including *American Chopper*, one of my favorite shows on Discovery Channel.[7]

The audition is at Pilgrim Films' offices in the Valley. The hallway is full of Middle Eastern-looking men and a few young blondes. I sign in and receive my sides. The dialogue is between a moderate Pakistani journalist and an extremist Muslim cleric. I'm not sure which they want me to read so I study both. When I'm invited into the conference room, I find two men at the other end of the table from me. One of them operates the camera. I read Hamoud's part. They both nod and ask me to read it again, this time with a heavier accent. I'm thinking, hm, that's a good sign. I read Hamoud's part again. They nod again and ask me to read Abu Fahd's role. I do, twice. I know I've done well. It felt right. These are both serious roles and that's what I like. I have trouble smiling or laughing on command because my face turns to wood.

That's two auditions I've gotten from submitting myself online at www.actorsaccess.com. The fee is $68 a year. I just need to land one part and it'll pay for itself. Seems like the perfect tool for actors who don't have agents.

☆

SUNDAY, DECEMBER 7, *DOG SHOW COMMERCIAL* EXTRA GIG
PRODUCTION COMPANY: CAN-DO PRODUCTIONS
WHO: DEBBY AT BACKGROUND TALENT
START AT 9:30
WHERE: GRAND OLYMPIC AUDITORIUM, 1801 S. GRAND, L.A., 90015
ROLE: SPECTATOR
SCENE: DOG SHOW
WARDROBE: BUSINESS CASUAL LIKE FIRST DATE, WEAR ONE AND BRING
TWO CHANGES. NO GREEN.
PAY: $80 FOR 10 HOURS

This is my second cattle call in a row and I'm not very happy about it. Once again I'm part of a huge group of people who have been called up to play an audience. This time we're make-believe dog enthusiasts, watching a make-believe dog show that will be the commercial vehicle for Eukanuba pet foods.

One guy in front of me is silently rehearsing lines. A young woman is reading a book about post-production. Every once in a while the acting show-dogs go by and we are directed to applaud. Dummies populate the back rows. Not idiots, but stuffed facsimiles of humans that are far enough from the camera and the lights to appear like actual people on film. It's weird to be sitting next to them. Makes for a cold reminder of the extra's place in this business. There oughta be a law.

There are two food tables set up no more than ten feet apart. One is for the cast and crew. The other is for us, the extras. There is quite a difference. Ouch. For that matter, we are getting paid $80 for ten hours' work. One of the other extras complains that the dogs are getting $500.

As an extra you have to overlook a number of indignities. You could argue that indignity is in the eye of the beholder and there's merit to that argument. Still, there's no ignoring the class society that is Hollywood. The hierarchy of the business seems almost as rigid as in the military. If you don't know your place it's only a matter of time before someone points it out to you.

On the way home I call Extras! Management and ask them not to book me on any more cattle calls. Ever.

☆

MONDAY, DECEMBER 8, *CENTURY CITY* EXTRA GIG
NETWORK: CBS
EPISODE: SWEET CHILD OF MINE, #5
WHEN: MON. 12/8 AND TUE. 12/9
START: 7:00 A.M.
WHERE: EL SEGUNDO STUDIOS, 2265 E. EL SEGUNDO BLVD.
ROLE: JUROR
SCENE: COURTROOM
WARDROBE: YEAR 2054, VERY MODERN DRESS, CLEAN LINES. NO BLACK.
WEAR ONE AND BRING TWO OTHER SELECTIONS. MOST MODERN SHOES,
DARK SUIT, 3 OR 4 BUTTONS, BRIGHT SHIRT.
PAY: $100, $108

Working as an extra is perfect for people who enjoy meeting colorful individualists and wackos. I use the term affectionately. We are all, in our way, wackos. Today I'm a juror in a futuristic courtroom drama called *Century City* that has been sold to CBS and will begin airing mid-season. It's a two-day call, so I get to know a number of the background actors quite well. I also get to chat with some of the principals and guest stars on the set, including Richard "John Boy" Thomas and Gregory Jbara, both affable men. Another guest star on this episode is Rebecca McFarland, who plays the demanding role of Mrs. Jansen. I'm so impressed with her performance that I approach her following the scene and tell her that.

This turns out to be an eleven-hour day, the highlights of which include Mary, a skinny, somewhat gawky woman in her forties who has a permanent expression of near-panic. She claims to be a psychic dog whisperer and apparently takes out-of-body excursions often. She says that she belongs to a commune in Oregon, takes something called BH3 and knows the guy who formulates it. I'm not sure what BH3 is but will be steering clear of it. When we get on the set, she and I sit in the jury together. At one point during a take (during the take!) she begins to poke her finger into the back of the man playing jury foreman. This guy is not an extra but an actual speaking actor. I'm bracing for a train wreck but he ignores her utterly. Later, Mary buttonholes the director on his way to the bathroom. She wants to discuss the episode, which deals with the ethically thorny issue of preselecting a child's personality before it is born. The director stops and listens politely for a few seconds then, when the necessary computations had taken place in his brain and confirmed that this woman will keep talking as long as he stands there, he says, "ah...gotta go!" and walks off. Mary turns to me and rambles on.

Then there's Chuck, an elderly man who likes to hover. I suffer from personal space deficiency (PSD). People immediately sense it and ask if they can move ahead of me in a queue, or approach for a chat, or hit me up for money. Chuck detects this and shuffles over. Now, with not so much as a how-do-you-do, he gets right up close and whispers, "I'll tell you this because I like you. I've been with a lot of women. I'm 68 years old and I still like to...You know." (Here he pokes me in the solar plexus and winks). "Sure, I need a little help now, like half a Viagra— Y'gotta look out for your prostrate [sic]." I introduce him to Mary.

Some sets are friendlier than others. I mean by this the degree to which extras are allowed to move about the set and mix with the principals. *Century City* is a fun show to work on for that reason. All the people involved are provided the same food. No one objects to my walking around the set, discreetly watching the monitors during shooting, or fraternizing with the talent. This is vastly better for us extras than, say, the arrangement on the *Dog Show Commercial* set. The only concession extras are asked to make here is to let the cast and crew eat first. Some principals grab a tray and sit right there at the long tables with everyone else. Others will take their tray to their trailer and eat alone. This is their prerogative, of course, and there's certainly lots for them to do, like memorize lines and prepare for the next scene.

Postscript: According to her alma mater, Rebecca McFarland has quit the business since that episode of "Century City." In addition to being a good actress, McFarland has the grit to say in an interview with Look@Tulane: "What it comes down to in Hollywood is, you get a job because you look right. It really has nothing to do with talent. I knew that and I worked that. I took care of myself, I wore the right outfits. But then I thought, 'This is what my life is about? Finding the right outfit?' It wasn't fun any more."[8]

Postscript II: According to Internet Movie Database (IMDB) at www.imdb.com, McFarland may have returned to the business of show, appearing in the movie "Play Dates" (2005) and on several TV programs. It would be a shame for someone this good not to act.

☆

WEDNESDAY, DECEMBER 10, *CROSSING JORDAN* EXTRA GIG
NETWORK: NBC
EPISODE: ALL THE NEWS THAT'S FIT TO PRINT, #54
START AT 12:30 P.M.
WHERE: UNIVERSAL STUDIOS
ROLE: DETECTIVE
SCENE: CENTRAL PRECINCT HALLWAY
WARDROBE: DARK SUIT
PAY: $54

Who is Brad English? You'd recognize him if you saw him because he's been on TV since the seventies. He's appeared as a guest star on everything from *Kojak* to *Dallas* to *Frasier* to *The Practice*. I meet him on the set of *Crossing Jordan*. He's a guy's guy, a big bear of a man with an easy disheveled manner and a casual charm. I recognize his face but have no idea who he is or what he's appeared in until we get to chatting. Turns out we both have lower back strain and are fighting to stay fit and keep our weight down. I tell him that Richard Thomas, whom I'd met on the set of *Century City*, keeps his weight where he wants it and stays looking trim by fasting one day a week. Name dropping? Who, me? I mention Brad because he seems to me the epitome of the working actor, an unpretentious professional who has done this work for a long time and is much like the rest of us, as opposed to the stereotype we carry in our minds of Hollywood actors. Most actors, those that are actually making a living in this business, are like Brad. They deal with the same issues as the rest of us.

I spend most of the day on the set with a gregarious and chatty black man in his forties who looks a lot like Lou Gossett Jr. This guy's story is amazing. A few years ago he was attacked outside his home, stabbed multiple times and shot four times by two assailants. Somehow he survived and looks no worse for the wear. He's indestructible—the 50 Cent of the extra world. The two of us are in the scene. We play detectives who walk through Central Precinct behind Dr. Mahesh "Bug" Vijayaraghavensatyanaryanamurthy (Ravi Kapoor) and Woody Hoyt

(Jerry O'Connell), two of the show's principals. Between takes I wind up talking to Ravi. He's originally from Liverpool and has only been in the U.S. for five years. I've spent some time in that part of England so we at least have the weather to talk about, agreeing quickly that southern California is a far gentler place to live, certainly warmer.

These conversations with the principals are helping me see what makes for a good actor. Watching them perform is better than school. There is nothing theoretical about it. What's happening right here is what winds up on TV or in the cinema. Seeing it in process and then seeing the final product is a great way to get an overall sense for how actors and directors collaborate in producing high-quality shows.

As I hang out with a few of the other extras outside the sound stage, someone says, "There goes Chad." "Who's Chad?" I ask. "He's one of Central Casting's union casting directors," replies one of the guys. So I march on over to Chad and ask the question that I had repeatedly been warned not to ask. "So," I say, casually ambivalent, like I'm asking for the time, "how does a person go about getting a SAG voucher on this show?" Chad head-fakes and ducks into the production trailer, where he knows I cannot follow. There must be something to the Almighty SAG Voucher question.

☆

THURSDAY, DECEMBER 11, *DEATH ON THE KALAHARI* AUDITION
TYPE OF PROJECT: SPOOF ON REALITY SHOWS
CASTING AGENT & EXECUTIVE PRODUCER: SHER SIMONE
LOCATION: IFP WEST, 8750 WILSHIRE BLVD, SECOND FLOOR[9]
LOS ANGELES, 90211
ROLE: FARMER JUSTIN, FARMER, HE AIN'T THE SHARPEST STICK IN THE PILE
BUT HE KNOWS ALL ABOUT PLANTS, "GROWIN' STUFF", AND HOW TO
READ THE WEATHER.[10]

Another audition through Actors Access. I'm one of the first people here, way ahead of my 3:25 p.m. appointment. Sher Simone arrives not long after and sets up the sign-in and size sheets. Another actor shows up. His call time is ahead of mine so he gets invited in first and is in there for a good ten minutes, quite a long time by audition standards. I'm next and have memorized the sides. There's quite a bit of dialogue. It surprises me a bit to find Sterling Tomas, who is the author and producer, in the studio. He's easy-going and friendly and asks me to read with Sher. I've rehearsed the part but can't concentrate. I just can't get into it and of course Sterling and Sher can see that. Nevertheless, they ask me to run through it twice more. Then the author says, "Excellent, thank you." Except that it wasn't.

Postscript: All quiet on the Kalahari.

Postscript II: As of October 2005, "Death on the Kalahari" is listed as a movie in development and a TV show in pre-production on Blue Palm's website at www.bluepalmproductions.com.

☆

THURSDAY, DECEMBER 11, *U101* AUDITION CALLBACK
PRODUCTION COMPANY: PILGRIM FILMS
TYPE OF PROJECT: INDUSTRIAL NON-UNION
CASTING AGENT: CARLA LEWIS, EXTRAS CASTING GUILD
LOCATION: 4730 WOODMAN AVENUE
SHERMAN OAKS 91423
ROLE: HAMOUD

I felt good about my chances when I left the first *U101* audition nearly a week ago. Sure enough, I've been invited for a callback. This time Jennifer, the young lady at the reception who is coordinating everything, recognizes and greets me warmly. That settles me down a bit. I'm given the same sides as last time but today I read for the director, Eddie Barbini. I Googled and IMDB'd him earlier. He's been at it for a long time and has amassed considerable credits. I'm a little intimidated. Surely if anyone can spot how green I am, it would be Eddie. He could laugh.

I walk in, shake hands and take my position at the end of the conference table, just like last time. I then read both parts, just like last time. Eddie says, "Thank you" and that's it. Perfect poker face.

☆

Friday, December 12, *NEC Commercial* Audition
Type of Project: Short Film
Production Company: Thin Man Pictures
Casting Agent: Anissa Williams Casting
Location: Casting Underground 1641 N. Ivar, Hollywood 90028
Role: Senior Scientist

Victor called. Anissa Williams, bless her, has invited me to read again, this time for a NEC short film. She had requested me for the Toyota Tundra audition earlier this month. Victor says it's a good sign when casting directors invite an actor back. It means that they're happy with his work. I'm a little surprised. I thought I had really blown the Tundra audition. This time I play Taggart, a senior scientist talking to a younger one. NEC is moving on to new technologies. I'm the old fart, the late-adopter. By the time I'm called in I've memorized my sides. Anissa reads the part of the younger man and I nail my lines. At the end she stands up, walks over, says, "Awesome" and high-fives me! I leave the place walking on air and excited about the possibility of getting my first commercial. So what if my best work is playing old farts.

At another studio the callback audition for Nexium IV is underway. I guess I won't be getting called back for that. *Note to self: return golf club to Big 5 store.*

☆

Tuesday, December 16, *JAG* Extra Gig
Network: CBS
Episode: People v. SecNav #196
When: 12/16, 12/17 and 12/18
Start at: 7:00 a.m.
Where: Dos Carlos Studios, Corner Mill and Conway
Role: Press and Foreign Dignitary
Scene: International Criminal Court
Pay: $90, $115 and $79

Three-day call. Nice. This is my second stint on *JAG* and a big episode in which the U.S. Secretary of the Navy appears in front of the International Criminal Court to defend himself against accusations of war crimes commission in Iraq. Art foreshadows Life.

A whole lot of us are here today: judges, dignitaries, press people, and of course the show's stars, Catherine Bell and David James Elliott. This is *JAG*'s ninth season and it shows in the efficiency of the cast and crew, which is not to say that things are serious—quite the opposite. Everyone seems to be enjoying themselves. The agitator in the group is unquestionably Elliott. Between takes he chats with various people, swears not infrequently and otherwise kids around. Catherine Bell is more reserved but friendly and lovely. Dean Stockwell, one of TV's most experienced actors, plays Secretary of the Navy. He's been in showbiz since the forties, with occasional sabbaticals, and has appeared in *Matinee Theater*, *The Twilight Zone*, *Dr. Kildare*, *Mission: Impossible*, *Bonanza*, and many other shows. Between scenes he retires to his trailer. A couple of times I walk by his open door and he appears to be napping. You must be one cool cucumber if you can nap between scenes. If there is one thing that sets good actors apart from the rest of us, it's that they seem utterly relaxed all the time on-set. Who knows what's going on inside, but they appear unconcerned in the slightest. Then, on "Action!" they smoothly shift gears into their character.

Being on a three-day shoot makes it possible to get to know the other extras. Among them, Nona gives me the following bit of advice: "If you really want to succeed at auditions, do exactly the opposite of the obvious action the script calls for. If it calls for anger, be sedate, if it calls for fear, laugh." I think that's from the George Costanza school of acting and will hold off trying it until I'm as famous as Jason Alexander.

There is a minor drama in the ranks of extras when a very old, very small Chinese man in the gallery issues a series of loud gastrointestinal objections during a very somber courtroom scene. Later he and his younger companion are quietly sent home. He doesn't seem to mind.

Easily the most fascinating individual I meet here is Jack Herman, 2nd AD and showman extraordinaire. Jack's responsibility is to manage the large gang of extras, about fifty of us. He has done this for years and has perfected his approach. He doesn't just choreograph our various comings and goings—the man entertains and edifies us. Most of the time his banter is light and amusing. Once in a while, though, if you're listening, he can part with some real insights. Among his choicest:

"If you're known as an extra, your chances of becoming a principal can be hurt. You may have to leave extra work behind. Odds are against you anyway. If one extra in this room makes it as a professional working actor, it's nothing short of a miracle. You gotta feed the kids. That's the decision you wind up making and the dream dies."

Jack can be frank and you may not like everything he says, but there is no question that the man knows his business and shoots from the hip. Think of it as tough love.

☆

MONDAY, JANUARY 5, *U101*. GOT THE PART! WOOOHOOOO!

Mike from Extras Casting Guild called to say that I've landed one of the principal roles on *U101*. I'll be playing Major Hafiz Mirza and should work at least three days. This is a non-union project so the pay is $200 per day. I'm so happy to have won an actual speaking role on an actual production that I'd have paid *them* for it.

So it is possible, even if you have no résumé and no training, to land a speaking role in a legitimate production. The trick is to go on as many auditions as you can and to prepare to the best of your ability, such as it is. All this time I've been worried about not getting a speaking part. Now I'm worried that I have. What if I'm late to the set? What if I can't remember my lines? What if I'm asked to smile? What if I have a panic attack and self-destruct in front of the whole cast and crew? A person could worry himself loony in this business.

☆

TUESDAY, JANUARY 6, *THREAT MATRIX* EXTRA GIG
NETWORK: ABC
EPISODE: EXTREMIST MAKEOVER, # 14
WHERE: DISNEY STUDIOS, 500 SOUTH BUENA VISTA, RIVERSIDE GATE
ROLE: PAKISTANI DIPLOMAT
SCENE: COURTYARD OF U.S. EMBASSY IN ISLAMABAD
PAY: $54

Some gigs are better than others. The ones I prefer involve some action and camera-time. Like sitting on a jury and reacting to the dialogue and the principals and the action. This is not one of them. I spend the whole day doing crosses well away from the camera. The only member of the cast that I recognize is Kelly Hu, who plays Lin. What's worse is that I bear a small indignity when I check in and report to Makeup. They say that I look perfect for the Pakistani Diplomat but that I could use a quick trim. As she cleans my neck with clippers the Makeup lady asks if I mind that she shave my spitter, my soul patch, that little tuft of hair growing immediately under my lower lip that I shape into an invert-ed triangle and that gives me the appearance of an artist, musician, drug dealer, pimp. It's my funky accessory, a Zappa tribute. But it also makes me look that much less like a cross between Saddam Hussein and Joseph Stalin. I say sure, even though I really want to say no way. But I learn a lesson: never again agree to any amount of manscaping for a non-speak-ing, non-featured, non-anything part.

Postscript: "Threat Matrix" was cancelled after shooting sixteen episodes and airing fourteen. Never did see it, won't take any of the blame. And anyway, I'm less excited now about the possibility of spot-ting myself on-screen for a nanosecond.

☆

WEDNESDAY, JANUARY 7, *CISCO COMMERCIAL* AUDITION
TYPE OF PROJECT: COMMERCIAL
CASTING AGENT: TLC, LOREE BOOTH
LOCATION: 6521 HOMEWOOD AVENUE, LOS ANGELES 90028
ROLE: CEO

I like auditioning for roles in a suit. I spent most of my working life as a suit. Understandably, these are the roles in which I am most at ease. Today I'm one of five CEOs, having dinner and commiserating about a network outage. The CEO using Cisco gear is quiet, until one of the oth-ers notes that. To which he says, "Our network did not go down," or something along those lines. The others make him pick up the check.

Postscript: I saw the commercial. The actors that were hired are per-fect for it. Still...You don't understand. I coulda had class. I coulda been a contender. I coulda been somebody, instead of a bum, which is what I am, let's face it. [Yes, I feel this way but the words are Terry's (Marlon Brando) in "On the Waterfront"].

☆

WEDNESDAY, JANUARY 7, *GREENLIGHT FINANCIAL COMMERCIAL*
AUDITION
TYPE OF PROJECT: COMMERCIAL
CASTING AGENT: MADILYN CLARK STUDIOS
LOCATION: 10852 BURBANK BOULEVARD, NORTH HOLLYWOOD, 91601
ROLE: GENERAL PUBLIC

Sometimes you know right away that things are not going to go your way on an audition. Like today. It takes me nearly two hours in gridlock to get to this building out in North Hollywood. The place looks like it could have been someone's house or a restaurant. It is just packed with people, among whom one young woman has brought her baby. There's no air in here. It's hot and stuffy and we're all fighting to get jammed together butt to kneecaps on the old furniture and folding chairs that line the narrow corridor. I go to sign up and realize that I don't have my headshots. Damn. Few things in life are more infuriating than one's own knuckleheadedness. Just then one of the lenses in my reading glasses just disappears. One minute it's there and the next it's not. I have two hopes of finding it in the brown, deep shag carpet–drum roll please–no hope and Bob Hope. On top of that, the sides make no sense at all. Mercifully, the casting director has realized that there are way too many people here to ever get caught up. Now she brings us in ten at a time and asks each to hold a name card and, when the camera is on us, react to the following statements:

"Bad credit?"

This is where we grimace and otherwise show dejection.

"But you fixed it!"

And this is where we beam with pride and joy.

I'll eat my shoe if I get a callback.

☆

THURSDAY, JANUARY 8, *IT AIN'T EASY* AUDITION
TYPE OF PROJECT: FEATURE FILM
CASTING AGENT: BALYNDAH BUMPUS
LOCATION: COLE STUDIOS, 6001 N. COLE, LOS ANGELES, 90038
ROLE: DETECTIVE

Several casting studios manage multiple projects simultaneously here, so the waiting area is crowded. Men playing detectives are being called in two at a time. I'm asked to read Detective #2 while the other man with me has Detective #1. I'm a little distracted and launch into his lines by mistake. You'd think that listening to simple instructions and following them is easy. Well, it isn't. In the heat of trying to remember the lines and morphing into someone else on very short notice, your mind tends to triage some things right out. Anyway, I apologize and we start over. I now have nothing to lose so put on a heavy *Scarface*-type accent. The other detective and I are talking to a badass perp being read by the casting coordinator. Detective #1 decides to embellish the script a bit as well. Most memorably, he unilaterally adds the word "Roadrunner" when addressing the bad guy. For example, "Listen, I know what you're up to" becomes "Listen, Roadrunner, I know what you're up to." Under most circumstances one word would not throw me but this particular word under these conditions slays me, so I laugh. A modest laugh. Sadly, I'm the only person in the room who thinks something is funny.

I'll eat my other shoe if I get a callback.

☆

MONDAY, JANUARY 12, *U101* PRINCIPAL PART
TYPE OF PROJECT: INDUSTRIAL FILM
CASTING AGENT: HEADQUARTERS CASTING
LOCATION 1: THE HERALD EXAMINER BUILDING, LOS ANGELES
LOCATION 2: CAL. STATE U., CHANNEL ISLANDS CAMPUS, CAMARILLO,
ROLE: MAJOR MIRZA
DATES: 1/12, 1/13, 1/16, AND 1/17
PAY: $200 PER DAY

Getting this part is an encouraging first proof that someone with no training, no experience, and no talent can land a speaking part in

Hollywood. Okay, so it's an industrial production and will never be broadcast, but that does not blunt my sense of accomplishment. And just three months after I started submitting myself for auditions. I had the faintest hope. *I'm on the...top of the wo-orld, lookin', down on creation...*

The first day of shooting is at the old Herald Examiner building on South Broadway and East 11th Street in downtown Los Angeles. This landmark, like his castle in San Simeon, was designed for William Randolph Hearst by Julia Morgan.

The other members of the principal cast are veterans of the trade and take in their stride the inadequacies of the location. There are no changing rooms so we occupy one of the many empty ones on the ground floor. All the little distractions fall away when we start shooting, except for the busy MTA buses that frequently pull in and out of the stop across the street. Every time one of them arrives or leaves, we have to hold the shoot until they're out of microphone range.

The remainder of the shoot is at the remote Channel Islands Campus of California State University. It's all the way in Camarillo, a long drive from Hermosa Beach. On the last day of shooting I am cruising to location on the 101 when traffic suddenly comes to a stop. Within minutes I'm at the accident and see two people on the roadway and a crumpled Harley under the rear bumper of a big white truck. I'm a motorcyclist; accidents like this one chill me. Not a good start to the day.

I play Major Mirza, swarthy Middle Eastern action hero. My men and I storm terrorist strongholds and roust evil-doers. In the last scene of the day I run across a courtyard with my squad of tough guys then race ahead and take forward position behind a barrel. I then signal them to follow. We do a number of takes. It's getting dark and cooler. Then on the fourth or fifth take I get to the barrel, skid on the damp grass and come up shins first under the front bumper of a big, white truck that is parked there, part of the set. It all happens very fast, as accidents do. My neck jerks and the back of my head connects with the ground. The pain in my leg wells up. A muscle in my side spasms. But the show must go on; no injury of mine is going to slow us down. I know it—drank the Kool-Aid. So I pick myself up, assure the director that I am okay, and do the shot one more time. Luckily that's it because now blood is seeping through my camo pants and my shin is swelling up. The set medic, a fire-fighter who moonlights on film productions, cleanses the scrape and bandages it up for me. The cast and crew shower me with kudos for bravery and toughness. Yup, you can't keep a good man down. Certainly not an actor of my caliber. But it has been a dangerous, off-balance day from the start. Ending it in one piece is my top priority.

I drive home very, very carefully, on the lookout for rogue bumpers on big, white trucks.

☆

WEDNESDAY, JANUARY 14, SORRY, I'M UNAVAILABLE TO AUDITION
CASTING: BOB MORONES CASTING
LOCATION: 4130 CAHUENGA, UNIVERSAL CITY
ROLE: CAUCASIAN MALE, JAMES BOND LOOK

Unfortunately, I have to turn this one down because I'm working on *U101* on the 17th, which is when this project is scheduled to shoot. It hurts to have to turn anything down. Who knows, this could be the one, the break that launches. But really, my chances of getting a part as a James Bond lookalike are remote, even if my mother thinks I can't lose.

☆

TUESDAY, JANUARY 20, *NAVY CIS* EXTRA GIG
NETWORK: CBS
EPISODE: ONE SHOT, ONE KILL #13
START AT: 6:30 A.M.
WHERE: LOS ANGELES GARMENT DISTRICT, DOWNTOWN
ROLE: NONDESCRIPT ATMOSPHERE
SCENE: STREET AND RECRUITING OFFICE
PAY: $54

At lunch in the big mess tent I overhear this conversation between two young men who are playing supporting roles in this episode:

Dude #1: I love bok choy.

Dude #2: Dude, yeah. So do I, totally.

Dude #1: So, uhm, do you live in a house or an apartment?

Dude #2: Dude, I live in a trailer!

Dude #1: Cool.

Dude #2: Yeah, it's a three-bedroom and two-bath and the view from my room is, like, the Pacific Ocean.

Dude #1: Sweet.

Dude #2: Oh yeah, I'm stoked. My roommate, y'know, owns it. Only problem is I can't stand his girlfriend.

Dude #1: She's dumb, huh?

Dude #2: Not exactly dumb, dude, y'know...I'm not sure how to explain it...Um...her parents are, like, super rich. She's from Santa Monica and, dude, she *knows* she's rich.

Dude #1: So what, she's snooty?

Dude #2: Naw, not really.

Dude #1: Stupid?

Dude #2: No, not stupid, exactly.

Dude #1: Some girls look smart but are really stupid.

Dude #2: Um...

Dude #1: Yeah, I dated this girl once, she was so frikkin' dumb but she was really hot so I dated her anyway. So, what was the deal with that chick, your roommate's girlfriend?

Dude #2: One time she asked me if my hair was wet–It was kinda greasy.

Dude #1: Dude, no way?

Dude #2: Yeah.

Dude #1: What does she care?

Dude #2: Totally.

Meantime, a grip is all the way up a telephone pole across the street bolting to it a safety harness for an actor who will later play a telephone company lineman. As the bolt bores into the wooden pole, it makes an excruciatingly tortured sound, like a squeaky door but many times more anguished. One of the guys in the crew shouts up to the grip on the pole: "Hey, leave that parrot alone!" Set humor–not fancy but it works.

I spend a lot of time today with Christie from Austin. She's studied acting and is serious about Hollywood. I admit that I'm trying to bluff my way to a career in showbiz. She says it's no good. Too many strong, trained, talented, good-looking actors out there. I'll get exposed for sure. In consolation she gives me the following tip: If you want your mouth to form natural and believable forms while you pantomime—something extras have to do a whole lot of—merely repeat the word "watermelon" continuously. Watermelon watermelon watermelon watermelon...She's right, though, I'm doomed.

Now we're shooting a scene on Broadway St. A dozen extras, including me, are hanging around waiting for the next take. It's taking forever. The camera is set up on a crane across the street taking a very wide shot. We busy ourselves by chatting with the storekeepers in this garment district. I buy myself an inexpensive black scarf and have a strange conversation with the lady who sells it to me. She follows me outside and froths into a litany of complaints about her husband whose waist, apparently, has gone from size 34 to size 44 since they were married three years ago. Just then her cell phone rings. It's him, asking her to come back inside the store.

When we finally get called for the shot, only one of the show's stars is involved: Sasha Alexander. She plays Kate Todd. We don't see Mark Harmon all day.

Who says background work isn't fun?

☆

THURSDAY, JANUARY 22, *JAG* EXTRA GIG
NETWORK: CBS
EPISODE: PERSIAN GULF, #198
WHEN: THU. 1/22 AND FRI. 1/23
START AT: 12:30 P.M.
WHERE: UNIVERSAL STUDIOS
ROLE: COFFEE HOUSE PATRON WITH CAR
SCENE: WASHINGTON D.C. IN WINTER, IRANIAN NEIGHBORHOOD
PAY: $144, $135

I'm sitting in my car, a 1988 Jaguar XJ6. Both of us, the car and me, have been hired as extras for this episode of *JAG*. There's a lot of activity on the set. We're shooting a Washington D.C. street scene. There are other extras with their cars parked at the curbs or waiting for "Action!"

It's taking a while to set up the scene. I keep busy disassembling the Jag's power antenna motor. It's been on the blink so I disconnected and pulled it from its bracket in the trunk and am now trying to figure out why the rotor that swallows or pushes up the antenna is jammed.

Since I am right there on-set in my car I figure I'll hear 1st AD Robert's call to roll camera, so I lose myself in my little mechanical project. A few minutes later I look up from my distraction and see that Robert is standing a couple of feet away looking suspiciously at what I'm doing. "Hey," I say, wondering why he's staring at me. "What is that?" Robert asks, "It looks like a bomb." Turns out he took one look at the power antenna, all encased in black plastic with a metal pipe sticking out, then he looked at me all Middle Eastern and, well, these are strange and jittery times we live in.

Not long after that, I'm still in the car by the curb when a couple of crew guys walk by. One of them says to the other: "Shush, do you hear that?" I look up and they're looking at my right front tire. I get out and walk around to them. By now Rick the audio guy has crouched by the tire. I crouch with him and, damn it, there's an audible hiss. Now a small crowd of grips and other crew gathers to see what's up. So much for keeping a low profile. Rick passes his palm across the surface of the sidewall and locates the leak. Every time he moves his finger from the spot the hissing resumes. He takes a piece of gum out of his mouth and sticks it on the source of the hiss. Clever, but it won't get me home. The crowd has swollen to about twenty cast and crew. We discuss. One guy says that he has a "tire patch in a can" thing. I say I could use it. "Well, It costs about ten bucks." I tell him I'll pay. Just then I remember that I also have one of those puncture seal cans in the trunk. As I'm rummaging back there the whole gang busts out guffawing. I've just been had. Royally! This is apparently Rick's trademark gag. He's conned everybody else on the lot with this little ruse. He does the hissing, not the tire. It's a simple yet beautiful practical joke and I laugh good-naturedly. I'm just sorry I won't be on this show long enough to get the bastard back!

☆

SATURDAY, JANUARY 31, *ANCHORMAN* EXTRA GIG
PRODUCTION COMPANY: DREAMWORKS PRODUCTIONS
PROJECT TYPE: FEATURE FILM
START AT: 7:00 A.M.
WHERE: GRIFFITH PARK
ROLE: TECHNICAL DIRECTOR IN A TV STUDIO
SCENE: NEWSCAST IN THE STUDIO
PAY: $54

It gets very cold up here in January. The high point of the day is running into my friend Ann-Marie the stuntwoman. They've got her in
Makeup and have teased her hair to 80s bigness. I make a crack about
it and the hair designer throws me out. Our group of extras spends eight
hours outdoors waiting to be called to the set. Finally we end up working all of forty-five minutes. I'm nowhere *near* the camera. Will Ferrell
and Christina Applegate play TV news anchors Ron Burgundy and
Veronica Corningstone respectively. There's a strange vibe on the set.
People are whispering and chuckling secretly. I don't know—I'm cold and
it's strange and I'm happy to get the hell out of there.

☆

MONDAY, FEBRUARY 2, *THE DA* EXTRA GIG
NETWORK: WB
EPISODE: THE PEOPLE VS. DR. OLIVER C. HANDLEY
START AT: 6:30 A.M.
WHERE: VALLEY PRESBYTERIAN HOSPITAL, VAN NUYS
ROLE: DOCTOR
SCENE: LOS ANGELES IN SUMMER
PAY: $111

I'm not a doctor, but I play one on TV. Always wanted to say that.
Also always wanted to say, "Well, Oprah, you're just gonna hafta discuss
that with my agent."

Today we're at the Valley Presbyterian Hospital in Van Nuys. This is
a working hospital. Real doctors and patients come and go. The reception desk is busy taking phone calls and directing traffic. The cast and
crew of *The DA* are in another, abandoned wing of the hospital. It was
closed following the big quake of '92. Structural degradation. Hm.

I arrive promptly for my 6:30 a.m. call time but it has been changed to 8:00 a.m. I neglected to call and double-check before I left home. It's a cold morning. The 2nd AD seems disoriented and is having a shouting match with one of the production coordinators so I shuffle back to my car and nap for an hour.

Holding is on the 6th floor of the abandoned wing. Other extras have staked out rooms and are sleeping or watching TV or grabbing snacks from the insubstantial craft services table. No coffee is served until the afternoon. That sours my mood and I spend most of the day alone.

The scene I'm in is a suicide. A woman has jumped from one of the hospital windows and is splayed out on the second floor overhang with fake blood spilling down to the street below. I rush out into the street with three other doctors and an orderly. We all look up and react to the scene. A dozen takes later the "dead" actress begins stiffening up from the cold so we call it quits.

Extra work is very time consuming and interferes with just about everything else. It's true. Some gigs I've worked on have gone twelve hours. Most extras you ask will tell you that they prefer a very short day, maybe four hours, or a very long day, like twelve. Eight hours is the worst because you neither get paid for hours you haven't worked—the minimum is eight hours—nor do you get overtime pay.

Postscript: The DA first aired in March '04 and was cancelled in April '04. Not my fault.

☆

TUESDAY, FEBRUARY 3, *HOLLYWOOD DIVISION* EXTRA GIG
NETWORK: UNIVERSAL
TYPE OF PROJECT: TV PILOT
EPISODE: ONE MORE NIGHT IN HOLLYWOOD
START AT: 6:30 A.M.
WHERE: L.A. CONVENTION CENTER
ROLE: PRINT REPORTER/DOCTOR
SCENES: RESTAURANT AND AIRPORT
PAY: $156

We started out at La Cucina restaurant on Melrose and Martel where I meet the remarkable Jenny Wilke, extra extraordinaire. Jenny has a lot to say about showbiz and she ought to know; she's been at it for ten years and has seen just about every conceivable situation. Jenny has no illusions about this business. She knows that no one is indispensable, least of all extras. We discuss the benefits and drawbacks of working as background. It's not hard work, as a rule. The money can be pretty good; enough to make ends meet if you live simply and work regularly. The biggest downside is the unpredictability of finding work and, when you do find it, the long hours in Holding.

After the restaurant scene we all head back to the convention center and shoot an airport terminal scene. I stroll around the place and stumble onto a shoot that's going on in one of the larger halls. A number of young women in scanty leotards are doing a shaky breaky kind of dance. I join a small crowd of onlookers until we are shooed away by a severe and very unhappy production assistant. "Go to Holding," she orders.

☆

WEDNESDAY FEBRUARY 11, *CENTURY CITY* EXTRA GIG
EPISODE: ONLY YOU #108
WHEN: FEB 10, FEB 11
START AT: 2:00 P.M., 7:30 A.M.
WHERE: EL SEGUNDO STUDIOS, 2265 E. EL SEGUNDO BLVD.
ROLE: COURTROOM GALLERY MEMBER
SCENE: COURTROOM
PAY: $60, $130

On the first day of this gig I sit around Holding for six hours, ready to go on-set, nothing left to read, tired of talking to my fellow extras-in-waiting. The red on-air light keeps coming on and the bell keeps sounding but we don't get called. Whatever it is they're shooting in there, they obviously don't need us. So I decide to get some exercise and begin a Hajj-like circumnavigation of El Segundo Studio. Production studios have a lane demarcated along the inside of the building's walls. It's a three-foot wide walkway that's kept clear so people can get from one end of the studio to the other without stumbling through the snarl of crew and sets and equipment that always clutters up the place. It takes two minutes to go around this one. I turn and go back. Then, again. Like that until one of the 2nd ADs expresses his fervent wish that I would stay in Holding. This happens a lot. It is the 2nd AD's job to ensure that extras are ready at a moment's notice as needed. On days like this, when hours pass without us being called up at all, we naturally get restless and make their job that much more difficult.

On the second day the extras work a lot. We are on-set most of the day. Hector Elizondo, the marquee name on this show, is here today. He makes an effort to get to know at least the extras in the first rows of the gallery and jury box. Nice man, utterly unpretentious and, like Dean Stockwell, a stalwart presence in showbiz for many decades. He has credits that reach all the way back to 1963, with roles in nearly a hundred movies—including a wonderful starring role as Martin Naranjo in *Tortilla Soup* (2001)—and TV appearances on *All in the Family*, *The Rockford Files*, *Hill Street Blues*, and *The West Wing*.

Suddenly, in the middle of a take, a young woman sitting in the gallery immediately behind him has a wild coughing fit. She tries to stifle it but instead explodes in breathless hacking and looks ready to pass out. Elizondo is with her right away, comforting and insisting that she not feel at all bad for scrapping the shot. The whole company responds like that, including the other stars and the director. This is the real Hollywood.

Back in Holding, our eclectic gathering of extras passes the time in wait. Here's a budding comic whose best gag is to appear to be brutally cracking his own neck when in fact he has an empty plastic bottle that he is surreptitiously crushing under his arm for sound effects. There's twenty-something Marisse, combing her hair all day long and talking to boys on her cell phone. And Alex with his portable DVD player, watching movies, oblivious to the rest of us. "What're you watching?" I ask on our way back to Holding. "Today it's *Ocean's Eleven*," he replies. "Yesterday it was *Dogma*." And Jenny knits while a quiet elderly woman in thick glasses just sits and looks at her clasped hands resting in her lap.

Postscript: I didn't know it at the time but that was the last of "Century City." Eight episodes were shot but only four aired before the show is cancelled. This business is brutal.

☆

WEDNESDAY FEBRUARY 18, *THE FORMULA* AUDITION
TYPE OF PROJECT: MUSIC VIDEO
CASTING AGENT: ANISSA WILLIAMS, CASTING UNDERGROUND
LOCATION: 1641 NORTH IVAR
ROLE: MR. ANUGEST

As I understand it this audition is for a hip-hop music video. When Victor calls to let me know I've been called in he has very little information and seems hurried. He just says that they want to see me in a suit. I download the sides and have my lines memorized when I go in. Three young producers are in the room. I read the part. They like my slim reading glasses. "Thanks, that was great."

Postscript: I sent Anissa a card thanking her for thinking of me again. This is the third time I've auditioned for her. Haven't heard from her since. This business is unfathomable.

☆

MONDAY, FEBRUARY 23, *24* EXTRA GIG
NETWORK: 20TH CENTURY FOX
EPISODE: 8:00 TO 9:00 A.M., DAY 3, #56
WHEN: FEB. 23 FITTING & FEB. 24 SHOOT
START AT: 9:30 A.M.
WHERE: 6250 CANOGA AVENUE, WOODLAND HILLS
ROLE: ARMS DEALER
PAY: $29 & $115

Hallelujah! My very first SAG voucher. Extras! Management called a couple of days ago to ask if I would be willing to work today if the gig were for a union voucher, even though I had told them I would be unavailable. Of course I would, I said, a little breathlessly. Joining SAG is one of my target milestones, even though I've learned that being a union actor is not necessarily good news, since there isn't that much work to go around. It's now exactly three months since I did my first extra gig on *JAG*. I've spoken to some people who have been doing background work for years without getting a single SAG voucher. On the other hand I've met a couple who got all three vouchers in one week.

Even better is that this gig on *24* will consist of two short days. The first is a fitting and does not count toward the three union vouchers I need. I drive to Woodland Hills and spend a couple of hours getting fitted to play, sorry to say, an arms dealer. I had a feeling this might happen. I look Arab, or Latino. Regardless, I don't look like your typical WASP and therefore, particularly under the circumstances—Bin Laden, Iraq, 9/11—there is a great deal of demand for actors who can play the bad Arab. I'm avoiding it. Not much call for good Arabs, though.

The shoot itself the next day lasts a half-hour. It's a still photo shoot in which I supply Stephen Saunders (Paul Blackthorne) with an attaché case that contains a bomb and biological agent. The production's second unit photographs us walking down a hallway, making the handoff. The shots are intended to look like they were made clandestinely. Finally, I am asked to stand against a wall for mug shots. In the course of the shoot Paul asks where I'm from and I say Beirut. Turns out he had visited Lebanon and Jordan in '94 so that gave us something to talk about. Of course like all such set conversations, this one is brief.

☆

WEDNESDAY, MARCH 1, *VISA COMMERCIAL* AUDITION
TYPE OF PROJECT: COMMERCIAL/PRINT
CASTING AGENT: RODEO CASTING, BRITT ENGGREN
LOCATION: 7013 WILLOUGHBY AVENUE, LOS ANGELES, 90038
ROLE: BLUE COLLAR WORKER

I'm whiling away a couple of hours at Java Man, waiting for the traffic into L.A. to subside. Rush hour is all damn day on the 405! It's at a standstill if there's an accident. Java Man has one of the free hot spots in Hermosa Beach. If your computer is properly equipped, you can connect wirelessly to the Internet. It's a beautiful thing.

Victor called last Friday night to say that I have an audition today at noon for a Visa print ad. There will be three million people there competing for this gig. Victor pointed out that, if I get it, it pays two thousand dollars. I head up Aviation and decide at the last minute to take the 105 east and the 110 north. Luck is on my side today. It's 11:05 when I leave Hermosa and I arrive at Rodeo Casting at 11:35, twenty-five minutes early. That's record time. Two young women are hanging over a low adobe wall that separates the house from the street, having a smoke. They say hi and I hi back before heading up the stairs to the first floor where I fill out the sign-up sheet and hand my headshot to the blonde, who has finished her cigarette. She ushers me into the studio where a young, shaggy photographer takes a couple of shots of me and says "Thanks." That's it. Most auditions are like this, very quick. Even the one that got me a callback and eventually a lead part as Major Mirza with Pilgrim Films. Let's keep 'em moving; busy, busy, busy. Whoever says New York is faster than L.A. ought to try showbiz.

So far I've had thirteen auditions and landed one part. Other actors tell me that's a really good hit rate. Maybe so, but this is no business for people who can't take no for an answer. It's for people who *won't* take no for an answer. Tsk.

☆

WEDNESDAY, MARCH 3, *THE PRINCESS DIARIES II* EXTRA GIG
NETWORK: UNIVERSAL STUDIOS
PRODUCTION COMPANY: BOTTOM OF THE TENTH
PROJECT TYPE: FEATURE FILM
WHEN: MARCH 3 AND MARCH 4
START AT: 11:00 A.M.
WHERE: DISNEY STUDIOS, 500 SOUTH BUENA VISTA, BURBANK 91521
ROLE: EAST INDIAN DIGNITARY
SCENE: WEDDING PHOTO
PAY: $29 & $115

Extras! Management called yesterday saying that I would have a fitting today to play an Indian dignitary on Friday. When I arrive at 922 Vine Street and report to Mary Ellen, she asks if I'm union. Well, I'm not yet, but I understood this to be a SAG gig, just like last week's. So to avoid any misunderstanding or, heaven forbid, getting a non-union voucher, I say yes. She asks again a few minutes later and I say yes, again. She gives me a SAG voucher. Now I feel a little guilty that I may have misled her. Like I've snuck into the fancy, exclusive club in my old brown shoes.

In any case, she hands me over to a lushly bearded young man for the fitting. He leads me to the back where several people are busy sewing and rearranging garments on hangers and doing other Wardrobe doings. I'm guided into a curtained-off area of the big room and given my clothes: a down to mid-calf black jacket with gold embroidery running the length of the front; black pants, black shoes and a T-shirt to wear underneath. When I emerge everyone agrees that I look fabulous and we take a Polaroid for the record, then I'm off. The whole thing takes twenty minutes. In Hollywood everyone often tells everyone else that they look fabulous. People who have not tried to work in showbiz might find that peculiar, or even laughable. But actually the mutual admiration maintains the necessary amount of hot air inside the showbiz balloon. Without constant praise, our plump but delicate egos would deflate.

The next day shoot on *Princess Diaries II* is brief. Of the nearly seven hours I spend at the studio, six are passed waiting. When we're finally called to the set, we wait some more while the crew makes last-minute adjustments. Finally all is ready and Anne Hathaway is summoned. She arrives, introduces herself and shakes hands with all six of us extras. It's a nice touch to take the time and be civil. Not all stars are this gracious but most are.

Some of my colleagues in the extras contingent were complaining earlier that it's a waste of money having us just sit there. I happened to be reading a small book called *Hollywood Chronicles*, by L.D. Silva, in which he calculates that on a $50 million dollar movie with a fifty-day shooting schedule, "the meter runs at $1,667 per minute." I share this with the group and point out that the six of us are costing the production company a paltry $720 for the whole day. Only the big guy with the facial scar finds this gripping. "Thanks, Cliffy," he says.

☆

THURSDAY, MARCH 4, CALL FROM CARLA LEWIS RE *JIMMY KIMMEL LIVE*

My mobile phone trills while I'm napping by the pool. I love living in Socal. It snowed today on the East Coast. I pick up and it's Carla Lewis from Extras Casting Guild. She wants to know if I'm available tonight to do the *Jimmy Kimmel Live* show. They want me to play Osama bin Laden! It's an AFTRA under-five role. I have a prior commitment that I cannot get out of so I beg off. On the one hand I feel bad that I am passing up an opportunity and letting down a casting director, particularly one who has thought of me on other roles. On the other I'm relieved because, once again, I don't want to play the bad Arab. Certainly not *that* bad Arab.

This brings to mind *Reel Bad Arabs: How Hollywood Vilifies a People* by Jack G. Shaheen, Interlink Publishing Group, 2001. It's a huge volume in which Shaheen argues Arabs are overwhelmingly cast in bad-person parts. He's right. How come the Finns never get fingered.

☆

FRIDAY, MARCH 5, *THE INDICATOR*, MISSED AUDITION
PRODUCTION COMPANY: GAN HANADA
ROLE: DETECTIVE RAMIREZ, 40-45 YEAR-OLD PUERTO RICAN

I had submitted myself for this audition and received a call inviting me to come in. Unfortunately, the day coincided with the *Princess Diaries II* shoot; I could not get there in time and, for the first time, had to call and apologize. Having a schedule conflict is an uptown problem. It's a lot worse having a wide-open calendar and nowhere to go.

☆

THURSDAY, MARCH 11, *GEORGE LOPEZ SHOW* EXTRA GIG
NETWORK: WARNER BROTHERS
PROJECT TYPE: TV SITCOM
EPISODE: THE ART OF BOXING
START AT: 7:00 A.M.
WHERE: WARNER BROTHERS STUDIOS, 4000 WARNER BLVD., STAGE 4
ROLE: BOXING TRAINER
SCENE: BOXING CLUB AND MATCH
PAY: $69

It's a foggy morning in L.A. The drive from Hermosa Beach at 5:30 this morning is pleasant for the absence of traffic and the softening of all edges that fog brings on. I arrive at Warner Brothers Studios in Burbank by 6:15, nearly an hour ahead of my call time. The parking lot is across Forest Lawn Drive from the WB campus. Just down the road, Bette Davis, Queen of Warner Brothers, lies in final repose, keeping a posthumous eye on the studio. There's eucalyptus in the air.

One of the other extras, Seth, is already here. We strike up a conversation while waiting at the stage door. He is a process server as well as an actor. He did extra work when he was younger and is back at it now in his mid-forties. Just when I think we've run out of small talk, Seth mentions that he has disposed of his firearm because his ex-wife keeps siccing the cops on him and he's worried that one of these days they're going to find it. You meet interesting folks doing background work.

This is my first sitcom and there is quite a bit of difference from one-hour dramas. For one thing, four cameras are working at the same time. The director is Joe Regalbuto. Joe's had a long and impressive career in showbiz, including many directing credits, but I remember him most as Frank Fontana from *Murphy Brown*. The atmosphere on the set is light and casual. Joe laughs each time one of the principals delivers a funny line. So does the rest of the crew. I figure that's the protocol so laugh along with them, even when the lines aren't that funny but clearly intended to be. Plus, this gives the actors the pause that will later be occupied by the laugh track. Sitcoms without laugh tracks could be desolate affairs. That's just the way it is.

In the first scene I'm a boxing trainer working with a couple of young boys on their moves. They're eleven. Alex is smaller and more attentive. Adrian keeps drifting off and fidgeting with a nail he's picked up off the floor. At the end of the day Alex comes up and asks for my autograph. Two young women, laughers, are watching from the bleachers. We all get a kick out of the kid thinking I'm somebody. Says Hyacinth Bucket on BBC's *Keeping Up Appearances*: "This could be the day that I'm mistaken for someone important."[11]

Incidentally, laughers are extras who are hired expressly for the purpose of laughing off-camera to emphasize gags and supplement the pre-recorded laugh track. Why do producers feel the need to hire laughers instead of relying on volunteer audiences? Because here's what could happen if they count on an uncoached audience:

> "The audience turned up to be bloody awful. For starters we had a Moronic Laugher among them. That's always bad news: some idiot with a very loud, inane laugh, who goes on baying or cackling or shrieking at something long after everybody else has stopped, or starts up when nobody else is laughing, in the lull between two gags."[12]

Laila Ali (Mohamad Ali's daughter) and her husband Johnny (Yahya) McClain are on the set today. She's a guest star and Johnny, who is also her manager, is the fight coordinator. Laila "She Bee Stingin'" is an attractive, friendly woman. Still, after seeing her spar I'm sure I would not want to upset her in any way. Yahya is also pleasant and seems to enjoy working with the kids.[13]

The second scene is fight night. I'm at ringside, cheering our guys on. During a break, while Seth and I stand by the door chatting, Sandra Bullock comes in right behind me. As she enters she apologizes to no one in particular for coming straight from the gym in her sweats. I say, "No sweat." She smiles and gives me a friendly oh-aren't-we-the-clever-fellow look. Or maybe I imagned that. I ask Seth what she's doing here and he tells me she's one of the producers.

Apparently, this is the fiftieth episode of the show and at the end of the day the crew and principals have a celebration to commemorate the occasion. Sandra gives George Lopez a congratulatory hug. He wells up as he says a few words to the hundred or so cast and crew gathered in the studio. The whole thing is very familial and touching. Say what you want about Hollywood glitz and glam—most of the time this is hard work, long hours, team effort. You don't get to be as big as Lopez and Bullock by sitting on your butt.

☆

FRIDAY, APRIL 9, PILGRIM FILMS, *COLORADO PROJECT* AUDITION
TYPE OF PROJECT: INDUSTRIAL FILM
PRODUCTION COMPANY: PILGRIM FILMS
CASTING AGENT: RICHARD COURTNEY
LOCATION: 4730 WOODMAN AVE., SHERMAN OAKS 91423
ROLE: COUGHLIN

Nice to be back at Pilgrim. My nephews Tarek and Malek are in town and Tracy takes the day off so we all drive to the Valley. While they wait, I read for the part of Coughlin. Richard Courtney is one of the most hospitable casting directors in town. He always takes the time to greet actors warmly. I feel a certain confidence, having already worked for Pilgrim, and can see how an actor can gradually build a base of employers. Get a part, do well, get invited back. Or get a part, bomb, adios.

On the way home I get a call from Victor. I have an audition for a Novartis commercial. Here we go again. Do I love or hate auditions? Both, probably. Must maintain perspective. Relax. Breathe. This could be my first national commercial. Money. Fame. Money.

☆

SATURDAY, APRIL 10, *NOVARTIS COMMERCIAL* AUDITION
PRODUCTION COMPANY: CROSSROADS FILMS
CASTING AGENT: LIEN COWAN CASTING
LOCATION: 7461 BEVERLY BOULEVARD, LOS ANGELES 90036
ROLE: MIDDLE-AGED MAN CONCERNED ABOUT HIS BLOOD PRESSURE

It's strangely quiet when I arrive for this audition. The casting coordinator, Annabella, is in a good mood, not at all stressed and harried as casting people can get in the course of their day. Soon a few other actors arrive and she brings us into the studio four at a time. We line up against the wall, face the camera, slate and, on her request, ad-lib some stuff about whatever comes to mind. She then asks each of us to respond to four questions regarding blood pressure. "Thanks, that was great." I leave with no real sense of how I did, except that I felt relaxed during the audition and did not hesitate or butcher any words. I think I also made a funny. Somehow it's all a blur, like shooting the Zambezi.

Victor calls later in the day to say that I've been invited for a callback. I'm glad to hear it but gone are the days when I got excited about callbacks. The odds are just too long. The secret to contentment, as Catherine Deneuve says in *Indochine* (1992), is *"L'indifférence."*

☆

MONDAY, APRIL 12, *NOVARTIS COMMERCIAL* CALLBACK
PRODUCTION COMPANY: CROSSROADS FILMS
CASTING AGENT: LIEN COWAN CASTING
LOCATION: 7461 BEVERLY BOULEVARD, LOS ANGELES 90036
ROLE: MIDDLE-AGED MAN CONCERNED ABOUT HIS BLOOD PRESSURE

It's a zoo at Lien Cowan Casting on this Easter Monday. There are many, many people on this callback, or *all*back, as one of the guys sardonically calls it. I'm pressed for time because I have a Pilgrim Films callback in the valley at 12:30. When I arrive at Lien Cowan it is immediately obvious that they are running quite late. This is a very different scene from when I was here last week. I weigh my options and decide that it's a safer bet to ditch the Novartis audition, particularly since there are so many actors here. I'm reasonably optimistic about my chances of landing a part with Pilgrim Films, since I've already worked with them in the past. As a last resort I plead my case to James, one of the casting coordinators. He is sympathetic and sends me in with a group of people earlier than I would have otherwise gone. The five of us wait inside the studio. Several production people are here. The director, Mark Pellington, who had been out of the room, hits me with the door when he comes in. He apologizes profusely and I accept just as profusely. After all, this is the man who decides whether or not I get the part. I ask if he wants to hit me with the door again. He chuckles. The actors line up and slate, then we each enter the camera frame and pantomime our morning ablutions in an imaginary bathroom. I go first and when I finish, Pellington says, "Perfect!" I discount the remark, figuring he still feels guilty about whacking me with the door. The other actors in the room go through their auditions then we all exit and I rush off to the Pilgrim audition. *L'indifférence*, I tell myself.

☆

MONDAY, APRIL 12, PILGRIM FILMS. *COLORADO PROJECT* CALLBACK
TYPE OF PROJECT: INDUSTRIAL
PRODUCTION COMPANY: PILGRIM FILMS
CASTING AGENT: RICHARD COURTNEY
LOCATION: 4730 WOODMAN AVE., SHERMAN OAKS 91423
ROLE: COUGHLIN

The traffic is not terrible today, thankfully, so I make it to the Valley in decent time but am still late for my second audition of the day. I change in the parking lot into my suit. Upstairs I run into Eddie Barbini, the director whom I met on the *U101* project. Eddie says, "Hey, Buddy," and I'm sure that he recognizes me even if he cannot come up with my name. I wonder if he remembers the accident with the big, white truck and my heroic recovery. Richard Courtney, the casting director who ran the first cut is here for the callback. As usual, Richard has a kind word for everybody. I read the part of Coughlin again and Richard says, "Well, you can't ask for much more than that!" Good one. I wonder if casting directors have an arsenal of one-liners with which to conclude an audition. They should. Richard seems to. His remarks are always substantial. I'm tired of "Thanks, that was great."

Two auditions in one day. If I lived nearer Hollywood I could do three or four. Not that most people get the chance to go on three or four auditions in one day.

Postscript: I'm writing this many months later because I have just had my most rewarding post-audition experience. I'm at Allison Jones Casting. They're looking for Saddam lookalikes, four of them, to work on "Arrested Development." The idea of a casting agency waiting room full of pseudo-Saddams kills me, so I'm in a good mood, ready for a laugh. But there's only one guy here when I arrive. He looks nothing like Saddam and is, in fact, Iranian. But hey, this is Hollywood.

In the story the faux despots all live in the same apartment in pre-Shock-and-Awe Baghdad, waiting to be called on to stand in for the genuine despot. It's a hilarious possibility. I get called in and read the lines of all four Saddams. The casting director, Michael, takes me through it again. I think his name is Michael, could have been Steven—sometimes, under audition stress, I forget simple things like names. I wait for "Thanks, that was great." But it doesn't come. Instead, Michael actually asks me a question:

"No résumé, huh?"

"Nope. I haven't done much. Mostly industrial stuff, commercials."

"How long have you been in the business?"

"Oh, a couple of years."

"You should be working more. You have a good look. As many shows as need Middle Eastern guys these days—let's see—who's your agent?"

"Kruglov."

"Hm. He should be sending you on lots of auditions. You have good instincts. Here's a guy that read earlier today. Lots of under-fives, and you're a better actor. You'd be happy with small roles here and there. Why weren't you in 'Syriana'?"

"Um, I understood that some of these films are packaged. My agent may never even have had access to the breakdowns."

"I doubt that. You should talk to him."

Now that's feedback. There's a place for Michael in showbiz heaven.

☆

TUESDAY APRIL 13, WHEN IT RAINS...

"...Hot in Hollywood is about as hot as it gets. And we are fizzing and steaming and burning up the track."[14]

Man, lots of good news today! Victor calls to say that I've booked the Novartis commercial and just a few minutes later Richard Courtney calls to offer me the part of the U.S. Ambassador on the *Colorado Project*. Well, it isn't quite that straightforward. Victor actually called me three times today. The first time was in the morning to let me know that Crossroads Films had put me on "Availability," or "Avail" in the industry's jargon. This means that, although they are not booking me, they still want me to be available on the days of the shoot. He calls again in the early afternoon to say that it's between me and one other guy for the final slot on the commercial. I hate waiting for news. Finally, right around 6:00 p.m., Victor calls with the good news. I'm booked. It's a big deal. This is a union project so I'm Taft-Hartleyed into SAG. Also, I'll make about four thousand dollars for the shoot, with the possibility of more if the commercial eventually airs.

And to think I nearly ditched the callback!

☆

FRIDAY APRIL 16 THROUGH TUESDAY APRIL 20, *NOVARTIS COMMERCIAL*
TYPE OF PROJECT: NATIONAL COMMERCIAL
CASTING AGENT: LIEN COWAN
PRODUCTION COMPANY: CROSSROADS FILMS
LOCATION: MULTIPLE, LOS ANGELES,
ROLE: MIDDLE-AGED MAN CONCERNED ABOUT HIS BLOOD PRESSURE
PAY: $3,478

There's a bunch of heavy hitters on this production. The director, Mark Pellington, has worked with stars like James Earl Jones, Tim Robbins, Demi Moore, Whoopi Goldberg, Ben Affleck and Kevin Bacon. In 1992, Billboard Video Music Awards named him Best Director for the Pearl Jam music video *Jeremy*. The following year Pellington won four MTV Video Awards, including Best Director, also for *Jeremy*. He has been nominated for a Grammy, has written, produced, and acted. This man is very talented and accomplished and yet, as he directs this commercial for Novartis, mixes easily with all of us on the set and has an easy fraternal manner about him, more like the pool guy than an award-winning director. I keep looking for the proverbial Hollywood megalomaniacs but have yet to come across one. Quite the reverse, really. There is a higher degree of courtesy on film and TV sets than existed in many corporate boardrooms during my stint in that world.

The actors on this project are all veterans. They include Sherman Howard, whom I recognize and who has worked on *Dallas, Miami Vice, L.A. Law* and more recent shows like *Cold Case* and *Las Vegas*.

I also meet Denise Dowse. She has a long list of credits to her name, having appeared in countless TV and film projects, most recently as the sultry Marlene in *Ray* and Principal Garrison in *Coach Carter*.

Nevertheless, these veterans' talents are largely wasted here. The work is not challenging and consists of walking down streets and out of house doors and exiting elevators in downtown office buildings. There is no dialog at all. It's like being an extra except that we get $500 a day during the week and $1000 a day on weekend days. It adds up to nearly $4,000 in four days. It would take sixty eight-hour days of non-union work to make that. No one is complaining and, anyway, we're all certain that Pellington will weave magic.

Postscript: The Novartis commercial never aired, so I have no idea what the final product would have looked like. Also, visions of dancing dollar bills from residuals were replaced with the more enduring satisfaction of having made it into SAG and earned enough from this one gig to get a couple of dental crowns.

☆

WEDNESDAY, APRIL 21, *COLORADO PROJECT*
TYPE OF PROJECT: INDUSTRIAL
CASTING AGENT: RICHARD COURTNEY
PRODUCTION COMPANY: PILGRIM FILMS
LOCATION: DOS CARLOS STUDIOS, LOS ANGELES
ROLE: U.S. AMBASSADOR TO CONTADORA
PAY: $200

In this production, I play the U.S. Ambassador to a fictitious Latin American country. The shoot is at Dos Carlos Studios. I worked here once before on a *JAG* episode. Many of the same people from the *U101* project are here, including the director and the producer. I do one scene in which I am seated behind a heavy wood desk in a big leather chair, debriefing U.S. brass about possible terrorist activity. Between the time I received the script two days ago and this morning, all my lines were cut. Eddie agrees, however, that it would bring nice closure to the scene if I could say something at the end. So I say, "Any guess as to target or type of device?" We do the scene a dozen or so times then get coverage. I'm done in a couple of hours. That's $100 per hour. Far better than a kick in the head. It's also encouraging to get called back by a director with whom I had worked in the past. Victor says that the surest way to success in Hollywood is in developing relationships with a handful of casting agencies and directors. If the people you work with once like you, they'll call you again. If they don't..."Thanks, that was great!"

☆

WEDNESDAY, APRIL 28, *AMERICAN EXPRESS COMMERCIAL* AUDITION
TYPE OF PROJECT: COMMERCIAL
PRODUCTION COMPANY: CROSSROADS FILMS
CASTING AGENT: LIEN COWAN CASTING
LOCATION: 7461 BEVERLY BLVD., LOS ANGELES
ROLE: PLUMBER

Victor called yesterday afternoon to say that I had this audition. I assumed they wanted me to play a dapper businessman and asked Victor if I should wear a dark suit. He chuckled, "No! You are *plommer*." My very first audition back in November was a cold read at Daniel Hoff Agency, where I was asked to describe myself in terms of a recognizable brand. "American Express!" I cried, thinking style, jet-setting, Coronas, tuxedos, savoir-faire. The irony in my being asked to play a plumber instead of a mogul is nearly as comical as it is depressing. Why can't I be a mogul?

I arrive one hour early and there is just a handful of people at the casting studio. Then I notice that the commercial's storyboard is posted along with a list of people auditioning today. They're seeing people from 10:00 a.m. until 2:00 p.m. The list has sixty names on it. Fifteen people an hour. We are invited in two at a time and asked to improvise with plumbing and electrical tools that have been provided for that purpose. No dialogue at all. Nobody asks me to smile. No worries.

After the audition I go to Insomnia Café on Beverly Boulevard and spend ten dollars on two hours of WiFi while I wait for my lunch appointment with Victor. Every patron here is working on a screenplay.

☆

WEDNESDAY, APRIL 28, LUNCH WITH VICTOR

Now that Victor and I have consummated our relationship with the Novartis commercial, I figure it's time we got to know each other better. So I invite him to lunch at Buddha's Belly, which is right next door to his office.

Victor was born in the good ole USSR and lived in Odessa until he was twenty-nine. He has had a very colorful and interesting professional life, including stints as a train conductor. For the past eighteen years he has been a talent agent in L.A. I tell him that I'm working on a book for people who want to try their hand at acting in Hollywood and ask if he would be willing to let me share his insights. He agrees. Victor's insights are of the pull-no-punches variety. What is the most important thing about acting in commercials? Victor will tell you it's your look.

I order the black cod and it's very good. Somebody who's somebody is in the corner booth. You can tell because all the energy in the room is sucked into that corner. Everybody looks then looks away. I have no idea who the woman is but when the waiter goes by with her lunch I note that she, also, had ordered the black cod.

☆

THURSDAY, APRIL 29, ASK FOR THE ORDER AUDITION
TYPE OF PROJECT: INDUSTRIAL TRAINING FILM
PRODUCTION COMPANY: AMERICAN MEDIA
CASTING AGENT: BELSHE CASTING
LOCATION: LOS ALAMITOS
ROLE: MR. SANCHEZ, BUSINESS EXECUTIVE

One thing about going on auditions is you really get to know Los Angeles. This one is at a theater in Los Alamitos. Judy Belshe is running the auditions on her own. She is seeing us two at a time. I audition for the role of an executive being pitched a product. No camera, just a read-through with an actress who plays the salesperson. Judy says she likes what we did with the scene but wants to see a few other people before making her mind up. Callbacks are on Wednesday of next week and I fully expect to be invited back. After all, I'm no longer nobody. Just yesterday I had lunch with a famous person at Buddha's Belly. (Good Food. Good Fortune). We both had the black cod.

☆

SATURDAY, MAY 1, *AMERICAN EXPRESS COMMERCIAL* CALLBACK

Victor called to say that I've been called back for the Amex audition. They're seeing people three at a time today. When my threesome goes in, the director, Nick Lewin, introduces himself and shakes hands with each of us. One of the other actors, a portly fellow in a plumber uniform complete with a "Fred" nametag says, "I've done this for a very long time and this is the first time that a director has shaken my hand." Puhlease! Everybody laughs and applauds. One of the producers in the room says, "That's why we love him." Nick sets up the scene: I work for the owner of this hair salon. The other two guys are electricians doing work at the salon. It's total improvisation. No sweat. Been there, done it. The scene comes naturally even if I am a little too much of a hard-ass to the other two actors. I may have stepped on their lines, as well, interrupting, making it real. It felt good. "Fred" goes up to the director and kisses his ring. Not really. That might've been a little over the top.

☆

MONDAY, MAY 3, DON'T LEAVE HOME WITHOUT IT!

Victor Calls. I got the American Express job. *I'm on fire!* First the Novartis gig and now this. A month ago I was sure I'd never land a commercial. Now I'm booked on two. Victor is right: it's all about look. There could not have been many people auditioning for this commercial with less experience and training than I have.

☆

TUESDAY, MAY 4, *AMERICAN EXPRESS COMMERCIAL* FITTING
TYPE OF PROJECT: COMMERCIAL
PRODUCTION COMPANY: CROSSROADS FILMS
CASTING AGENT: LIEN COWAN CASTING
LOCATION: 8630 PINE TREE PLACE, LOS ANGELES, 90069
ROLE: PLUMBER

The Crossroads Films business offices are in a mansion just off Sunset
Boulevard. The director is coming down the stairs from the upper floor
just as I walk into the mansion's foyer. I flash on Gloria Swanson in
Sunset Boulevard. He recognizes me and I recognize him and call out,
"Hi, Chris." Trouble is, of course, that's not his name. My Swanson cutaway discombobulated me. His name is Nick Lewin. This only registers
after he looks at me quizzically and shoots through into another room.

*Note to Self: Always remember the director's name and if you don't,
just say, "Hey, Buddy."*

☆

WEDNESDAY, MAY 5, *NISSAN COMMERCIAL* AUDITION
CASTING AGENT: NOVA CASTING, MILLA NOVA
LOCATION: 2545 BEVERLY BLVD., SANTA MONICA, 90405
ROLE: CUSTOMER

The breakdown on www.actorsaccess.com reads as follows: Latino
male, mid-40s, tall, handsome, well-educated, successful, confident.
Does not need to speak Spanish...Well, I'm well-educated.

Milla Nova, the casting director, is also a client of Victor Kruglov, my
agent. She and I play a scene where we're a couple discussing a car. She's
great. I suck. She should give herself the part of the woman in the project. Still, I leave expecting to be called back just on the strength of my
look, which I think is perfect for the part.

*Postscript: Never heard back. Is it impossible to predict callbacks? I
really expected to get called back for this one. On the other hand, I
would not have bet a wooden nickel that I'd be called back and get the
Novartis and American Express jobs.*

☆

THURSDAY, MAY 6, *ASK FOR THE ORDER* CALLBACK
TYPE OF PROJECT: INDUSTRIAL TRAINING FILM
PRODUCTION COMPANY: AMERICAN MEDIA
LOCATION: CHELSEA STUDIOS, 11530 VENTURA BLVD., STUDIO CITY
ROLE: MR. SANCHEZ, BUSINESS EXECUTIVE

There is a roomful of people in the casting studio, including the producer and Tim Armstrong, the director. Judy Belshe is here as well. They're seeing us two at a time. I read with an actor named Steve. Tim asks us to improvise for a while and everyone behind the camera seems delighted. Of course this is meaningless because we don't know who else has been here before us and who will come next and what's really going on in the mind of the director.

I do know that I'm getting a little tired. It's been a busy couple of weeks of jobs and auditions. The trouble with auditions is that you don't get paid to do them but you incur expenses and, what's more, spend a lot of time coming and going and preparing for them. When I started out doing this I was totally focused on getting calls to audition. Then I wanted a speaking part. Then a commercial. Now I see how difficult it must be to do this long-term. It wears you down, beats you up, knocks you sideways. Sort of an omni-directional whup-ass.

☆

FRIDAY, MAY 7, *AMERICAN EXPRESS COMMERCIAL* SHOOT
TYPE OF PROJECT: COMMERCIAL
CASTING AGENT: LIEN COWAN
ROLE: PLUMBER
PAY: $1,200

The star of this commercial is Jonathan Antin, who is a real Beverly Hills and Hollywood stylist to the rich and famous and wannabe rich and famous. The ad is part of the *Do You Know Me?* series that American Express has run over the years. In it Jonathan appears to be signing autographs for an unseen throng. The off-camera fans thrust their books and notepads at him. As the camera pulls back, however, it becomes obvious that he is actually signing vendors' invoices. The other five guys and I, dressed as plumbers and electricians, are gathered around Jonathan getting our invoices signed. That's the general idea.

The ad is running in conjunction with the opening of a new Jonathan salon in Beverly Hills.

It sounds simple enough but it takes all day to shoot. Late in the afternoon one of the assistant directors runs into the steel counterweight at the base of a boom that supports a heavy spotlight. We're all hanging out on the set waiting for the next take when we hear a THUP-WHUMP-UNGH! She drops on her back like she's been whacked with a baseball bat. By the time we get to her a large bump, and I mean large, like lemon-sized, has inflated on her forehead. She is taken away to hospital. The topic of conversation for the rest of the day is accidents. Despite rigorous SAG safety guidelines, they happen all too often. Many are minor, such as mine on the set of *U101*. A few are fatal like Vic Morrow's on the *The Twilight Zone* and Brandon Lee's on *The Crow*.[15]

☆

MONDAY, MAY 10, *ME AND YOU AND EVERYONE WE KNOW* AUDITION
TYPE OF PROJECT: FEATURE FILM
PRODUCER: GINA KWON
CASTING AGENT: MEG MORMAN CASTING
LOCATION: 3000 W. OLYMPIC BLVD., SANTA MONICA 90404
ROLE: ARTIST

Here's the breakdown as it was posted on www.actorsaccess.com:
[ARTIST] 30-45. Male. Middle Eastern. This artist is exhausted and dirty from setting up a museum installation. When Nancy realizes the exhibit isn't what she'd expected, the Artist ends the conversation with what Nancy suspects is an outright lie...1 speech & 5 lines, 1 scene (25).

When I show up at the audition I immediately see that I cannot compete. That's the kiss of death for an actor. There is a hallway full of übersexual men here, waiting to audition. There isn't a himbo in the bunch. They're all young, sharp, more Middle Eastern and more arty than me. Still, I stay and do a pretty good read with Meg Morman. She has been involved in some high-profile projects in the past including *The Italian Job*. Maybe she'll see my potential and call me back.

Postscript: Nope. My potential remains incognito.

☆

MONDAY, MAY 10, CLOSING THE DEAL ON *ASK FOR THE ORDER*

Judy Belshe just called. Armstrong Pictures is booking me to play one of the supporting roles on *Ask for the Order*. The shoot is on May 16.

☆

TUESDAY, MAY 11, THANK YOU LIEN COWAN

On Victor's advice I pay a visit to Michael Lien and deliver a nice gourmet basket in appreciation for the Novartis and American Express auditions that turned into jobs. Michael congratulates me on landing two national commercials in a row. I say, "It's dumb luck." He does not dispute.

☆

WEDNESDAY, MAY 12, RECEIVED CHECK FOR *NOVARTIS COMMERCIAL*

It's always nice to get money in the mail. The Novartis check is for $3,049 after taxes. Victor's cut is 15% of gross, which is $520. I can see how being a talent agent could be quite lucrative.

☆

Wednesday, May 12, *Targeted: Osama bin Laden*, Voice-Over
Type of Project: Documentary
Casting Agent: Carla Lewis, Headquarters Casting
Production Company: Wild Eyes Productions
Location: Oracle Post, 3232 Nebraska Avenue, Santa Monica 90404
Role: Afghani
Pay: $54

Wild Eyes Productions has made hard-hitting documentaries in some of the world's most dangerous hot spots. When Headquarters Casting calls to ask if I can do two hours of voice-over for $54, I jump at the chance.

At the studio I meet a Lebanese Armenian named Misak who is also here for the voice-over. This is his first and he tries to get some tips from me. I'm sure that I'm a huge disappointment when I inform him that it's my first as well. Soon we're led into the control room where we meet the engineer, Chad. He says we're playing the translators on a project called *Targeted: Osama bin Laden*.

Maria Wye Berry, the producer, arrives and sends me to the recording booth where I read Sharrif and Gul.

After the session I give her a copy of my book, *Away From My Desk*, and inscribe it as follows: "For the intrepid documentarians at Wild Eyes." I also give her my business card, hoping that I'll hear from Wild Eyes again. I've always wanted to be a documentarian. I even have a degree in TV production. Just haven't gotten to it yet. Maybe next year.

☆

Wednesday, May 12, Received SAG Eligibility Letter

Dear Applicant:
We are pleased to inform you that you are eligible to join Screen Actors Guild based on employment under Screen Actors Guild. Enclosed please find the documents you submitted as proof of employment. If you have not scheduled an appointment to join, please contact our office at 323-549-6769 at your convenience.

☆

TUESDAY, MAY 18, *REVENGE* AUDITION
TYPE OF PROJECT: NON-UNION FEATURE FILM
PRODUCTION COMPANY: PIBERA PICTURES
CASTING AGENT: DEBBIE WALSH CASTING
LOCATION: PLAYERS SPACE, 4934 LANKERSHIM BLVD, N. HOLLYWOOD
ROLE: PANCHO

My props for this audition are a ninety-five-cent cigar and oversized sunglasses. That's as close as I'm coming to a Groucho Marx impersonation. Pancho is listed in the breakdowns as a Hispanic mob boss in his forties to fifties. When I walk in I find myself in the waiting room of a small theater. I can hear a man reading Pancho's lines in the back. What can I say? The guy is perfect for the part, with just the right accent and a raspy, hacking voice. Unless he's 6'2" and blond, I can't imagine why they would want to hear anyone else read for Pancho. And sure enough, when the guy emerges, he looks just like a Hispanic mob boss ought to. He nods, gurgles, "Good luck" as though wishing me a slow death and leaves. Still, I focus on my plan and do the very best job I can. Debbie Walsh is here and so is the writer/producer, Ben Kobby. When I finish Ben says, "That was just great, thanks." It's almost better when they say nothing at all. I'm still wondering if casting directors have a list of things to say to gracefully end an audition. Maybe I'll write a little booklet: *A Hundred and One Innocuous Dismissals for Casting Agents*. It will contain gems like, "Thank you so much, it's not often we see such unusual work." Or, "Excellent, excellent—I felt something." Or even, "You kiddin' me?"

☆

WEDNESDAY MAY 16, *ASK FOR THE ORDER* GIG
TYPE OF PROJECT: INDUSTRIAL
CASTING AGENT: JUDY BELSHE
PRODUCTION COMPANY: AMERICAN MEDIA
LOCATION: CERRITOS PUBLIC LIBRARY, CERRITOS
ROLE: CORPORATE MANAGER
PAY: $250 + 10%

The city of Cerritos must be loaded. This library is outfitted in modern, sleek furnishings, more like a corporate HQ. I arrive a little early so make my way in with the crew and find a leather recliner on the second floor in which to wait to be called to Wardrobe and Makeup.

The scene is a corporate boardroom. We are a group of managers discussing a software project. The antagonist is a cantankerous old fart, Jenkins, who is against the consensus opinion that we buy the software. My line is: "Look, there's no point in leasing. We've got the money in the budget, Why not buy it?" Yes, it's not much, but I'm here and I'm working.

The peculiar thing about this production is that the client, Art Bauer, a noted sales trainer and producer of corporate training programs through his company American Media, is also very involved in directing the shoot. He explains when all the actors get on the set that he and Tim Armstrong would both be providing direction. In fact, while Tim handles directing the crew, Art also directs the cast. They seem to get along fine but I can imagine how this arrangement could lead to drama.

Postscript: The biggest reward for me from doing this gig is meeting Tim Armstrong. He would hire me again and also agree to an interview in which he shared a director's insights into showbiz.

☆

THURSDAY, MAY 20, *STRONG MEDICINE* EXTRA GIG
NETWORK: LIFETIME TELEVISION
EPISODE: "FRACTURED" # 505
START AT: 11:00 A.M.
WHERE: STRONG MEDICINE STAGE, 5933 SLAUSON AVE., CULVER CITY
ROLE: DOCTOR, HEAD OF DEPARTMENT
SCENE: DEPARTMENT HEAD MEETING
PAY: $124

The stars of this show are almost all new to me, except Patricia Richardson. She is best known, to me at least, for her role as Tim Allen's wife in *Home Improvement*. That show ran during the nineties and provided predictable chuckles. Her dry sense of humor made the perfect foil for Allen's slapstick. On *Strong Medicine* she plays Dr. Andy Campbell. The other female headliner on the show is Rosa Blasi, who plays Dr. Luisa 'Lu' Delgado.

I'm SAG now so get $124 a day, compared to $54 when I was non-union. This makes the stultifying waits in Holding 129.63% more tolerable.

Three other extras are in the scene, two men and a woman. We all play doctors, department heads. The scene we're in includes Blasi, Richardson, Philip Casnoff as Chief of Staff Dr. Robert Jackson and Richard Biggs as Dr. Norton. We're in a conference room discussing the recent deaths of geriatric patients and the suspicion that these were mercy killings. Richard Biggs sits to my left, munching on a bagel. Everyone on the set is funny and friendly. Rosa Blasi is especially animated. This is my idea of a fun gig.

☆

SUNDAY, MAY 23, *REVENGE* CALLBACK
TYPE OF PROJECT: FEATURE FILM
PRODUCTION COMPANY: PIBERA PICTURES
CASTING AGENT: DEBBIE WALSH CASTING
LOCATION: PLAYERS SPACE, 4934 LANKERSHIM BLVD, N. HOLLYWOOD
ROLE: PANCHO

I am mildly surprised to hear back from Debbie Walsh since that guy who read the part before me seemed like a shoo-in. Nevertheless, I make the trek all the way to North Hollywood. The cigar I used for the last audition is still in the glove compartment so I repeat my first performance complete with props. This time I feel very little love from Debbie and Ben and a second man—could be the director, Matt Cimber—who sits as far from the stage as he possibly can. If this really is Matt Cimber, IMDB credits him with directing Jayne Mansfield and Orson Welles in their last pictures. Probably just coincidence.

Postscript: I never heard back from Pibera Pictures or from Debbie Walsh. Funny thing, I was unable to find anything more about "Revenge."

☆

WEDNESDAY, MAY 26, GOTTA PAY THE MAN

Mailed Victor a check for $41, his cut from the *Ask for the Order* job. Even though I submitted myself for this job, I pay Victor because I believe it is the fair thing to do. Having representation is essential to being credible when self-submitting. I figure he deserves his 15% commission on any job I get, as long as I'm listing him as my agent. The exception is extra work that for one thing doesn't pay much and, for another, is not contingent in any way on having an agent.

☆

SATURDAY, MAY 29, SEAN MURPHY PHOTOGRAPHY AUDITION
TYPE OF PROJECT: PRINT COMMERCIAL
LOCATION: 1804 FLOWER STREET, GLENDALE 91201
ROLE: TURKEY GUY

Victor calls to say that I have an audition. It's a print job that pays two thousand dollars.

"What's it for, Victor?" I ask.

"Toorkey guy," he says.

"Turkey guy? What's that?"

"They're looking for Khispanic male in early forties. Must
be funny but not too much character. That's it."

When Victor says "That's it," he means it. So I drive out to Glendale, find the studio and sign in. A young man who seems blissfully disinterested in everybody says, "Smile" and shoots me twice. I'm caught precisely in mid-grimace. I have zero chance of getting it, whatever the hell *it* is, unless they're looking for a guy who appears to be in severe pain.

☆

TUESDAY, JUNE 1, *STRONG MEDICINE* RECALL EXTRA GIG
NETWORK: LIFETIME TELEVISION
EPISODE: "FRACTURED" # 505
START AT: 9:30 A.M.
WHERE: STRONG MEDICINE STAGE, 5933 SLAUSON AVE., CULVER CITY
ROLE: DOCTOR, HEAD OF DEPARTMENT
SCENE: DEPARTMENT HEAD MEETING
PAY: $124

I did not think much of it when I was called to work on *Strong Medicine* again. In fact I was a little excited, thinking that maybe they liked me so much that they wanted to make me a regular extra. It would make sense, wouldn't it? After all, I played a department head on the hospital staff. Surely that's a guy you'd see around the place on a recurring basis. No? In any case, the possibility is good for some first class daydreaming.

Not long after arriving on the set I learn we're reshooting the same episode, "Fractured." Sadly, Richard Biggs, who sat to my left while we shot this scene last week, has passed away from a massive stroke. He was forty-four.

The mood is understandably somber on the set, but the show goes on. People die all the time but there is something different, something impossible about the death of a man who appeared to be in perfect health and who, just a couple of days ago, sat next to me having a bagel and playing a doctor on TV.

☆

WEDNESDAY, JUNE 2, WHERE DOES THE TIME GO?

A year ago today I had my photo shoot with Joan Lauren in Marina del Rey. Looking back on the year I feel that the most important thing to launching a career as an actor in Hollywood is stamina and perseverance. I've spent an awful lot of time auditioning and preparing. I've landed a handful of jobs. It may not seem like much but it is quite a bit above average for an actor's first year. The two national commercials, Novartis and American Express, are the biggest scores in terms of money. The industrial projects, however, have been the most valuable in terms of experience.

Emotionally, it's been just what I expected. High highs and low lows. Jorge Luis Borges said it somewhat more eloquently: "I knew states of happiness and darkness that transcend common human experience." Well, okay, maybe that's a little too big. But the constant current for the year has been electric. I've felt somehow more in the moment, more immediate, more likely to spontaneously combust.

All in all, it has not been a bad year.

☆

TUESDAY, JUNE 8, *SONY COMMERCIAL* AUDITION
CASTING AGENT: TLC CASTING
LOCATION: 6521 HOMEWOOD AVE., LOS ANGELES 90028
ROLE: BUSINESS EXECUTIVE

This is my second visit to TLC Casting. The first was five months ago when I auditioned for the part of CEO on a Cisco commercial. This audition is more of the same. I play a business executive and arrive appropriately dressed in suit and tie. Only a couple of other actors are here so we get into a conversation in the comfortable waiting room with the casting director, Leland Williams. Leland is in good form and has something to say about everything from Abraham to Taoism. Interesting man, low-key. You'd have to be if you want to be a casting director.

TLC Casting is in an older house and has one of the friendliest and most comfortable waiting rooms in the business. They always have drinking water available as well as little sugar candies. Leland seems to know many of the actors who come in. Makes sense. Casting directors like to work with the same talent. This one feels a lot like a mom-and-pop agency.

☆

WEDNESDAY, JUNE 9, SAG ORIENTATION
LOCATION: SAG HEADQUARTERS,
5757 WILSHIRE BOULEVARD, LOS ANGELES 90036

New SAG members are invited to an orientation in which they are indoctrinated and advised and edified. Today I'm here with about fifty other new members, listening to the irrepressible Lee Garlington explain to us the ins and outs of SAG. Lee is the consummate working actor and has been part of the Hollywood scene for more than twenty years. She has a long list of credits in TV, including roles in *Hill Street Blues*, *Murphy Brown*, *Friends*, *Everwood* and, very recently, *Desperate Housewives*. Her film credits include *Psycho II*, *Field of Dreams*, *One Hour Photo*, and *Sum of All Fears*.

She begins by asking for a show of hands and we learn that only three people in the audience, including me, have a theatrical agent. Lee is not surprised and points out that the two toughest hurdles in showbiz are getting into SAG and getting an agent. During the three hours that we spend with her, she presents loads of useful information about SAG and also brings in other speakers from the guild to cover specific areas.

The most entertaining thing about this orientation, however, is Lee's knack for cutting to the gist of the issues.

She summarizes a typical newcomer's experience in L.A. as follows, and I paraphrase: they spend the first year crying, the second writing their own movie or starting an improvisation group, and the third year finally working in showbiz. This was her experience, in any case, but she has for years now been an active and busy working actor. Lee averages ten to twelve jobs a year. She's in the top 1% of earners in the business.

Here's a handful of her many wise witticisms:

★ It's called Show Business and not Show Art for a reason.

★ L.A. is the town of the quick yes and the slow no, according to Lee's agent, Lori Rothman.

★ This is a business that eats its young and throws away its old.

★ The three biggies in showbiz are:

• Never be late.

• Never walk off the set.

• Keep track of pay stubs and residuals.

★ In this business you get paid to wait. You act for free.

☆

THURSDAY, JUNE 10, *HARASSMENT AND DIVERSITY*, AUDITION CALLBACK
TYPE OF PROJECT: INDUSTRIAL, CORPORATE TRAINING FILM
PRODUCTION COMPANY: KANTOLA PRODUCTIONS
CASTING AGENT: JUDY BELSHE
LOCATION: CHELSEA STUDIOS, 11530 VENTURA BLVD, STUDIO CITY, 91604
ROLE: CORPORATE EXECUTIVE

Judy Belshe called to invite me directly to the callback for this new industrial. She explains that when she has already worked with an actor whom she believes would be good for a particular part, she will bring them in again without the first audition. I drive out to Chelsea Studios in the Valley and join two dozen men and women waiting to audition. The subject of the film is workplace discrimination and harassment.

Tim Armstrong is directing this training video and is here with Steve Kantola and a couple of other people. When I walk in with two other actors Tim recognizes and introduces me to Steve. After we play through the scene a couple of times, Tim thanks us. Ordinarily this means we all leave but in this case he and I wind up having a short conversation about travel and other things. I suppose if a person stayed in the business long enough, they would eventually build a network of directors and casting directors who know them and their work and call on them again and again. I can see working with Tim on more projects but am now SAG and can only do union work.

☆

MONDAY, JUNE 14, *TASTY FOODS COMMERCIAL* AUDITION
CASTING AGENT: SAMUEL WARREN CASTING
LOCATION: 2244 4TH AVENUE, SAN DIEGO 92101
ROLE: MIDDLE EASTERN FARMER

The breakdown for this project reads as follows:

Airing only in the Middle East
　　Non-Union
　　Casting Director: Samuel Warren
　　Interviews: Week of 6/7
　　Interview Location: San Diego
　　Shoots: TBD
　　Rate: $400 incl. agency
No Lines

Casting for a Middle Eastern family of 4 and a farmer.

[Farmer] 50-60, Middle Eastern type or look...

When I sent in my submission I included a standard headshot. Sam Warren called and invited me to come to San Diego for the audition, so I guess I pass for a farmer in the Middle East.

And yes, I drive all the way to San Diego for a non-union audition. There's a lot wrong with this picture. First of all, it's a hell of a long way to go for any audition, particularly when there will be no residuals if I get the gig. Second, I am now a member of SAG, whose Rule One is: Never Take Non-Union Work! Why do I go anyway? Because I'm thinking that it may be a worthwhile move to go Financial Core but I will not send a letter to that effect to SAG until I've been offered a non-union gig that merits the move. Also, I'm still not sure I know what Financial Core means!

It's a lovely day in San Diego and a nice crowd of families is gathered outside the studio, waiting to be called in. Sam Warren recognizes me from my photo and comes over to say hi. Then the client goes over the storyboard with me. I play a farmer who emerges from his house and looks out over his fields with satisfaction. We do a couple of takes. Ten minutes, tops. As far as I can tell I'm the only person here auditioning for the farmer role. I drive back to L.A. The whole thing has taken six hours. What was I thinking?

Postscript: I did not get offered this gig, which fact, though disappointing, was something of a relief because I could continue to defer my decision on staying a full member of SAG or going Financial Core.

☆

WEDNESDAY, JUNE 16, *IN THE MORNING* AUDITION
TYPE OF PROJECT: SHORT FILM
PRODUCTION COMPANY: IN THE MORNING PRODUCTIONS
CASTING AGENT: DANIELLE LURIE
LOCATION: AMELIA'S CAFÉ, VENICE
ROLE: CHEF

I meet Danielle at Amelia's cafe on Main Street in Santa Monica. Turns out she is the writer and co-producer of this short film that deals with the issue of honor killings. It was inspired by the true story of a Turkish young woman who had been raped and whose family later killed her to expunge the dishonor of the rape. Barbaric in any language.

Danielle has me read the chef's two lines and asks if I can act. Good question. I flash on Dorothy Parker's famous comment about Katharine Hepburn: "She runs the gamut of emotions from A to B." For a moment I contemplate borrowing it. Instead I reply that I can but—always better to be honest—have a limited range. Some actors can do anything asked of them. I am more comfortable in serious roles. I don't do comedy. Danielle seems satisfied that I can handle the part and gives me the script in English and Turkish and also a tape on which my lines have been recorded in both languages.

Postscript: Unfortunately it becomes clear, later in the day, that I have a number of conflicts with the rehearsal and the shoot. I call Danielle back and beg off.

Postscript II: "In The Morning" premiered as a ten-minute short at the 2005 Sundance Film Festival. It received excellent reviews. Danielle is now working on the feature film version of the short. It'll be first-rate.

☆

SATURDAY, JUNE 19, LIEN COWAN COMMERCIALS WORKSHOP

Finally broke down and signed up for a class. Victor, whose office is one floor up from Lien Cowan's on Beverly Boulevard, recommended this one. Jon Smet and Jan Bina, who are also casting directors for Lien Cowan, deliver the class.

Most of the students are in their early twenties. That makes me the relic in the room. Jan and Jon kick off the workshop with a very inform- ative introduction in which, among other things, they claim that 75% of people brought in by casting directors are already known to them. They ought to know. If this is true, even if it's half true, it really underscores the importance of developing rapport with the casting community.

We spend the bulk of the day teaming up in twos and threes and going through various audition situations and improvisations. Following each set of performances, the whole gang gathers in one room and screens them one by one, providing constructive criticism and feedback to the actors involved. Jan and Jon weigh in with their own tips and an invaluable list of dos and don'ts.[16]

The fee for the class is $125 and it's a bargain at that.

☆

THURSDAY, JUNE 24, LUNCH WITH VICTOR

Having lunch at Buddha's Belly again. Victor has warmed up a great deal to me since we first met and now shares his savvy freely. Today we discuss whether or not it makes sense for me to opt for Financial Core status with SAG. We agree that, unless I'm offered a very lucrative non- union job, I will maintain my status as a full member in SAG.

At one point, Victor suddenly leaves the table to give his card to a young blonde walking her dogs. When he comes back to the table he reports that she said it was good timing since her manager had just died! There is something mildly ambulance-chasingish about all this.

☆

MONDAY, JUNE 28, *HARASSMENT & DIVERSITY: RESPECTING DIFFERENCES*
TYPE OF PROJECT: INDUSTRIAL TRAINING VIDEO
CASTING AGENT: JUDY BELSHE
PRODUCTION COMPANY: KANTOLA PRODUCTIONS[17]
LOCATION: IRWINDALE
ROLE: BUSINESS EXECUTIVE
PAY: $450

Today's shoot is at Edison CTAC offices in Irwindale. Man, do I know my way around now! I'm in three scenes and play the Senior VP in the story. I know my lines and feel good and relaxed and ready to go. Then out of the blue, as I'm sitting across the desk from another actor preparing to deliver my lines, I suddenly feel very anxious. I always have a little nervousness before a scene but this is different. My heart is racing, I'm short of breath and mildly concerned—well, perhaps not mildly—that this is where I crash and burn. It's difficult to overestimate oxygen and right now I'm not getting enough. I grab the arm of the chair I'm in, take two very deep breaths and the moment passes. I go on to do the scene without incident. *Note to self: No more triple Americanos before going on-set.*

Postscript: "Harassment & Diversity: Respecting Differences" won a Telly Award. Kantola Productions sent me a copy of the tape. I liked me in it.Does this make me an award-winning actor?

☆

TUESDAY, JUNE 29, OUTGRADED FROM THE AMEX COMMERCIAL

Victor calls earlier today to say that he has received a letter notifying us that I've been cut from this ad.

Postscript: The ad aired on local stations. Of the five who were hired to play service and delivery people, only one survived the editing. I remember when I first met him at the Crossroads Films offices. This was the very first audition he had ever been to. He books the job and gets in the commercial. That's showbiz!

☆

MONDAY, AUGUST 16, LUNCH WITH VICTOR

I've been away for nearly six weeks so I contact Victor as soon as I get back to town and we meet for lunch. We're at Buddha's Belly, as usual. The Wayan brothers are at the next table. They seem to be having as much fun off-screen as they do on. Victor says business is slow. He attributes the decline to the rampant growth of reality shows. The good news is that Novartis must still be thinking about airing the ad because Crossroads Films has paid to extend the exclusivity period by another thirteen weeks. That's the way it works in commercials. If the ad has not run within thirteen weeks of his last day of employment, the actor is free to work for competing advertisers unless a new exclusivity period is paid for. Good thing Novartis paid up because competing advertisers are beating down my door. In this case the fee amounts to about $520. Free money. Victor of course gets $80, his 15% commission.

Postscript: When it came time thirteen weeks later for another renewal, and we didn't receive a check, we figured the ad was dead. As of right now that continues to be the case but I have a small hope that the footage will someday be used and that I'll experience the joy that is a residual check.

☆

TUESDAY, AUGUST 17, *MALCOLM IN THE MIDDLE* EXTRA GIG
NETWORK: FOX
START AT: 3:00 P.M.
WHERE: 4024 RATFORD AVENUE, 91604, STAGE 21, COLFAX LOT PARKING
ROLE: AFGHANI MAN
SCENE: ON BOARD AIRPLANE
PAY: $118

I miss extra work. There is something relaxing about hanging out with a bunch of new people every day and collaborating on a movie or TV show. Also, even if I am merely an extra and my contribution to the show is negligible and even though I can be replaced at a moment's notice, I am still hanging out with stars and actors and learning from them.[18] I mean, here I am and there, not three feet from me, is Jane Kaczmarek playing Lois, Malcolm's mother on the show. Jane is no slouch! She has been in showbiz since the early eighties with starring or guest starring roles on *St. Elsewhere, Hill Street Blues, Frasier* and *The Simpsons*, as well as numerous movies.[19] How can you not learn something watching her work?

I play an Afghani man on an airplane. Wardrobe puts me in a white turban over my navy blue suit. One of the other extras, Gladys, says I look like I've been transplanted from Madras. Let's hope the show's audience doesn't think so, since Madras is in India.

☆

THURSDAY, AUGUST 26, *BILLIONAIRES FOR BUSH*[20]
PROJECT TYPE: MUSIC VIDEO
EXECUTIVE PRODUCER: FELONIUS AX (AKA CLIFFORD J. TASNER)
PRODUCER: G MONEY (AKA CATHY GESUALDO)
PRODUCER: KENT NICHOLS
DIRECTOR: CECIL B. D'MILLION (AKA MILES SONENBAUM)

Not sure what to make of this. Kent calls to ask me to play one of the billionaires in the music video. Unfortunately I could not make it. I think that this was a very low—if any—pay political video so I didn't lose much sleep over it.

Postscript: The music video "The Billionaires Are In the House" is available for download at www.billionairesforbush.com. Looks like it would have been fun!

☆

THURSDAY, SEPTEMBER 9, *FORD COMMERCIAL* AUDITION
TYPE OF PROJECT: TV COMMERCIAL
CASTING AGENT: LIEN COWAN CASTING
LOCATION: 7461 BEVERLY BOULEVARD, LOS ANGELES, 90036
ROLE: MALE DRIVER

Lien Cowan Casting studios are becoming very familiar. This is the fifth audition I've done here. The commercial is for Ford. I'm paired with an actress and we drive our imaginary Ford as the world outside falls apart with all sorts of trouble. Inside the car we're serene and safe and that's the look we're both asked to convey. If you find yourself in a similar audition, I hope that you are not, like I am, concerned that looking serene and looking stoned are not that different. I do my best and even look contentedly at my partner and she looks at me and, for a moment, I can imagine this would look good on the air.

Postscript: I saw the ad when it aired. The actors chosen for the roles looked to me like an affluent though not too-rich white couple somewhere in their forties. They exuded an air of exquisite Americanness. I couldn't do that if my life depended on it.

☆

WEDNESDAY, SEPTEMBER 15, *STATE FARM COMMERCIAL* AUDITION
TYPE OF PROJECT: TV COMMERCIAL
CASTING AGENT: LIEN COWAN
LOCATION: 7461 BEVERLY BOULEVARD, LOS ANGELES 90036
ROLE: JUST A GUY

Long live Lien Cowan! Here I am again and this time Jon Smet is running the auditions. It's an acting exercise in which I improvise with a number of props that are in the room, including a soccer ball and an old, clunky calculator. On my way out I run into one of the guys I worked with on the Novartis commercial. Also here is Anne-Marie

Johnson. You'd recognize her if you saw her. She has done a lot of great work in TV and film but I remember her most as Althea Tibbs on the 1988 TV series *In The Heat of the Night*. Anne-Marie has been an actress for nearly thirty years, has more than fifty TV and twenty film credits and yet here she is, in the same room as me, auditioning. Just doesn't seem right.

☆

SUNDAY, SEPTEMBER 19, *TEXACO COMMERCIAL* AUDITION
TYPE OF PROJECT: COMMERCIAL PRINT
CASTING AGENT: ALICE ELLIS CASTING
LOCATION: SPORTSMAN'S LODGE, 12825 VENTURA BOULEVARD
ROLE: WORKING MAN

Painless. Stopped in more than an hour ahead of my appointment, dressed in denim shirt over a white Polo shirt. The casting coordinator asked that I take the denim shirt off because they were no longer looking for a working man but for an executive in casual dress.

Postscript: Victor called on 9/24 to say that Alice Ellis Casting had called and that the production company wanted me on avail for the days of the shoot, 9/25, 9/26, and 9/27. Later Alice Ellis called to say that she would not know anything more until Monday the 27th since the client was on the East Coast. I never heard from her again but Victor called to say that none of the people who had been put on avail were called in. Something's wrong with this picture.

☆

MONDAY, SEPTEMBER 20, TURNED DOWN ROLE OF RAMON LOPEZ
BECAUSE AM NOW SAG

Richard Courtney from Pilgrim Films called and left a message offering me the part of Ramon Lopez in yet another film they're doing. I turn down the part because it's a non-union project and I am now SAG. I don't want to jeopardize my SAG status for a $200-a-day gig, even if I'd very much enjoy working with Pilgrim Films again. Financial Core keeps coming up as an option but I'm still not sure what the implications would be. When I call SAG and ask, they explain that by declaring myself Financial Core, I am effectively withdrawing from the union and therefore eligible for none of the potential benefits. I can still work union projects and SAG cannot prevent me from doing so, but I'll bet that a SAG signatory production company would rather hire a full SAG member than a Financial Core actor, even if they both get the same pay. Finally, the lady I speak with at SAG emphasizes the point that once I go Financial Core, there is no guarantee that I'll be readmitted into the union. Long story short, she scares me—so I think I'll just play it safe for now. If Tarantino wants me to play a Lebanese psycho in a non-union production, I'll reconsider.

☆

SUNDAY, OCTOBER 10, *SOCCOM III* AUDITION
TYPE OF PROJECT: VIDEO GAME
CASTING AGENT: BRIDGET BORGIN
LOCATION: SANTA MONICA STUDIOS, 3025 OLYMPIC, 90404
ROLE: BENITO SALAZA ZAIAS

Victor calls to tell me about this audition. He usually sends me on things for which I have a decent chance. This one is an exception. The character is described in the breakdowns as having a Napoleon complex. Wouldn't that have to be a shorter actor? I go anyway, certain that it will go nowhere.

Postscript: It goes nowhere.

☆

MONDAY, OCTOBER 1, *AMEX MOTORCYCLE BUILDER* AUDITION
TYPE OF PROJECT: TV COMMERCIAL
CASTING AGENT: LIEN COWAN CASTING
LOCATION: 7461 BEVERLY BOULEVARD, LOS ANGELES, 90036
ROLE: MOTORCYCLE BUILDER

The breakdown calls for someone outgoing, personable, in jeans, T-shirt or work shirt. There are no sides. Instead the casting coordinator asks about my experience with motorcycles. Well, it so happens I've been riding for a few years and so tell him about crossing the U.S. and Canada and Europe and New Zealand entirely by motorcycle. He is

impressed. I think he even said wow. Now he asks what sort of motor-
bikes I ride. I tell him that it's either BMW or Honda touring bikes for
me and a cold chill immediately descends on our little conversation.
They're looking for a Harley man, I'm sure of it.

"Thank you, that was great."

☆

MONDAY, OCTOBER 18, *OFFICE DEPOT COMMERCIAL* AUDITION
TYPE OF PROJECT: TV COMMERCIAL
CASTING AGENT: LIEN COWAN CASTING
LOCATION: 7461 BEVERLY BOULEVARD, LOS ANGELES
ROLE: GIFT RECIPIENT

It's nice to keep getting auditions but three of the last five have been
from Lien Cowan. On the one hand it's good to know that they like me.
On the other I'd like to hear from other casting directors.

This audition consisted of me walking up to a gift-wrapped box and
reacting to it. I'm happy to have received a gift—not too happy, just
happy. I'm in my favorite navy blue suit. After doing the gift-reaction bit
I turn, look into the camera and describe my feelings. Sheesh.

☆

WEDNESDAY, OCTOBER 20, *MAZDA COMMERCIAL* AUDITION
TYPE OF PROJECT: TV COMMERCIAL
CASTING AGENT: WESTSIDE CASTING, STEVE BURDICK
LOCATION: 2050 S BUNDY, LOS ANGELES, 90025
ROLE: AUTO ENGINEER

This one turns out to be fun. They're seeing the actors three at a time.
We're all playing auto engineers working for Mazda competitors Honda,
Nissan and Toyota. These engineers are watching a video of a Mazda
automobile being put through its paces.

Nissan Engineer: This could be trouble.

Toyota Engineer: Yup, real trouble.

Honda Engineer: We're gonna have to drive this bad boy.

The other two engineers look reproachfully at him.

Honda Engineer: You know...for testing purposes...

It's a cute scene and I feel like I did a good job in it.

Postscript: The ad aired and Charles Emmett is in it. The man has been in every other commercial I've seen lately. We met on the set of the Novartis commercial. It's great to see how well he's doing.

☆

WEDNESDAY, OCTOBER 20, *T-MOBILE COMMERCIAL* AUDITION
TYPE OF PROJECT: TV COMMERCIAL
CASTING AGENT: WESTSIDE CASTING
LOCATION: 2050 S BUNDY, LOS ANGELES, 90025
ROLE: TAILOR

I sneak into this. On my way to the Mazda audition Victor calls to say that this T-Mobile audition is at the same location and to see if I can get in. This is interesting: crashing an audition. Turns out it's easy. I sign-up, fill out a size card and bam! I'm in.

☆

FRIDAY, OCTOBER 22, DIRECT TO CALLBACK AUDITION FOR *REASONABLE DOUBT*

Carrie calls from *Reasonable Doubt* to invite me directly to a callback audition for the next episode of this Discovery Channel crime mystery. Again I have to decline because of my union status. *Reasonable Doubt* is a non-union show.

☆

MONDAY, NOVEMBER 1, *DOMINO* EXTRA GIG
TYPE OF PROJECT: FEATURE FILM
START AT: 10:00 A.M.
WHERE: DOWNTOWN LOS ANGELES
ROLE: FASHION SHOW AUDIENCE MEMBER
SCENE: FASHION SHOW
PAY: $152

I drive to downtown L.A. and park at the lot on 4th and Main as instructed. I then join a rabble of extras on a big bus that takes us to Sunset and Argyle in Hollywood, where we sit until 3:30 p.m., have a tasty catered lunch, then get bused back to 4th and Main. We sit around some more. It gets dark. Somebody gets hurt. She fell but is okay. The brief and minor crisis breaks the monotony of the day. Eventually we all get invited into the old building where a fashion runway scene is set up.

Keira Knightley (the most desirable single woman in Britain) is the star.[21] In this scene she is one of several catwalk models. Scantily clad, muscular young men escort the women up and down the platform. The guys are in costumes that evoke the Village People. In the scene's climax Knightly spins around suddenly and yanks another model by her hair to the floor. We, the extras, gasp appropriately. The biggest challenge is not coughing. The crew is using movie smoke and, for added authenticity, or just because they don't care, a couple of them including the DP are smoking big cigars in this stuffy old hall. To object would be really Church-Lady-like, so I keep my trap shut and skip every other breath.

☆

DECEMBER 24, CHRISTMAS EVE, RETIREMENT

George Burns said, "I can't retire—I'm booked." Wouldn't want that to happen to me. Yes, the risk is negligible but I think I'll call it a career. Unless Victor calls.

☆

1. Joan Lauren Photography, 310-451-4021, http://www.joanlauren.com.

2. Imagestarter, 4849 Laurel Canyon Blvd., North Hollywood, 91607. 818-506-7010.

3. This is how the listing appeared in the Casting Networks database. In other databases it also appeared as Alese Marshall Model and Commercial Agency. Their Verizon phone book entry reads: Alese Marshall Model-TV Commercial-Acting School & Agency, 23639 Hawthorne Blvd, Torrance, CA 90505, 310-378-1223, http://www.alesemarshallstudios.biz.

4. Extras! Management, 207 South Flower Street, Burbank, CA 91502. 818-972-9474. Kids Management provides same service for kids.

5. See appendix B, "Casting Agencies" for representative list.

6. Extras Casting Guild, Hollywood OS, 400 South Beverly Drive, Suite 307, Beverly Hills, CA 90212, 310-289-9400. See their book *"Extra" Work for Brain Surgeons.*

7. Pilgrim Films, 4730 Woodman Ave., Suite 300, Sherman Oaks, CA 91423. 818-728-8800.

8. Jason Eness, "Close a Door, Open a Window," Look@Tulane, February 24, 2005, http://www2.tulane.edu/feature_curtain_e.cfm.

9. IFP is a not-for-profit service organization dedicated to providing resources, information and avenues of communication for its members: independent filmmakers, industry professionals and independent film enthusiasts. It is committed to the idea that independent film is an important art form and a powerful voice in our society. http://www.ifp.org/nav/about.php.

10. From casting call breakdowns.

11. Hyacinth Bucket (Bouquet) on *Keeping Up Appearances*, BBC Television.

12. Lodge, *Therapy*, 77.

13. Laila's record as of December 2005 is as follows: won 22 (19 K.O.s); lost 0; drawn 0. Source: BoxRec at http://www.boxrec.com.

14. Phillips, *You'll Never Eat Lunch...*, 146.

15. Showbiz is roughly in the middle of the range of incidence of non-fatal occupational injuries and illnesses. The most dangerous is Justice, Public and Safety Activities, with a rate of 16 cases per 100 during 2003. The safest is Professional, Scientific and Technical Services, with a rate of 1.9 cases per 100. Arts, Entertainment and Recreation comes in at 5.8 cases per 100. Source: Bureau of Labor Statistics, U.S. Department of Labor, Survey of Occupational Injuries and Illnesses, in cooperation with participating State agencies.

16. Jan and Jon generously agreed to let me incorporate their dos and don'ts in this book. They appear in chapter 7, "Auditions".

17. 55 Sunnyside Avenue, Mill Valley CA 94941. 800-989-8273. http://www.kantola.com.

18. How replaceable are extras? I worked on one set where the director

was unhappy with the selection of women he had for a particular shot. The scene called for a young couple to drive up to a restaurant in a Ferrari. He tried the shot with three different female extras then stopped everything while the extra casting agency sent to the location a tall slinky young model-type who fit the bill. The whole thing took a half-hour.

19. http://www.tv.com/jane-kaczmarek.

20. *Billionaires for Bush* is a grass-roots organization that seeks to expose and parody politicians who cater to special and money interests.

21. http://www.tv.com/keira-knightley.

☆

EPILOGUE

I love acting. It is so much more
than life.

— Oscar Wilde

☆

Love has got to stop somewhere short of suicide.

—Sam Dodsworth (Walter
Huston) in William Wyler's
Dodsworth, (1936).

☆

☆

IT HAS been anything but dull trying to get into showbiz in Hollywood. Here's a review of the main events in my so-called career so far:

Career Milestones

June 2 . . . . .Photo shoot

October 30 . . . . .Mailed headshots to agent list

November 7 . . . . .Got an agent

November 17 . . . . .First audition

December 1 . . . . .First extra gig

January 5 . . . . .Booked first lead part

February 23 . . . . .Received first SAG voucher

April 13 . . . . .Booked Novartis commercial

April 21 . . . . .Booked supporting role on industrial

May 3 . . . . .Booked American Express commercial

May 12 . . . . .Joined SAG

May 12 . . . . .Booked first voice-over

May 16 . . . . .Booked supporting role on industrial

June 28 . . . . .Booked lead part on industrial

There it is, a year's worth of testing and being tested by Hollywood. I made a plan, followed it, and often reworked it until it evolved into the roadmap in this book. Another way of assessing my results is by the numbers:

Career Stats

★ Earned $9,350 of which $6,000 was from SAG work.

★ Paid my agent $970.

★ Spent $800 on headshots in two printings.

★ Spent $1,500 to join SAG.

★ Spent $400 in calling service and registration fees.

★ Submitted myself online for 170 projects.

★ Auditioned for forty-two parts.

★ Booked four industrial productions.

★ Booked two national commercials.

★ My hit-rate was one role for every seven auditions and approximately one audition for every eight submissions.

★ Worked as background on thirty or so TV shows and five feature films.

★ Turned down three parts, one for a short film, one for a TV skit, and one for an industrial video.

★ Turned down about twenty background gigs.

Are the above results typical? Is this what you have to look forward to in the first couple of years of your Hollywood career? Let's do the math.

The Bureau of Labor Statistics (BLS) estimates that SAG members earn an average of $5,000 per year. My earnings in Hollywood during one full year were above average. That should be encouraging to you. If I can do it, ill-prepared as I am, then your prospects could be better.

What about the number of auditions I got? This is where the math starts to get a bit fuzzy, because there are no reliable figures for things like how many people are trying to be actors, or how many auditions are held in a particular year. Still, we can extrapolate from available data and say a couple of incantations and see what we get.

Here goes.

Casting Networks (also known as L.A. Casting) reports that, from January through October 2005, approximately 676,000 auditions had been obtained by actors using their site. That works out to about 2,250 auditions a day. (I'm not discounting Sundays. This throws the numbers off a little but we're already in the *Twilight Zone* anyway). Here's where we make a bold statistical leap: let's stipulate that 2,250 accounts for 25% of all auditions in the country. Then approximately 10,000 auditions a day occur nationwide. We can do a sanity check here by estimating the total number of auditions differently. The Casting Society of America has about 360 members. If each of these agencies works an average of 200 days a year and conducts 50 auditions a day, that works out to 3,600,000 auditions a year or 9,860 per calendar-day, not too far from our earlier result of 10,000. Let's accept 10,000 as the number of auditions that take place each day nationwide. We also know from SAG's *2004 Casting Report* that there were 41,000 SAG roles cast in 2004. If we assume that this accounts for 25% of the total number of union and non-union roles cast during the year, then that total would be 164,000 roles, or about 450 per calendar day.

Okay...breathe.

The above number crunching suggests that for every 10,000 auditions, 450 roles are cast, which makes the average hit-rate one role for every 22 auditions. Mine was 1 for 7. Your audition hit-rate will be somewhere between 1 for 5 and 1 for 30. Yes, that's a wide spread, but this analysis requires a healthy margin of error. At least now you have some baseline against which to compare your expectations.

So much for the essential numbers. There is much more to learn, however, and the experience of working in Hollywood offers rewards that are not readily quantifiable.

Among these rewards is working alongside accomplished veterans of the art, as well as with beginners who, not seldom, were on their very first gig. I learned that actors are some of the toughest and most courageous people I've met. They are also among the most tragic, motivated as they are by a cocktail of stimulants: fame, fear, immortality, adulation, money and variety. An actor constantly seeks out and faces his or her fears, pushing through them, competing for roles and becoming someone else for a while.

I also learned why people continue to be drawn to this altar. Moth to a flame comes to mind. The process of auditioning, getting called back for a second audition, winning that part and then performing it is dangerous, thrilling, addictive. Each time the actor is living a new and different reality. It calls on all his courage to go after and compete for the part. Then it calls for all his talent and all his intellect to learn that part and play it well. There is no limit to how well a role can be played, nor to the variety with which it can be interpreted. That is why the greatest stories are told and retold.

I learned that this is not a career that you can fake. You can't phone in a performance, as they say about the bad ones. The nearly immortal George Burns knew this, as you can deduce from the calculated absurdity in his famous words: "The secret of acting is sincerity. If you can fake that, you've got it made." You really can't fake it. You have to be committed and smart and trained and talented. If you're not you'll be found out soon enough and you'll have to get better or go broke or get lost.

I learned that it is a treacherous profession because, perhaps more so than most other professions, it promotes what William James, in a letter to H. G. Wells, calls "…the exclusive worship of the bitch-goddess Success."[1]

And finally, I learned that it can be done. You can make a living as an actor in Hollywood. Young or old, tall or short, whatever your race, whatever your face. You can become a star. Just don't imagine it'll be quick. It certainly won't be easy.

Break a leg.

☆

1. Henry James, Editor, *Letters of William James, Vols. 1 and 2 (1920),* (Montana: Kessinger Publishing, August 1, 2003).

☆

APPENDIXES

Acting is the expression of a
neurotic impulse—it's a bum's
life. The principal benefit acting
has afforded me is the money
to pay for my psychoanalysis.

— Marlon Brando

☆

We're actors—we're the opposite of people.

— Tom Stoppard

☆

☆

THE FOLLOWING appendixes include various resources that are available to the beginning actor. They are not exhaustive and I encourage you to supplement them with your own research.

Service providers are listed when they are leaders in their field or have otherwise distinguished themselves.

☆

APPENDIX A — AGENTS

Association of Talent Agents (ATA),
www.agentassociation.com,
Offers a free list of ATA member agencies.
Casting Networks Los Angeles,
www.lacasting.com
Offers a free list of over two hundred area talent agencies.

Select Los Angeles Talent Agencies

• **Abrams Artists Agency,** 9200 Sunset Blvd., #1130, Los Angeles, CA 90069, Phone: 310-859-0625.

• **Agency for the Performing Arts,** 9200 Sunset Blvd., #900, Los Angeles, CA 90028, Phone: 310-273-0744.

• **Broder, Webb, Chevrin, Silbermann,** 9242 Beverly Blvd., #200, Beverly Hills, CA 90210, Phone: 310-281-3400.

• **Creative Artists Agency (CAA),** 9830 Wilshire Blvd., Beverly Hills, CA 90212, Phone: 310-288-4545.

• **Endeavor Agency,** 9601 Wilshire Blvd., 3rd Fl., Beverly Hills,CA 90212, Phone: 310-248-2000.

- **Gersh Agency**, 232 N. Canon Dr., Beverly Hills, CA 90210, 310-274-6611.
- **Innovative Artists**, 1505 10th St., Santa Monica, CA 90401, 310-656-0400.
- **International Creative Management (ICM)**, 8942 Wilshire Blvd., Beverly Hills, CA 90211, 310-550-4000.
- **Kazarian/Spencer**, 11969 Ventura Blvd., 3rd Flr., Studio City, CA 91604, 818-769-9111.
- **Paradigm**, 360 N. Crescent Dr., Beverly Hills, CA 90210, 310-288-8000.
- **United Talent Agency (UTA)**, 9560 Wilshire Blvd., 5th Flr., Beverly Hills, CA 90212, 310-273-6700.
- **William Morris Agency (WMA)**, 151 El Camino Dr., Beverly Hills, CA 90212, 310-859-4000.

☆

APPENDIX B — CASTING AGENCIES

Select Los Angeles Casting Agencies

- **Sande Alessi Casting**, PO Box 19190, Encino, CA 91416, 818-623-7040.
- **The Casting Connection**, 200 S. La Brea Ave., 2nd Fl., Los Angeles, CA 90036, 310-508-3033.
- **Central Casting, Entertainment Partners**, 220 S. Flower St., Burbank, CA 91502, 818-562-2700.
- **Alice Ellis Casting**, 310-314-1488.
- **Danielle Eskinazi Casting**, 1641 N. Ivar St., Hollywood, CA 90028, 323-461-8353.
- **Headquarters Casting**, 400 S. Beverly Dr., Beverly Hills, CA 90212, 310-556-9006.
- **Lien Cowan Casting**, 7461 Beverly Blvd., Ste. 203, Los Angeles, CA 90036, 323-937-0411
- **Mimi Webb Miller Casting**, 2050 Bundy, Los Angeles, CA 90025, 310-452-0863.

- **Prime Casting**, 6430 Sunset Blvd., Ste. 425, Hollywood, CA 90028, 323-962-0377.

- **Rodeo Casting**, 7013 Willoughby Ave., Hollywood, CA 90038, 323-969-9125.

- **Sheila Manning Casting**, 332 S. Beverly Dr., Beverly Hills, CA 90212, 310-557-9990.

- **TLC Booth, Inc.**, 6521 Homewood Ave., Hollywood, CA 90028, 323-464-2788.

- **Vicki Goggin & Associates Casting**, 451 N. La Cienega Blvd., Los Angeles, CA 90048, 310-492-6540.

- **Anissa Williams Casting**, 6605 Hollywood Blvd., #218, Hollywood, CA 90028, 323-856-8001.

- **Zane/Pillsbury Casting**, 585 N. Larchmont Blvd., Los Angeles, CA 90004, 323-769-9191.

☆

APPENDIX C — ONLINE RESOURCES

- **Academy of Motion Picture Arts and Sciences**, www.acadpd.org.
- **Academy Players Directory**, www.playersdirectory.com
- **Acting Site**, www.actorsite.com.
- **Actor Source**, www.actorsource.com.
- **Actor's Access**, www.actorsaccess.com.
- **Actor's Checklist**, www.actorschecklist.com.
- **Actors' Equity Association**, www.actorsequity.org.
- **American Film Institute**, www.afionline.org.
- **Backstage.com**, www.backstage.com.
- **Breakdown Services, Ltd.**, www.breakdownservices.com.
- **Casting Networks**, www.lacasting.com.
- **Central Casting**, www.entertainmentpartners.com.
- **Entertainment Careers Net**, www.entertainmentcareers.net.

- Film, TV, Commercial Employment Network, www.employnow.com.
- Hollywood Creative Directory Online, www.hcdonline.com.
- Internet Movie Database (IMDB), www.imdb.com.
- LA411.com, www.la411.com
- National Academy of Television Arts & Sciences Job Bank, www.emmyonline.org/jobbank.asp.
- Screen Actors Guild, www.sag.org.
- Showbiz Jobs, www.showbizjobs.com.
- TVI Actors Studios, www.tvistudios.com.

☆

APPENDIX D — PHOTOGRAPHERS

In addition to the photographers listed here, check Appendix B, "Online Resources." Some of the sites listed there offer lists of area photographers.

Select Los Angeles Photographers

- Kevyn Major Howard, www.headshot-photography.com.
- Hollywood Headshot Studio, www.hollywoodheadshotstudio.com.
- Joan Lauren Photography, www.joanlauren.com.
- Nino Via Photography, www.ninovia.com.
- Elliot Photography, www.elliotphotography.com.
- Todd Tyler Photography, www.toddtyler.com.
- Digital Headshots, www.digitalheadshots.la.
- PhotosAndVideo.net, www.photosandvideo.net.

☆

APPENDIX E — PRINTERS

- **Argentum Photo Lab**
1050 Cahuenga Blvd., Hollywood, CA 90038,
323-461-2775, www.argentum.com.
- **Duplicate Photo**
1518 N. Highland Ave., Hollywood, CA 90028,
323-466-7544, www.duplicate.com.
- **Final Print**
1952 N. Van Ness Ave., Los Angeles, CA 90068,
323-466-0566, www.finalprint.com.
- **Focus Foto Finishers**
138 S. La Brea Ave., Los Angeles, CA 90036,
323-934-0013, www.focusdi.com.
- **Genesis Printing Los Angeles**
5872 W. Pico Blvd., Los Angeles, CA 90019,
323-965-7935, www.genesis-printing.com.
- **Grand Prints**
6143 Laurelgrove Ave., N. Hollywood, CA 91606-4618,
818-763-5743, www.grandprints.com.
- **Graphic Reproductions**
1421 N. La Brea Ave., Hollywood, CA 90028,
323-874-4335, www.graphicreproductions.com.
- **Imagestarter**
1016 W. Magnolia Blvd., Burbank, CA 91506,
818-506-7010, www.imagestarter.com.
- **Paper Chase Printing**
7176 W. Sunset Blvd., Los Angeles, CA 90046,
323-874-2300, www.paperchase.net.
- **Photomax Lab**
7190 W. Sunset Blvd., Los Angeles, CA 90046-4415,
323-850-0200, www.photomaxlab.net.
- **Reproductions**
3499 Cahuenga Blvd. West, Los Angeles, CA 90068,
323-845-9595, www.reproductions.com.

☆

APPENDIX F — PUBLICATIONS

- **Back Stage West**
5055 Wilshire Blvd, Los Angeles CA 90036,
323-525-2356, www.backstage.com.
- **Cinescape**
PO Box 807, Venice, CA 90294,
310-399-8001, www.cinescape.com.
- **Filmmaker**
104 West 29th Street, 12th Floor,
New York, NY 10001,
212-563-0211, www.filmmakermagazine.com.
- **Hollywood Reporter**
5055 Wilshire Blvd.,
Los Angeles, CA 90036-4396,
323-525-2000, www.hollywoodreporter.com.
- **LA411**
5700 Wilshire Blvd., Ste. 120,
Los Angeles, CA 90036,
800-545-2411, www.la411.com.
- **Variety**
5700 Wilshire Blvd., Suite 120,
Los Angeles, CA 90036,
323-857-6600, www.variety.com.

☆

APPENDIX G — SAMPLE RÉSUMÉ

Jean Luc Lamirande

456 Batata St., Los Angeles, CA 90555

SAG, AFTRA

Height: 5'10"   Weight: 170 lbs.   Hair: Brown   Eyes: Brown

TV & Film

Dark of Night	2006	Sam	CNM
Dr. Looney	2005	Matt	MCN
Spend It Now	2004	Scrooge	Fly By Night Films

Theater

Hamlet	Hamlet	Duke of Sandwich Playhouse
Hamlet	Ophelia	Bozart Triage
Three Men	Tom	Damfaroff Broadway Company

Commercials

On request

Training

Actor's Boot Camp	Igor Soreshins	2003
Improvisation Workshop	Mackie Tupp	1999
Method Madness	Vigo Knotts	1987

Special Skills

Tap dancing, ballroom dancing, motorcycling, child rearing, proficient cellist, fire-eater, juggler.

Languages

Fluent in English and German. Semi-fluent in Urdu and Dutch.

Agent

Jennifer Lane   555-333-3333 Beverly Hills

☆

APPENDIX H — SCHOOLS

There are many acting schools, workshops and personal coaches in Los Angeles. The list that follows selects a representative sampling. Check the sites in appendix C, "Online Resources," for additional schools.

Select Acting Schools and Workshops

• **Actors Asylum**, "If you're crazy enough to be in this business, you need to be committed."

818-679-1467, www.actorsasylum.com.

• **Actors Center**

1720 20th St., Santa Monica, CA 90404,

310-459-5064, www.actorscenter.com.

• **Actorswork**

Secret Rose Theater, 11246 Magnolia Blvd., North Hollywood, CA.

www.actorswork.com.

• **The Acting Corps**

5508 Cahuenga Boulevard, North Hollywood, CA 91601,

818-753-2800, www.theactingcorps.com.

• **Acting Place**

8879 West Pico Blvd., Los Angeles, CA 90035,

866-478-4886, www.actingplace.com.

• **Actors Workshop**

949-855-4444, www.TheActorsWorkshop.com.

• **Actors Workout Studio**

4735 Lankershim Blvd., N. Hollywood, CA 91602,

www.actorsworkout.com.

• **Allen Garfield's The Actors Shelter**

Suite #463, 289 S. Robertson Blvd., Beverly Hills 90211

310-838-4115.

- **Amy Lyndon's Cold Reading Technique Classes**

www.coldreadingclasses.com.

- **Angela Campolla Acting Studio**

Loudmouth Studios, 11340 Moorpark St., Studio City, 91604,

818-761-4098, www.auditionacting.com.

- **Anita Jesse Studio**

1501 N. Gardner Street, Hollywood, CA 90046,

323-876-2870, www.anitajessestudio.com.

- **Bernard Hiller's Studio**

13816 Califa St., Valley Glen 91401,

www.bernardhiller.com.

- **The Beverly Hills Playhouse**

254 S. Robertson Boulevard, Beverly Hills, CA 90212,

310-855-1556, www.katselas.com.

- **David Kagen's School of Film Acting**

6442 Coldwater Canyon Ave, North Hollywood,

818-752-9678, www.davidkagen.com.

- **Dennis Lavalle Actors Workshop**

4645 Van Nuys Blvd., Ste. 202, Sherman Oaks, CA 91403,

818-788-2183, www.lavalleactorsworkshop.com.

- **Hollywood Actor's Studio**

323-460-2580, www.actingconnection.com.

- **Joel Asher Studio**, Sherman Oaks, CA,

818-785-1551, www.joel-asher-studio.com.

- **The JRose Studio**

323-799-1183, www.jrosestudio.com.

- **The Lee Strasberg Theater Institute**

7936 Santa Monica Blvd., Los Angeles, CA 90046,

323-650-7777, www.santamonicaplayhouse.com.

- **M. K. Lewis Workshops**

1513 Sixth St., Santa Monica, CA 90401,

310-826-8118, www.mklewisworkshops.com.

- **The Larry Moss Studio Edgemar Center for the Arts**
2437 Main St., Santa Monica, CA 90405,
310-829-9692, www.edgemar.com.
- **Margie Haber Cold Reading Workshops**
971 N. La Cienega Blvd., Los Angeles, CA 90069,
310-854-0870, www.margiehaber.com.
- **Michael Chekhov Studio**
818-761-5404, www.chekhov.net.
- **The Network Studio**
14542 Ventura Blvd. Suite 203, Sherman Oaks, CA 91403,
818-939-1608, www.thenetworkstudio.com.
- **Playhouse West School And Repertory Theater**
4250 Lankershim Blvd., N. Hollywood, CA 91602,
818-881-6520.
- **Ruskin School of Acting**
3021 Airport Avenue, Studio 113, Santa Monica, CA 90405,
310-390-4212, www.ruskinschool.com.
- **Santa Monica Playhouse Actors' Workshop**
1211 4th St., Santa Monica, CA 90401,
310-394-9779.
- **Screen Actors Studio**
Westside Casting Studios, 2050 S. Bundy Dr.,
310-358-5942, www.screenactorsstudio.com.
- **Weist-Barron-Hill Acting for Television and Film**
4300 W. Magnolia Blvd., Burbank, CA 91505,
818-846-5595, www.weistbarronhillacting.com.
- **Judith Weston Acting Studio**
3402 Motor Avenue, Los Angeles, CA 90034,
310-392-2444, www.judithweston.com.

☆

Appendix I — Studios

Hollywood's Big Ten studios are owned by six umbrella organizations as follows:

Big Ten Studios

- Warner Bros., owned by Time Warner
- New Line Cinema, owned by Time Warner
- Sony Pictures Studios, owned by Sony
- MGM (Metro-Goldwyn-Mayer), owned by Sony
- Walt Disney/Touchstone Pictures, owned by Disney
- Miramax/Dimension Films, owned by Disney
- 20th Century Fox, owned by News Corporation
- DreamWorks SKG
- Paramount Pictures, owned by Viacom
- Universal Studios, owned by NBC Universal

The following is a list of many TV and film studios in the Los Angeles area. Although these studios account for most of the productions in the area, the list is not exhaustive. There are estimates of over 120 sound stages in Los Angeles.

Select Los Angeles Sound Stages

- **ABC Studios**, 4151 Prospect Ave., Hollywood, CA 90027, 310-557-4305, Thomas Guide: Page 594 A-4.
- **CBS Television City**, 7800 Beverly Blvd., Los Angeles, CA 90036, 213-852-2345, Thomas Guide: Page 633 B-1.
- **Century Studio**, 3322 La Cienega Pl., Los Angeles, CA 90016, 310-287-3608. Thomas Guide: Page 633 A-7.
- **Culver Studios**, 9336 W. Washington Blvd., Culver City, CA 90230, 310-202-1234, Thomas Guide:Page 672 H-1.
- **Dos Carlos Stages**, 1360 E. 6th Street, Los Angeles, CA 90021, 213-306-4555, Thomas Guide: Page 634 H-6.
- **Fox Television**, 5746 W. Sunset Blvd., Hollywood, CA 90028, Thomas Guide: Page 593 G-5.

- **Glendale Studios**, 1239 S. Glendale Ave, Glendale, CA 91205, 818-550-6000, Thomas Guide: Page 564 E-7.
- **Hollywood Center**, 1041 N. Las Palmas, Hollywood, CA 90038, 213-469-5000, Thomas Guide: Page 593 E-6.
- **Hollywood Stage**, 6650 Santa Monica Blvd., Hollywood, CA 90038, 323-466-4393. Thomas Guide: Page 593 A-6.
- **KCAL TV-Channel 9**, 5515 Melrose Ave., Los Angeles, CA 90038, 213-467-5459, Thomas Guide: Page 593 G-6.
- **KCBS, Channel 2**, 6121 Sunset Blvd., Hollywood, CA 90028, 213-460-3000, Thomas Guide: Page 593 F-4.
- **KCOP, UPN, Channel 13**, 915 N. La Brea, Los Angeles, CA 90038, Thomas Guide: Page 593 D-6.
- **KTLA Channel 5**, 5842 Sunset Blvd., Hollywood, CA 90028, 213-460-5500, Thomas Guide: Page 593 G-4.
- **Lindsey Studios**, 25241 Avenue Stanford, Valencia, CA 91355, 805-257-9292, Thomas Guide: Page 4550 C-1.
- **Mack Sennett Stage**, 1215 Bates Avenue, Los Angeles, CA 90029, 323-660-8466. Thomas Guide: Page 594 B-5.
- **NBC Channel 4**, 3000 W. Alameda Ave., Burbank, CA 91523, 818-840-4444, Thomas Guide: Page 563 E-4.
- **NBC-Hollywood**, 1420 N. Beachwood, Hollywood, CA 90028, 213-469-5000, Thomas Guide: Page 593 G-4.
- **Paramount Pictures**, 5555 Melrose Ave., Los Angeles, CA 90038, 213-956-5000, Thomas Guide: Page 593 G-6.
- **Raleigh Studios**, 5300 Melrose Ave., Hollywood, CA 90004, 213-466-3111, Thomas Guide: Page 593 G-7.
- **Ren-Mar Studios**, 846 N. Cahuenga Blvd., Hollywood, CA 90038, 213-463-0808, Thomas Guide: Page 593 F-6.
- **Santa Clarita Studios**, 25135 Anza Drive, Valencia, CA 91355, 562-294-2000, Thomas Guide: Page 4550 D-1.
- **Sony Studios**, 10202 W. Washington Blvd., Culver City, CA 90232, 310-244-4000, Thomas Guide: Page 672 F-2.
- **Sunset-Gower Studios**, 1438 N. Gower St., Hollywood, CA 90028, 213-467-1001, Thomas Guide: Page 593 G-4.
- **Twentieth Century Fox**, 10200 Pico Blvd., Culver City, CA 90067, 310-369-1000, Thomas Guide: Page 632 E-4.
- **Universal**, 100 Universal City Plaza, Universal City, CA 91608, 818-777-1000, Thomas Guide: Page 563 D-5.

• **Walt Disney Studios**, 500 S. Buena Vista Street, Burbank, CA 91506, 818-560-1000, Thomas Guide: Page 563 F-3.

• **Warner Hollywood,** 1041 N. Formosa, Hollywood, CA 90046, 213-850-2500 Thomas Guide: Page 593 D6.

• **Warner Bros. Studios**, 4000 Warner Blvd., Burbank, CA 91522, 818-954-6000, Thomas Guide: Page 563 D4.

☆

GLOSSARY

"Film" is a foreign word that
means "wait."

— Ernst Lubisch

☆

☆

A

1st AD. First Assistant Director.

2nd 2nd. Second Second Assistant Director.

2nd AD. Second Assistant Director.

¾ shots. Photo from head to mid-thigh.

3-D. A film that, when viewed through special glasses, appears to be in three dimensions. Wooooooo.

8x10. Headshot.

ACE. American Cinema Editors.

AD. Assistant Director. See also 1st AD and 2nd AD.

ADR editor. The individual responsible for ADR, generally reports to the Supervising Sound Editor.

ADR. Automated Dialogue Replacement.

ASC. American Society of Cinematographers.

Abby (Abner) Singer. Legendary production manager whose claim to fame is having the second to last shot of the day named after him.

above-the-line. Production budgets are divided into two major sections. The first section, appearing above an actual line in the budget, deals with the VIPs, including producers, directors, writers and principal actors. The second half, appearing below the line, deals with the rest of us. See also **below-the-line**.

Academy of Motion Picture Arts and Sciences (AMPAS). The organization that awards Oscars at its annual Academy Awards show.

action. What directors say to cue actors to begin a scene. "Background action" sometimes used to cue extras separately. Also a term applied generally to the sequence of events in a production.

Actors' Equity Association (AEA). The union for theater actors.

actorvist. An actor who is also an activist. The late Ossie Davis for one.

ad-lib. Dialogue that is unprepared and unrehearsed. Improvisation.

adaptation. In film, the rewriting of a book in screenplay form.

additional photography. A reshoot that requires cast and crew to return to a previously shot scene. See also **pickup**.

adjustment. An increase in an actor's base pay rate.

advertising agency. Creates advertising campaigns for clients, coordinates production.

AEA. Actors' Equity Association. Sometimes just "Equity." The union for stage actors.

aerial shot. A shot of a scene taken from high overhead.

AFI. American Film Institute.

AFM. American Federation of Musicians.

AFTRA. American Federation of Television and Radio Artists, union for broadcast, public and cable TV; radio and sound recordings.

agent or agency. The individual or company that secures bookings and negotiates compensation for actors in return for a percentage of their wages.

AGVA. American Guild of Variety Artists.

airbrush. A technique employed by photo labs to remove imperfections from photos. Often used on glamour shots and headshots.

Alan Smithee. An alias used by directors who refuse to have their name on a movie, generally because they are embarrassed by it. Satirized exquisitely in Joe Eszterhas' *Burn Hollywood Burn* (1998).

A-list. The list in any business that contains the big hitters, the stars of that business. An A-list director of photography, for example.

Alliance of Motion Picture and Television Producers (AMPTP). A trade association that serves production companies and studios and negotiates, on their behalf, labor agreements with performers unions.

ambient light. The diffused light that surrounds an object or scene in a film. Can in fact be natural or simulated using soft floods.

American Cinema Editors (ACE). Society of film editors. Film editors are voted into the honorary society based on their achievements in the industry.

American Federation of Musicians (AFM). The union representing musicians and arrangers.

American Federation of Television and Radio Artists (AFTRA). The union representing performers of radio, voice-over and TV programs that are shot on video. Most sitcoms are AFTRA productions.

American Guild of Variety Artists (AGVA). The union representing nightclub and variety show performers, as well as others in related productions.

American Society of Cinematographers (ASC). Honorary, by invitation society of cinematographers.

AMPAS. Academy of Motion Picture Arts and Sciences.

AMPTP. Alliance of Motion Picture and Television Producers.

animation. Creating moving pictures from a series of drawings.

answer print. The multiple versions of a film copied from the master original for distribution to theaters.

antagonist. The bad guy. See also **protagonist**.

anti-hero. The bad good-guy. A leading man or woman who does not fit the stereotype of a protagonist but to whom the audience is attracted. Stanley Kowalski on *A Streetcar Named Desire*.

apple box. Originally just that, apple boxes that were used on sets to raise objects or in place of chairs. Now manufactured in various sizes for that purpose.

arc shot. A shot in which the camera traces an arc or circle around the actor or scene.

art department. That subgroup of the production team that is primarily responsible for the visual aspects and overall look of a project.

art director. The individual who directs set design, construction and dressing.

artifact. An unplanned and undesirable sound or visual element that appears on film or video.

assembly. The earliest stage in editing, where clips of film are put together in the same order as the script.

assistant director (AD). See 1st AD and 2nd AD.

associate producer. Often a producer who has been involved in the hands-on production work.

atmosphere. One of many terms used for background actors. This one is relatively inoffensive.

audition. An opportunity to try out for a role by reading from a script or otherwise performing. Auditions are typically taped by casting directors and shown to directors and producers who then select candidates for callbacks.

auteur. French for "author." A term applied by movie critics to directors who imprint a project with their distinctive artistic values, transcending the script and eclipsing the original author.

automated dialogue replacement (ADR). The activity of replacing and manipulating dialogue in post-production.

avail. An actor's non-contractual agreement to remain available to work on a particular production. The actor is only paid if he works or is put on hold. See also **hold**.

B

back lot. An outdoor setting on a studio campus that is used for shooting exterior scenes like a city street.

backstory. Events that preceded the beginning of a movie's story but were instrumental in bringing it about. Often surmised from dialogue and consequent events.

back to one. The director's cue for all performers and crew to resume the scene from its very beginning.

backdrop. Large screens on which background settings are painted or printed.

back-end. Any contingency compensation that is paid after a project has been completed and distributed. A share of the profits. As opposed to up-front.

background. A term referring to the area behind the principal performers. Also synonym for extras and sometimes the set itself.

background cross. An actor's move across a scene behind other actors.

backlight. To light a subject from behind so that it appears in silhouette.

barn doors. Metal flaps on light fixtures that regulate the width and breadth of the beam.

beat. In screenwriting, a discrete sequence. Hence the beat outline, which is a skeletal view of a script. On the set a beat can be a brief pause. The director might say, "On 'Action!', wait a beat then enter."

beat outline. A chronological list of scenes that make up a screenplay.

bed. The soundtrack underlying voice-overs and additional sounds.

below-the-line. Production budgets are divided into two sections. The first, appearing above an actual line in the budget, includes producers, directors, writers and principal actors. The second, appearing below the line, includes everyone else. See also **above-the-line**.

best boy. Second in command, used primarily to designate the assistant to the gaffer (chief electrician) and sometimes to the key grip.

Big Ten. In Hollywood refers to the ten biggest studios. 20th Century Fox, Buena Vista, Dreamworks SKG, New Line Cinema, MGM, Miramax/Dimension Films, Paramount Pictures, Sony Pictures, Universal Studios, Warner Brothers.

bigature. Replicas that are so large, they cease to be **miniatures**.

billboard. A large sign usually attached to buildings or posts by the side of highways. In showbiz, a term signifying emphasis on a certain element in a script.

billing. Indicates an actor's stature in a particular production. See also **placement**.

bio. Abbreviation for "biography."

biography. Much like a résumé, describes an actor's experience.

biopic. A picture about someone's life. A movie biography like *Ali*, *Ray*, and *Alexander*.

bit. Bit part.

bit part. Not often heard these days, but traditionally a small speaking part.

blacklist. A large group of over three hundred Hollywood actors, writers and directors whose careers in movies were stopped cold or badly damaged by the Red Scare of the late forties and early fifties.

blocking. The choreography of actors' physical movements in a scene. See **mark**.

blocking rehearsal. A rehearsal during which the actors' movements and positions are practiced and marked on the set.

blooper. A mistake by the actor or a member of the crew during filming that results in a funny or embarrassing situation that is captured on film or tape, often trotted out in later years on shows like *TV's Bloopers & Practical Jokes*.

blowup. An enlarged copy of a photo.

blue screen. A plain blue backdrop against which actors perform. The blue is electronically replaced by other backgrounds. Best seen in TV weather reports, where the announcer actually stands in front of a blue screen. Viewers see various maps and images that replace the blue screen. Also green screen.

B-movie. A low-budget production.

B.O. Short for box office. Also body odor.

body shot. A photo that shows an actor's or model's entire body. Typically used as one of the images on the back of a zed card.

Bollywood. The prolific movie business in Bombay, India.

bomb. A movie that does very badly at the box office.

book. A portfolio that contains an actor's photos or a casting director's talent pool.

book (verb). To get hired for a role.

book out. Notifying your agent, calling service, or casting agency that you are unavailable to work certain dates.

bookends. A movie's opening and closing scenes when they are closely linked and provide visual or contextual brackets.

booker. Individual at an agency responsible for setting appointments for actors and models.

booking. A firm offer to work a specific job.

boom. A telescoping pole that is used to hold a light, a camera or microphone above the set.

boom operator. Operates the boom microphone.

bootleg. An unauthorized copy of a film, TV show, or piece of music.

Botox. Botulinum toxin. Well, it's a toxin and it is used to treat blepharospasm, strabismus, and cervical dystonia. 'Nuf said.

box office. Industry term for ticket sales.

break. What most actors spend most of their time hoping for. A part that sets their careers on the road to stardom.

breakaway. A prop that is designed to break easily, like a chair used in a saloon fight.

breakdown. A listing of roles and parts in a particular production, used by agents and casting directors to match with the right actors for those parts.

Breakdown Services. A private company that dominates the business of providing breakdowns to Hollywood casting agencies

breakdown sheet. A sheet that lists all the particulars of a scene, including location, characters and time of day. Breakdown sheets are summarized on strips, which are then used in a stripboard to organize the overall shooting schedule. See also **stripboard**.

bridging shot. A shot that links two other shots.

broad. A kind of floodlight. Also an adjective that is used to characterize an over-the-top performance by an actor.

bump. An increase in compensation given to a background actor in consideration of special activity or being featured. Generally added as a notation on the actor's voucher by the 2nd AD.

bury. Place someone or something such that they are not easily seen in a scene.

business affairs. The department within a studio that is responsible for putting together the complex deals and budgets behind film and TV productions.

bust shot. A shot in which only an actor's head and torso are in the camera frame.

buyout. The money paid to an actor, in advance, as compensation for future use of a particular production. This arrangement waives the actor's claim to residuals.

buzz. Publicity, sizzle, people talking about someone or something.

buzz track. White noise or the non-specific room tone that characterizes a set.

C

CU. Short for close-up.

CAA. Creative Artists Agency. One of the largest talent agencies in L.A. Founded by Mike Ovitz.

California Child Actor's Bill. See Coogan Laws.

call. Appointment.

call sheet. A detailed schedule of the day's activities, scenes, actors and crew. Often produced by the 2nd AD and distributed, sometimes more than once a day depending on revisions, to the members of the company.

call time. The actual time an individual is to report to the set.

callback. Second interview after an audition. An indication that the individuals deciding whom to hire for a particular part have placed you on the short list.

calling service. A company that is retained by a background actor to call casting work lines on his behalf and set up gigs.

cameo. A brief part ordinarily played by a recognizable actor. Alfred Hitchcock often gave himself walk-on cameos in his movies. He's the portly fellow in the back.

camera. Comes in two technologies, film and video. No camera, no movie.

camera left. The area to the left of the camera as seen from the camera operator's point of view.

camera operator. Works for the director of photography and physically operates the camera.

camera ready. Dressed and made-up and otherwise prepared to go onset. Extras are often expected to report to set camera ready.

camera right. The area to the right of the camera as seen from the camera operator's point of view.

camp. Over the top and intentionally flamboyant comedy. Possibly the opposite of dry or cerebral humor.

can. A can is a round container, made from metal or plastic and used to store film reels. Two cans make a French dance.

canting. Tipping the camera at an angle, creating an effect often used in cinéma vérité.

captions. Text that is overlaid on film or video to provide translation or other information.

CARA. Classification and Ratings Administration.

cartoon. Short animated film.

cast. Collective term for the performers in a production. Also used as a verb. To cast a project is to find the talent to fill the roles in that project.

castable. Refers to a project that is appealing to big-name actors. An attractive project that is easy to cast.

casting. Choosing models and actors for a specific job.

casting couch. Industry shorthand for exchanging sex for parts in movies or TV shows. No longer as widely practiced as in earlier years, owing mostly to heightened awareness of sexual harassment issues in the workplace. That, or people ain't talkin'.

casting director. The individual responsible for finding the talent for a show or print ad or any other project. Can be independent and retained by the production company on a job-by-job basis or can be an employee of a large production company.

caterer. An individual or company that prepares and provides meals on production sets.

cattle call. An audition or assignment involving a large number of applicants or actors.

censor. To edit a work of art by removing portions of it that offend public- or state-defined standards of propriety.

certificate. In motion pictures the rating that is given to a movie by the Classification And Ratings Administration (CARA).

CGI. Computer-generated imagery.

change. Refers to wardrobe changes that are required by the show. If these are the actor's own clothes, additional compensation is paid.

character. One of the people described in a script.

character actor. Nice way of saying "not the star." An actor who is cast in supporting roles. Often the best and busiest actors in the business.

character arc. In screenwriting the evolution that a character undergoes in the course of a story.

character study. A film that focuses on the interaction between its main characters as opposed to plot twists and action sequences.

cheat. To move or adjust one's position in order to accommodate camera placement; almost always on director's orders.

check the gate. The director's command to the camera crew at the end of a shot with which he is satisfied. The gate is that part of the camera through which film passes during exposure. If there is no problem with the gate the director can move on to the next scene.

checking in. What an extra does on arrival at the set, normally with the 2nd AD.

chick flick. A movie that appeals primarily to women. Slang, of course, and when uttered by a man, usually damning.

choker. Showbiz-speak for an extreme close-up.

chops. More specifically: acting chops. Industry jargon for prior acting assignments. See also **creds**.

chroma key. Especially in television, refers to the computerized replacement of a blue or green backdrop with an electronic image from another source. See also **blue screen** and **green screen**.

cinéma vérité. French for "reality cinema," a style of filmmaking that is spartan, uncontrived and lacks formal directorial guidance. Often a documentary-style character study. Arguably the grandmère of reality TV. Or not.

cinematographer. Otherwise known as the director of photography.

clapboard. A board with a hinged top that produces a clapping sound. Used to mark the beginning of a shot with a visual and aural cue. Also called a **slate**.

class A spot. A commercial that airs during prime time on a major national network. The schedule of residual payments is highest for this kind of spot. See also class B spot.

class B spot. A commercial that airs in a secondary market.

Classification and Ratings Administration. A division of the MPAA, responsible for viewing and rating motion pictures.

claymation. A compound word, or portmanteau, made up from "clay" and "animation." The art of animating clay figures and sets in the making of a movie or TV program.

click track. A sound track that produces metronomic clicks, often played in musicians' ears to help them stay on the beat.

cliffhanger. A highly suspenseful story.

climax. The point of greatest tension in a story, arrived at via multiple conflicts and resolved through catharsis and denouement.

clip. A length of film or videotape; a short portion of a program.

close captioned. A system that shows dialogue as text subtitles in real time for the benefit of the hearing-impaired.

close-up. A shot that focuses on a small detail of the scene, such as an actor's face or a particular prop. See also **choker**.

cold reading. Reading for a casting director from an unfamiliar script or dialogue.

color timer. A highly specialized individual who manipulates the various color characteristics of a film, in postproduction, to meet the artistic intentions of the director and director of photography.

colored pages. Edited versions of a script.

commercial. An ad or other message paid for by an enterprise to promote its goods or services.

commissary. The cafeteria on a studio lot.

commission. A percentage of an actor's or model's wages that is paid to their agent or manager.

composite card, comp card. A card that shows an actor or model in various poses and includes their essential measurements. Seldom used by actors. See also **zed card**.

computer-generated imagery. The technique of creating realistic looking creatures and objects using computers and specialized software.

concept meeting. A meeting of the senior creative producers, director and casting director to discuss and specify the look of the characters in a script.

conflict. In commercials, the situation in which an actor has already appeared in an ad for a competitor's product. In general, a reference to schedule overlaps.

console. The desktop equipment at which a sound or video mixer manages levels and inputs from various sources such as cameras and microphones.

contact sheet. Thumbnail reproductions of a photo shoot, used to view an entire series of photos and select the best for enlargement and printing.

continuity. Maintaining the look and position of a character or setting throughout a scene or movie. Making sure that the star does not appear clean-shaven in the dining room, then bearded ten minutes later in the den. Spotting failures in continuity can be a fun way to turn a terrible film into rich entertainment.

control booth. Also control room. Especially in TV and radio, the room in which the director and other production personnel manage the various inputs from cameras and microphones and issue commands to the camera operators and actors.

Coogan laws. Named for Jackie Coogan (1914-1984) who began acting as a child and achieved early fame in Charlie Chaplin's *The Kid* (1921). Coogan earned a pile of money but it was taken by his mother and stepfather. He sued in 1935 and the case brought about the California Child Actor's Bill.

co-producer. A member of the production management team.

copy. The script or any portion of it.

copyright. An individual or group's claim to intellectual property and to protection against unauthorized reproduction of that property.

copyright Infringement. The act of using intellectual property without proper authorization from the copyright holder.

copyright office. Department of the Library of Congress that administers copyright laws and issues and keeps a record of copyrights.

co-star. Somewhere between a starring and guest-starring role.

costume designer. Works with the director and creative producers in designing the costumes for a production. Is assisted by the key costumer.

cover set. An indoor set or a set on a sound stage that is used as a fallback in the event the location of a shoot becomes unavailable for any reason. Part of a defensive strategy known affectionately as CYA.

coverage. 1. Camera shots that capture close-ups or other angles of a scene and that are used to supplement the main camera view of the scene. 2. The job—usually performed by assistants hired expressly for that purpose—of reading scripts and providing summaries of them for harried senior creative executives to review.

crab. Sideways camera dolly.

craft services. The catering service on-set.

crane shot. A shot made with a camera that is elevated above the action on a crane. Normally used for very wide or establishment shots.

creative differences. Can be legitimate differences of opinion on important aspects of a project but sometimes face-saving Hollywood-speak to describe a reason for someone leaving a project.

creative executive. The title given to studio executives whose primary role is to find bankable scripts and do the deals that secure them for the studio.

creds. Short for credits.

credits. The list of project members and their titles, normally shown at the end of a film and presented in order of importance. Producer and director always list first.

crew. A general term referring to all production personnel on a set, excluding the cast. Cast and crew means everybody.

critic. A person who reviews films and TV shows. "What good are they," said Mel Brooks about critics, "if they can't make music with their hind legs."

cross. The act of walking or running across the foreground or background while the principals enact the scene.

crosscutting. Cutting back and forth between two scenes, creating the effect that they are contemporaneous.

crossover. A show that appeals to audiences with differing tastes.

crowd shot. A shot of a large gathering of people.

cue. An indication or signal to the actor to take a specific action like deliver a line, enter the scene, or exit. Most often this is the end of another actor's line.

cue cards. Large cards held up for actors to read while they are performing or auditioning. Some directors refuse to allow these on the grounds that they weaken an actor's performance.

cult film. A film that appeals to a small but very loyal following. Jim Sharman's 1975 *The Rocky Horror Picture Show* is an enduring example. So are all Monty Python movies.

cut. The command called out by the director to stop action and filming on the set. The end of a shot.

cutaway. A shot of an object or other scene or actor that is not part of the present action but is related to it.

cutter. Film editor.

cyclorama. A concave backdrop used to simulate the sky and other backgrounds in studio shoots.

D

DP. Director of photography, also cinematographer or, in video productions, videographer. In charge of camera and lighting departments.

dailies. The first positive prints made from raw footage that is shot on the set, later viewed by the director and film editor and others and used in assembling the final version of the production. Also called **rushes**.

day player. An actor hired to play a part for one day only.

day shot. Daylight scene.

day-for-night shot. A shot made during the day but lit so as to appear as though it were shot at night. Often *looks* like a shot made during the day but lit so as to appear as though it were shot at night.

day-out-of-days. A schedule that lists all the characters in a production and, for each day, indicates whether they are working (W), traveling (T), on hold (H), or in their final day (F). It shows at a glance the cast's activity on a production.

deadpan. Expressionless, as in deadpan humor.

decoupage. The order of shots in a film. See also **beat outline**.

demo tape. A video or audiotape that showcases an actor or their voice.

denouement. In classic plots, the denouement is the stage that follows the climax and in which the author ties up all the loose ends.

deuce. A certain type of lamp used on-set.

development. The phase and process during which a script goes from being picked up or optioned to receiving a **green light**.

development hell. A painful and interminable period of development.

DGA. Directors Guild of America.

dialect. Variation of a language typical of a region or country. Cockney is a dialect of English.

dialect coach. Helps talent perfect dialects that are called for in a production.

dialogue. Lines in a script that are written for the actors to speak

diffusion. The effect created when a source of light is not focused. A floodlight produces diffuse lighting whereas a spotlight produces focused lighting.

dimmer board. A console from which individual fixtures on the set are controlled.

director. The individual in charge of turning a script into a visual program. Responsible for all creative elements of a project on-set. Also oversees post-production to ensure that the final product is consistent with his artistic vision.

director of photography (DP). Works hand-in-hand with the director in capturing the action on film with the desired look and qualities. Also **cinematographer.**

director's cut. A version of the film that differs in some way from the final cut. Usually a rougher cut that has not been cleaned up by the studio.

Directors Guild of America (DGA). The union representing directors, unit production managers (UPMs) and select other individuals who work on TV or movie productions.

dissolve. A transition from one visual to the next during which the two are temporarily superimposed as one fades and the other intensifies.

distribution. The final logistical stage in the TV and film business, consists of placing the production with theaters and networks for viewing and broadcast. In film, distribution is dominated by the major studios.

distributor. An organization that owns or manages a distribution network.

documentary. A non-fiction production that recounts events in a journalistic manner. Examples include Michael Moore's *Bowling for Columbine* and Ken Burns' *Civil War.*

dolly. A wheeled cart on which the camera is mounted to ease moving it around the set. A dolly shot has the camera moving, often on rails, while recording the action.

dolly grip. The grip who is responsible for moving the camera and ensuring that the start and stop marks on a shot are observed.

double. The actor or performer who stands in for the principal, particularly during stunts or when, for whatever reason, the principal is unavailable.

dress the set. Add accessories and props to complete a set.

dresser. A personal assistant to big-name actors, assists them in making wardrobe changes. *The Dresser* is the title and subject of a 1983 movie starring Albert Finney.

dry run. A rehearsal without cameras running, often used to finalize movement and blocking.

dubbing. Adding a soundtrack to a film or video program in post-production. A movie can be dubbed into another language in lieu of subtitles.

Dutch tilt. A shot in which the camera is angled against the horizontal axis, often used in art house films and in shots where a suggestion of instability is called for.

dupe. Short for "duplicate," usually referring to a copy of a film or videotape.

E

ear prompter. Known in the business as "the ear." A recording device worn by the actor that feeds him lines from the script through a hidden earpiece.

ECU. Extreme close-up.

editing. In film and video, any act of cutting from, adding to, or otherwise amending and manipulating existing images and sound.

editor. In film or video, the individual who cuts and reassembles a program until it meets with the director's approval.

editing on the fly. Editing in real time when post-production editing is not possible.

eight-by-ten. Photo most often used as an actor's calling card. See also **headshot.**

eighteen-to-play-younger. An often-seen casting call for an actor who is eighteen but looks younger.

employer of record. The company responsible for paying an actor and tracking withholding taxes and other deductions.

end title credits. Credits shown at the end of a television show or film.

epic. A film that deals with a sweeping historical story and employs a cast of thousands. See Moustapha Akkad's *The Message* (1976) and Mel Gibson's *The Passion of the Christ* (2004).

epilogue. A brief final segment that concludes a film or program and provides additional information about the outcome of events.

episodic. A production that is presented in episodes over a period of time, like television sitcoms and hour-long dramas.

Equity. Short for Actors' Equity Association.

Equity waiver. Theaters that seat fewer than ninety-nine people and are exempt from Actors' Equity Association contract provisions and obligations.

escort. Companion. Now a euphemism for a professional who receives money for fraternizing with strangers and possibly undressing in the process. Not a brilliant career choice. See *The Wedding Date* (2005) for a syrupy take on how that might work out.

establishing shot. A camera shot that shows the overall scene where the action will be taking place.

executive in charge of production. Oversees day-to-day production activities, particularly in television.

executive producer. The individual most often responsible for securing the funding for a production. Also a credit sometimes given a writer.

experimental film. A film whose primary purpose is to challenge accepted filmmaking assumptions with no regard for commercial success.

exposition. Those parts of a screenplay or production that describe the background and circumstances against which events take place.

EXT. Short for exterior; a scene that takes place outdoors. As opposed to INT. or interior. These abbreviations occur in the screenplay and on the daily call sheet.

exterior shot. A scene that takes place outdoors. See also **interior shot**.

extra. Also **background** actor. An actor who has no speaking part.

eyeline. An imaginary line that traces the direction of an actor's gaze.

F

fade in. The gradual appearance of an image from a black screen.

fade out. A gradual darkening of the image on the screen until it disappears.

farce. Lowbrow humor, often physical and goofy. Richard Lester's *A Funny Thing Happened on the Way to the Forum* (1966) is a good example.

favor. What a camera does when it gives more prominence to one actor over another in a particular scene.

feature. A typical full-length movie, lasting anywhere from ninety minutes to three hours.

featured. Describes an actor who plays an important though not starring part on a production.

field of view. That part of a scene that is visible through the lens.

film noir. A movie with dark subject matter, characters, and even look. Emerged in the early forties with such classics as Michael Curtiz's *Mildred Pierce* (1945) starring Joan Crawford, or John Huston's *Key Largo* (1948), with Bogey and Bacall. A more recent example is Frank Miller's *Sin City* (2005).

filmic time. Time as measured by events in a movie. Usually, filmic time is shorter than real time. In other words, events that might take years to occur in life are presented in 120 minutes on-screen. See **real time.**

filmography. The body of film work credited to an actor, director, or other motion picture professional.

final cut. That version of a movie that is released to the theaters.

Financial Core. A much-maligned status that a union member can elect and that allows them to take non-union work while preventing the union from discriminating against them. Discussed in detail in chapter 10, "Performers Unions."

finder's fee. A sum paid to an individual in return for their finding and securing rights to a screenplay that a studio wants to produce.

fine cut. Next to last edited version of a movie. Approximates its final length and falls between the rough and the final cuts.

first assistant director. See 1st AD.

first reading. The very first audition to which an actor is invited. If it goes well, the actor may be invited for a second reading or a callback.

first team. The principal actors on a production. As opposed to second team, which is made up of the stand-ins.

fisheye. A wide-angle lens.

fitting. A booking during which an actor is fitted with a costume that they will wear in an upcoming shoot. Pays one quarter of the normal daily base rate.

flash frame. One or two clear frames resulting in a very brief bright flash. Used to create a visual pop between shots.

flashback. A scene that takes place in the past, inserted into a movie in order to inform the audience of the history that brought about the unfolding events. See also **flash-forward.**

flash-forward. A scene that takes place in the future but is inserted into the present action.

flat. A module that is used as part of a set construction. A wall.

flat rate. Non-hourly rate paid to a performer regardless of hours worked. Must exceed the state-mandated minimum wage.

flipper. False teeth used to temporarily replace lost teeth for child actors.

flop. A movie that fails at the box office.

focus puller. Works with the camera operator to ensure that the shot is in focus.

Foley editor. The individual who, in postproduction, is responsible for matching on-screen action with footsteps, hoof beats, clanks, thuds, and other sounds. Named after Jack Foley, one of the first to do this for a living.

footage. Generally used to denote some length of film or video.

forced call. A call time less than twelve hours after the previous day's dismissal time. Can trigger certain additional compensation for the actors and crew.

foreground. The area between the camera and the principal actor, as opposed to background, which is the area behind the actors.

fourth wall. The theoretical partition between an audience and the action on a screen. An actor can penetrate that partition between reality and make-believe by addressing the audience. An example of this is provided by Kevin Spacey's character Roger "Verbal" Kint in Bryan Singer's *The Usual Suspects* (1995).

fps. Frames per second.

frame. The smallest section of a reel of film. Each foot of 35mm film contains 16 frames. Each frame captures an image. The rapid progression of these discrete images is what creates the illusion of movement and action.

frames per second. The speed at which a film is exposed and replayed. 24 fps is the normal rate of exposing and running a film. Altering this rate is used to create the impression of slow motion and fast motion.

framing. A shot's composition, takes into account all the elements within the shot, including the actors, the set, and the space.

franchised agent. An agent, commercial, theatrical or otherwise, who is franchised by SAG or AFTRA.

free weeks. A term used in an actor's movie compensation contract that allows the production company to use that actor beyond the agreed term without additional payment. The actor's compensation is set at a higher initial rate in anticipation of such an overrun.

freelance. Working as a model or actor without agency representation or a direct studio affiliation.

freeze-frame. The effect achieved by repeating the same image for many frames. On the screen the action appears to be frozen, like a still shot.

French hours. On-set slang meaning no official meal stops. Food is available on-set all the time and actors and crew can eat whenever they wish, assuming of course they are not acting at the time!

Fresnel. A widely used spotlight, named for Augustin Fresnel (1788-1827). Pronounced "frah-nell."

f-stop. An inverted numerical scale designating the size of the aperture of a camera's iris. The larger the f-stop, the smaller the opening.

full length shot. A head-to-toe photo of an actor or model.

G

G. CARA film rating. General Audiences. All ages admitted.

gaffer. The head of the lighting department. He reports to the DP and is assisted by the best boy.

gate. The opening in a camera's mechanism at which a film is exposed to light.

genre. Category such as Western, Action, or Romantic Comedy.

go-and-see. A job interview, particularly in the modeling world.

gofer. The crewmember who runs various errands on the set, often a production assistant. Not a particularly nice thing to call anyone. "Assistant" is better.

Golden Age of Hollywood. The nineteen thirties and forties, during which the movie industry was powerful and influential and produced a large number of memorable films.

golden time. For SAG members, starts with the sixteenth hour of employment during any given day. Golden time pay is the base daily rate per hour. In other words, if a SAG extra's daily base rate is $120, their golden time compensation would be $120 per hour. Doesn't happen often but, when it does, Yippee!

grace. A twelve-minute delay in mealtime for which the production company is not penalized as long as the delay occurs because the crew is in the middle of a shot.

green light. The go-ahead for a movie production following development. This normally triggers the release of money and production resources.

green screen. See **blue screen.**

grip. A set worker whose primary role is moving and setting up electrical, lighting, and camera equipment. See also **hammers, dolly grip** and **key grip.**

groovy. A term of appreciation and admiration. Useful in the seventies. Now almost entirely displaced by "awesome."

guest star. An actor who has a bigger name and larger role than a featured actor.

guild. An organization that represents its members in matters of compensation and workplace safety but, unlike a union, does not secure work for them.

H

hair stylist. Works on hair changes.

ham. An actor who overplays a part that does not call for overplaying.

hammers. The grips with the hammers. The guys (or gals) who do all the miscellaneous work on the set that requires tool belts.

handheld shot. A shot made with a handheld camera, often used to create a real-life, unstaged effect. The *Blair Witch Project* exemplifies the technique.

hard-core. Refers to programs with explicit sexual content. See also **soft-core.** Also means serious. A hard-core cyclist is a dedicated athlete, not a XXX pedaler.

head. Lighting fixture. Alternatively the navy word for the honey wagon.

headbook. A talent agency's catalog of actors' headshots, sent to casting agents and producers for review and selection.

headroom. The space between the top of an actor's head and the upper edge of the screen frame.

headshot. Generally an 8"x10" photo of an actor's or model's head and shoulders. Also **8x10.**

helmer. Industry slang for director.

hiatus. Period during which TV series cease production. There are a couple of hiatus periods during the year, Christmastime and again April or May through July.

high concept. A term that describes movie ideas that can be stated in attractive sound bites. An example might be "suicidal down-and-out gambler makes an unbelievable comeback, gets the girl and discovers the true meaning of happiness."

high-angle shot. A shot in which the camera is positioned so that it is looking down at the subject.

high-definition. Also hi-def. A new TV standard with greater picture resolution.

hit the mark. An actor's ability to stand at the precise spot where they are supposed to on a set based on earlier blocking. This is important because the camera and lighting are set up on that basis.

hold. An actor who is put on hold by a production company is considered engaged and will be compensated even if he does not work on the day in question. See also **avail.**

Holding. The area on-set where background actors are expected to stay during the day so that the 2nd AD will know where to find them.

holding fee. The fee that a production company must pay an actor as long as it still is interested in possibly airing a commercial on which that actor worked. The holding fee extends the actor's commitment not to work for competing products. Generally thirteen-week periods. An actor's agent is responsible for tracking holding fees owed.

holding over. What a production is doing when it asks an actor to return to work at the end of his originally agreed schedule. For actors, unless there is a schedule conflict, this is good news. Producers and directors don't like having to do this because it means cost overruns.

Hollywood Ten. Alvah Bessie, Herbert Biberman, Lester Cole, Edward Dmytryk, Ring Lardner Jr, John Howard Lawson, Albert Maltz, Samuel Ornitz, Adrian Scott, Dalton Trumbo. The most visible of Hollywood's Blacklist. See also **blacklist.**

Hollywood Big Ten. Warner Brothers, New Line Cinema, Sony Pictures Studios, MGM, Paramount Pictures, Miramax/Dimension Films, 20th Century Fox, DreamWorks, Walt Disney Pictures/Touchstone Pictures, Universal Studios.

honey wagon. A somewhat nauseating euphemism for toilets on-set. Usually contained in a trailer that is parked on the production lot.

hook. The plot point at the end of a scene that makes viewers want to keep watching after the commercial.

horse opera. A Western.

hot dog. An actor who likes to show off. Also an American sausage.

hot mic. A microphone that is live.

hot set. A set that is dressed and has been or will be used. In order to maintain continuity, nothing on a hot set may be moved or otherwise disturbed.

hyphenates. Individuals whose titles include two or more components. For example. writer-producer, actor-model.

I

IATSE or IA. International Alliance of Theatrical Stage Employees.

IBEW. International Brotherhood of Electrical Workers.

IBT. International Brotherhood of Teamsters.

ICM. International Creative Management, one of the largest talent agencies in L.A.

IMAX. A film format that relies on an extra-wide gauge of film to capture very high-definition images that are then projected on huge screens in specially built auditoriums.

IMDB. Internet Movie Database. Excellent online resource for all things showbiz. www.imdb.com.

in the can. Completed and ready to be shown as in "it's in the can."

independent. Or "indie," or "independent production" is a production that is financed outside of the major studios.

independent studio. One of a large number of smaller studios, excluding the Big Ten. Among these are the following: Touchstone Pictures, Orion Pictures Corporation, Republic Pictures and others.

industrial. A program that is not intended for broadcast, often produced by a corporation or government entity.

insert. A shot that is inserted into other footage. See also **cutaway**.

INT. Short for interior.

intellectual property. Or IP for short. Any non-tangible asset that is protected by copyright and patent laws, including publications, inventions, films, and music.

intercom. A communications system, often wireless, that is used by the crew and production staff.

interior shot. A scene that takes place indoors.

International Alliance of Theatrical Stage Employees (IATSE). An overarching organization that represents below-the-line workers in showbiz. These include grips, costume designers, set designers and script supervisors, among others.

International Brotherhood of Electrical Workers (IBEW). Represents 750,000 workers in utilities, construction, telecommunications and television broadcast equipment operators and technicians.

International Brotherhood of Teamsters (IBT). The union representing transportation workers.

interstitial. An Internet ad that runs while you are going from one web page to the next.

iris. The camera's aperture that regulates the film's exposure to light.

J

jib arm. A mount that enables smoother movements of the camera.

juicer. Industry jargon for a lighting technician.

jump cut. A sudden cut from one shot to another, deliberately creating a sense of discontinuity.

K

key grip. The lead grip on a production.

key light. The primary light on an actor or some part of the set.

kick. A hard light aimed at the back of an actor's head. That could hurt.

kick-off. The beginning of production.

knee shot. A shot that frames the subject from the knees up.

L

last looks. 1st AD's warning to Wardrobe, Makeup and Props to inspect the scene and actors for the last time before shooting the scene. Final opportunity to head off wardrobe and other malfunctions.

laugh track. A pre-recorded tape of people laughing. Used in sitcoms in place of and sometimes in addition to a live audience.

laugher. An extra who is hired to sit in a live sitcom audience and laugh on cue.

lavalier. A clip-on microphone.

lead. Major part. Also leading man and leading lady.

leadman. The individual who heads up the swing gang.

libel. Publishing, in any medium, false and defamatory information about someone.

line producer. Coordinates hands-on day-to-day work in producing a project, such as managing vendors, logistics and schedules.

lines. An actor's portion of the dialogue.

lip sync. Matching mouth movement to prerecorded audio. Nearly perfected by Milli Vanilli.

loader. Responsible for loading film into the camera.

location. Literally where the production is shooting away from the studio. Examples include city streets, beaches, wilderness, etc.

logline. A very brief summary of a film's story. See also **high-concept**.

long shot. A camera shot that captures the subject from a distance. See also **wide shot** and **establishing shot.**

looping. The activity of synchronizing the audio track to the video or film following a shoot. This is done in the studio and is part of post-production.

loupe. Magnifying glass used to see slides and contact sheet images.

low-angle shot. A shot in which the camera is positioned so that it is looking up at the subject.

M

main title credits. Credits shown at the beginning of a film or TV show.

makeup artist. Applies and changes makeup for photo sessions and TV and film productions.

manager. An individual whose role is to direct the career of his actor clients. Different from agents in that he is not, by law, permitted to book his clients into jobs or to negotiate compensation.

mark. The spot on a set where the actor and camera begin and end their action in a scene. Often established during blocking rehearsals and marked with tape on the floor of the set.

marker! What the camera operator assistant calls out when he claps the slate board before the shot, thus establishing aural and visual cues.

martini. Last shot of the day. See **Abby Singer.**

meal penalty. Additional compensation paid to a performer if the production company is late in providing meals.

Method actor. An actor who practices Stanislavski's Method.

Method, The. A system of acting, developed by Constantin Stanislavski and refined by Lee Strasberg and others.

mimic. To copy the behavior of someone else. To impersonate.

miming. Short for pantomiming. Acting by using body movements, gestures and facial expressions, without speaking.

miniature. A detailed model that is built specifically for use in filming. Most useful in disaster movies where destruction of an actual city would be inconvenient and expensive. See also **bigature.**

miscast. Describes an actor who is selected to play a role for which they are not a good match. Anna Nicole Smith as Mother Teresa.

mixer. See **sound mixer.**

mockumentary. A spoof documentary, seemingly journalistic in style but intended to parody the subject matter. Rob Reiner's *This is Spinal Tap* (1984) is an example of the genre.

model release. Contract in which a model gives permission to use their photo as the client specifies. See also **release.**

monitor. One of a number of specialized TVs that are used by the production staff and the director to view the action during shooting.

monologue. A scene performed by one person that reflects a particular mood and demonstrates their acting talent.

montage. A sequence of short-duration shots linked together, usually over a continuous soundtrack. For example, juxtaposing images of a car going over a cliff, an empty bottle of Stoli, and a couple arguing, while the soundtrack plays Ozzy Osbourne's "Suicide Solution."

mood. The feeling that an actor projects to suit a specific role.

morph. Derived from "metamorphose." A computer-assisted change undergone by an actor or an object. Modern 3-D scanning and computer data manipulation technologies make almost any imaginable effect possible to enact on the screen.

motif. A theme such as music or visual element or concept that recurs in a film or video production and is integral to the story. An example would be the revenge motif prevalent in mobster movies.

motion picture. Feature film.

mouth noise. Undesirable and unintended noises that actors make when they speak, like pops and smacks. Can be avoided by making sure the actor has water available to keep their whistle wet. Failing that, mouth noise can be cleaned up in the editing process.

move on. Director's command for cast and crew to prepare for the next shot or scene.

musical. A movie that features a dominant soundtrack of songs. A recent and very successful example is Rob Marshall's *Chicago* (2002), starring Renée Zellweger and Catherine Zeta-Jones.

N

NAB. National Association of Broadcasters.

NABET. National Alliance of Broadcast Engineers and Technicians.

narrator. An individual, sometimes on-screen but often just in voice-over, who relates certain portions of a story. Commonly present in documentaries.

National Alliance of Broadcast Engineers and Technicians (NABET). Represents broadcast TV production personnel.

national commercial. A commercial that will air across the country. Highly desirable gig because of the potential for high residual payments when it does air.

NC-17. CARA film rating. No one 17 and under admitted.

negative cutter. The person who physically cuts the original film negative at the conclusion of the editing process in order to produce the master original from which answer prints for distribution are made. The negative cutter is rapidly being replaced by machines that do the work.

network TV. Refers to the national non-cable broadcasters including ABC, CBS, NBC, FOX and PBS (public non-commercial).

Nickelodeon. A cable channel with programming for kids. The term was coined in the late 19th century to describe small, neighborhood storefronts that charged a nickel to show silent movies.

night shot. A scene that supposedly takes place at night.

noise. Any unwanted sound.

non-linear editing. The ability to rearrange scenes and shots in postproduction. Increasingly the case as computer editing dominates film and television.

non-speaking role. A part that has no lines but receives credit, as opposed to an extra, who does not.

O

obligatory scene. A formula shot that is predictable in movies of a certain genre. Examples include the high-speed chase in Police Dramas and the shoot-out in Westerns.

off-camera. Refers to an actor who is in the scene and whose voice is heard but who is not seen on camera.

off-card. What a union actor is called when he is working on a non-union project. Not a smart thing to do as it can lead to expulsion from the union.

omnies. Sounds that are made by extras in unison. Although the background actors may be speaking in these group scenes, they are still considered extras. See also **walla**.

on a bell. Instruction from the 1st AD to the soundman to sound a bell that indicates the start or stop of a take.

on-camera. An actor who is in a scene and will be part of the camera's field of vision.

one-liner. A horse walks into a bar. Bartender says, "Why the long face?" A truly wise man never plays leapfrog with a unicorn. I went to a bookstore and asked the salesperson where the Self-Help section was. She said if she told me, it would defeat the purpose. I've got a million of 'em.

one-reeler. A ten- to twelve-minute film.

open call. Casting when the client sees all actors or models suitable for the part requested. Also referred to as open auditions or open casting calls. Also a session at which talent agencies, in search of new faces, see many actors and models.

option. The right to develop an intellectual property, such as a script. Usually time-bound and paid for.

outtakes. Shots that are not used in the final cut of a production. These are sometimes assembled in programs that are used to promote the final cut, or that are packaged along with the final cut on DVDs.

out time. The time at which an actor is released from the set and has his pay voucher signed by the 2nd AD.

overacting. Emoting and relying on broad gestures and mannerisms and possibly a theatrical voice. Whereas some of these techniques are desirable, even obligatory in the theater, TV and film call for a much more understated performance.

overcrank. To run film through a camera at a rate faster than the standard twenty-four frames per second (fps). The resulting action appears to be in slow motion. See **undercrank.**

over-the-shoulder. A shot in which the camera is on one performer while another is in the foreground and only their shoulder is in the frame. Often used for reaction shots.

overtime. Compensation paid to an employee if they stay beyond the agreed hours for which they are being paid. Overtime wages are a multiple of base pay.

P

PA. Production assistant.

packaging. Refers to the practice, employed by talent agencies, of combining multiple co-stars and supporting actors along with the star they contract out to a particular project.

pan. A side-to-side movement of the camera, considered amateurish if overdone. Also a bad review.

pantomiming. Acting out a scene without speaking, relying entirely on gestures and facial expressions. Extras are generally expected to pantomime. See also **mime.**

per diem. A daily allowance to cover food and other expenses, typically paid when a shoot is at a remote location rather than at a studio.

period piece. A production that is set in a past historical era.

PG. Parental Guidance Suggested. CARA rating. Some material may be inappropriate for children.

phoning it in. Refers to a particularly uninspired performance by an actor. Not a nice thing to be accused of.

photo double. An individual who resembles one of the lead actors and takes their place on some shots but does not speak.

pick-up. Recommencing a shoot somewhere in the middle of a scene. Typically done when all but a part of a scene has been successfully shot.

picture picked. Selected for a part from a headshot without an audition.

picture's up! An announcement made on the set by the 1st AD to alert the actors and crew that shooting of the scene will start shortly.

pilot. A prototype episode of a TV program. Almost always funded by a studio and produced for the purpose of testing the concept.

pirate. To make unauthorized copies of an intellectual property.

pitch. A presentation made to a potential independent or studio producer with the intent of convincing them to finance or produce a project. Also generic term for any form of selling.

placement. A term referring to where your credit appears relative to other credits.

plot. The main outline of a story. In feature films often structured into three acts of which the first lasts for thirty minutes and provides the set-up; the second lasts sixty minutes and provides the conflict; and the third lasts thirty minutes and provides climax and catharsis.

plot twist. A sudden and unexpected change in the storyline.

plus ten. Typical scale compensation for union actors. Also referred to as scale-plus-ten. The "ten" is 10%, the agent's commission.

point of view. Abbreviated as POV. Refers to the position of the camera on a shot. For example, if Superman is flying overhead and the script specifies "POV Superman," then the camera must shoot the scene as though it were looking through Superman's eyes.

porn. A genre of film and video programs that features explicit sexual acts.

portfolio. Main promotional tool for models. Consists of select photos in a vinyl or leather casebook, which show the models at their photogenic best, as well as samples of their work.

post-production. The phase in making movies and video programs that follows the actual shooting. In this stage a great number of activities are undertaken that produce the final product that an audience sees, including picture and sound synching, editing, and visual effects.

POV. Point of view.

premiere. A movie's first public viewing, often surrounded with a great deal of publicity and fanfare.

premise. The basic story idea. See also **high concept.**

pre-production. Activities that take place prior to the commencement of shooting. These can include scouting for locations and casting.

prequel. A movie that is released after the first or second installment of a series but includes events that took place prior in real time. An example is Renny Harlin's *Exorcist: The Beginning*, released in 2004. The events in this prequel precede those in the 1973 original, *The Exorcist.*

presence. The impact an individual actor makes. An actor with presence dominates a scene. Al Pacino and Meryl Streep have presence.

preview. A short film made up of shots from a feature film and used to advertise it before its release.

principal. A performer in a speaking role.

principal photography. The biggest chunk of shooting on a project. See also **second-unit photography.**

print. Describes a commercial that will primarily be produced in print media like magazines and newspapers. Also the command given by a director when he is happy with a shot.

printwork. Photography taken for catalog and mail order, books, brochures, ads for magazines or newspapers, magazine covers, commercial photography for household and business products and services.

producer. Catchall title referring to an individual who plays an essential role in making a production happen.

product placement. Advertising products by placing them in a movie or TV show for use by the characters. An important source of revenue for film and TV producers.

production. Refers to the entire process of making a film or video program. Can include writing the script at the start and doing the final touch-ups at the end. Production typically ends when the program is completed and ready for distribution and broadcast.

production assistant. Reports to the production manager and helps with everything on the set from handling paperwork to managing the lunch queue. Maybe the hardest-working people in showbiz, with the possible exception of James Brown.

production design. The overall look and artistic style of a production, including color attributes and visual quality.

production designer. Designs the physical set and all related visual aspects of a production, including costumes and props.

production executive. The studio executive who represents the studio in the course of a production, ensuring that the budget and schedule are adhered to.

production illustrator. An artist who renders the director's or director of photography's ideas in storyboards.

production manager. A producer who shares responsibility for line production. Similar in role to line producer.

production sound mixer. The individual on a set whose responsibility it is to capture the sounds collected during the production and ensure that they are of high quality.

promo. A short video production featuring highlights of a TV show and intended to publicize that show.

promotion. Publicity to advance a product, service or person.

proof sheet. Also **proofs.** A large sheet on which multiple photo thumbnails are printed and from which the client can select pictures for printing. Typically viewed with a loupe.

property master. Is responsible for managing the inventory of props and assigning them to actors as needed.

protagonist. The good guy. See also **antagonist.**

PSA. Public service announcement.

public relations. Creating an image of a product or service in the eyes of the public, mainly through the media.

public service announcement (PSA). A short program that is intended to educate or inform the public and not to sell anything. Generally funded by government.

publicist. An individual whose role is to cultivate interest in a client or a project while also managing the onslaught of unwanted attention. Sometimes referred to as "press agent."

Q

quartz light. A high-intensity set light.

quota quickie. A short, low-budget film whose primary purpose was to satisfy a law in the UK that required cinemas to include a certain percentage of British films in their showings.

quote. The compensation that an actor demands. Based on their last highest level of compensation. Relevant only to highly sought-after actors.

R

R. Restricted, CARA film rating. Under 17 requires accompanying parent or adult guardian.

rack focus. Shifting the on-screen focus of the camera lens from a distant to a closer object or vice versa.

range. An actor's ability to portray different emotions and conditions.

rates. Fees charged by actors and models. Rates can be negotiated by the unions, in which case they are referred to as "scale."

ratings. Labels assigned by the Rating Board of the Classification and Rating Administration (CARA) to help the public assess the content of movies: G: General, PG: Parental Guidance, PG-13: Parents Strongly Cautioned, R: Restricted, NC-17: No One Under 17.

raw stock. Unexposed film.

reaction shot. A shot that captures one actor's reaction to something another says or does. See also **over-the-shoulder.**

read-through. The act of reading through a script before acting it out. Normally involves the actors, director and producers and is intended to familiarize everyone with the material before the expensive work of shooting begins.

real time. Time in real life as measured in minutes, hours and days. Contrast with **filmic time.**

reality show. A TV show that features ordinary people, not actors, in ostensibly ordinary situations competing or otherwise interacting for the pleasure of the viewer. Can include eating bugs.

recall. Being called back for an extra day on a project.

recurring. Typically in TV, a role that figures into multiple episodes.

reenactment. The performance by actors of events, often crimes, that had taken place in fact.

regional. A commercial that only airs in a portion of the country.

release. A document that an actor signs agreeing to release the client from future monetary obligations in return for an upfront payment.

release date. The date on which a movie is shown in theaters.

residuals. Additional money paid to a performer when a program airs for the first time and every subsequent time. Residual rates are negotiated by the unions. Actors' residuals are also tracked by the unions.

resolution. The relative sharpness of a picture. Also the final sequence in a film, where conflicts that have built up throughout the story are resolved.

résumé. A summary of an individual's work experience, skills and education. In showbiz this includes credits from previous acting gigs.

retouch. To remove imperfections from photographs and film.

right-to-work. Designates certain states that have legislated an actor's right to do union and non-union work, limiting a union's power. California is not a right-to-work state.

rolling. What the camera operator announces to the director when the film in the camera is rolling and he is ready to shoot.

room tone. The ambient sound in a room when no one is speaking and no other noise is being made. Is used by sound mixers to lay down a baseline track. See also **wild track**.

rough cut. Essentially a first edited draft of a production.

run through. A practice run, typically when the cameras are not rolling. Some directors will ask actors to run through a scene while the camera is rolling because they think they might get relaxed performances out of them.

runaway production. A production that is shot in Canada or other lower-cost locations.

running time. The duration of a show.

rush call. A call for talent that comes at the last minute. Can be a good opportunity because fewer people will be available to compete for the gig.

rushes. See **dailies**.

S

SAG. Screen Actors Guild

SAGIndie. A SAG-sponsored organization whose charter is to help independent producers use SAG talent. To that end SAG recently ratified two low budget agreements, the Short Film Agreement and the Ultra Low Budget Agreement. Actor wages per these agreements are partially or totally deferred.

satire. A form of criticism that uses humor, parody and ridicule.

scale wage. Minimum wage set by the unions.

scene. The action and dialogue that takes place at the same time and location. For example. A courtroom scene, in which multiple shots cover the action.

scenery. A scene's background.

scene-stealer. An actor who, deliberately or not, takes the attention away from others in the scene.

score. The musical soundtrack of a movie.

scout. Person looking for prospective actors and models.

Screen Actors Guild (SAG). An organization representing actors who perform in TV or movie productions.

screen test. An audition during which the performer is filmed.

screening. Showing a movie.

screenplay. The standard format in which dialogue and descriptions are written for production as a movie or video program. Must adhere to very specific conventions of formatting. See also **script**.

script. Screenplay.

script supervisor. A key member of the production team whose primary responsibility is to ensure that there is continuity from one shot or scene to the next.

second second assistant director (2nd 2nd). On busy productions involving many actors and background players, a 2nd 2nd assists the 2nd AD in managing schedules and ensuring that all cast members are on-set and ready when needed.

second team. The stand-ins who are used in place of the stars while the crew sets up the lighting and camera for a scene.

second unit. A camera team that supplements the first unit.

second-unit director. The director of the second unit

second-unit photography. The footage that is shot by the second unit. See also **principal photography.**

sepia. A range of beige and brown hues that is reminiscent of the early days of photography. Now used to give images an antique look.

sequel. A production that picks up the story where a preceding one had left off.

sequencing. The process of arranging shots in a particular order in post-production. Part of the work of editing.

serial. A production that presents a story in discrete but thematically connected segments. An excellent example is USA Networks' *24*, starring Kiefer Sutherland. Each episode during the season depicts the action of one hour in real time.

session fee. An actor's compensation for a workday on a commercial. If the commercial airs, the actor will also receive **residuals**.

set. Arrangement of props and furniture in a TV or photo studio.

set decorator. The individual responsible for adding the elements to a set that make it look real, like curtains and photos and furniture.

set dressing. Props and other items placed in a set to make it consistent with the script. Set dressing can include furniture, drapes, art objects and plants.

setting. The historical, geographic, social and other attributes of a production. For example, a movie's setting could be Egypt during the decline of the Roman Empire.

set-up. The act of moving the camera and preparing or setting it up for the next shot.

sexploitation. A movie that uses nudity and other soft-core sexual content. Generally R-Rated.

SFX. Special effects.

shoot. A session during which film or video or still images are recorded in a studio or on location.

showcase. A stage production that features short performances by actors seeking to showcase their talents to an invited audience of talent agents and casting directors.

shuttle. A van or small bus that transports actors and crew from a parking location to the main shoot location.

side light. Directional lighting that illuminates the side of an actor or object. See also **kick**.

sides. Refers to the portion of the script that includes a particular actor's scenes and lines.

sign-in sheet. Lists the order in which actors arrive to audition.

signatory. A producer who adheres to union rules of employment and compensation.

silent film. Film of the pre-talkies era (1895-1928). Although these films did not have dialogue, they did have a musical accompaniment. The quintessential example is D. W. Griffith's 1915 epic *The Birth of a Nation*.

six-hanky film. Sobbing, snorting, tear-yanker like *Love Story* (1970).

size sheet. A card that an actor fills out at an audition listing height, clothing sizes, color hair and eyes. Casting coordinators collect these cards from the actors and attach them to their headshots and résumés.

slapstick. Physical comedy.

slate. To state your name on-camera before your audition.

slow-motion. On-screen action that is slowed down to a speed that allows real-time rapid action to be observed. Used extensively in TV sports coverage.

soft focus. The fuzzy image effect achieved by coating the camera lens with Vaseline or covering it with a fine mesh. Used to great effect in the romantic shots of the early talkies.

soft-core. Programs with non-explicit sexual content. Generally R-rated.

sound effects. Sounds made by Foley artists and taken from prerecorded sources to compliment soundtracks on a production.

soundstage. A warehouse-like building on a studio lot that is used for filming or taping programs in a soundproof environment. The major studios own vast lots on which tens of soundstages are used for multiple productions.

soundtrack. The audio portion of a program.

Spaghetti Western. A genre of mass-production Western movies that were very popular in the 60s and 70s. Examples include Sergio Leone's *The Good, the Bad and the Ugly* (1967), starring Clint Eastwood.

spec script. A script written without a previous commitment to produce.

special effects. Various activities that create a certain effect on-set, such as wind or smoke or flashing lights. Not to be mistaken for visual effects, which are generated off the set, most often by computer.

speed. The announcement made by the sound man when the audio recording system is in step with the camera and the scene can be shot and recorded.

spin. The practice of manipulating and sometimes distorting facts to achieve the greatest advantage for one's own agenda.

spin-off. A program that reuses some or all of the elements of a previous one. Sequels are an example of spin-offs. *Joey* is a spin-off from *Friends*.

split screen. A screen on which two or more images are shown in adjacent frames.

spokesperson. An actor chosen to explain the benefits and features of a product or service.

spoof. A parody. Jim Abraham and David Zucker's *Airplane* (1980) is a side-splitting example of the genre. Also anything by Monty Python.

spot. A TV commercial, most often thirty seconds but sometimes ten or sixty seconds long.

squibs. Packets of theatrical blood that are hidden in clothing and made to explode and simulate an actor being shot. Unrelated to *calamari*.

stage parent. An adult who fusses and watches too closely over a child performer and gets in the way of the shoot.

stand-in. Extras who take a principal's place on the set during lighting set up and other activities for which the principal himself does not need to be present. Their primary qualification is a rough resemblance to the actor they are standing in for.

star. The actor who tops the credits in a production.

Station 12. A SAG document certifying the status of an actor as a bona fide member. Producers must acquire this document before employing a SAG actor.

stats. Statistical information of a model or actor, including measurements, size, height, etc.

Steadycam. A harness system, carried by a specialized camera operator and allowing him to film action while moving with the subject.

still. Photograph.

stock footage. Archival film or video that can be reused in other productions as needed.

storyboard. Artwork that illustrates the main scenes of a production and is used by cast and crew to visualize the scenes.

straight man. A comic's sidekick, there to create openings for them to make jokes. Also a male person with limited color sense.

stripboard. A tool that is used by production personnel in scheduling the order in which scenes are shot. Each scene is represented by a strip that is inserted in a board in the slot that corresponds to its order in the shooting schedule. The strips can be pulled out and re-slotted to reflect needed changes in the schedule. Much of this work is now computerized.

strobe. Light fixture used by a photographer.

studio. An entity that is in the business of producing film and video programming. See **Big Ten**. Also the physical location where productions take place.

studio system. The monopoly that dominated movie making in the first half of the twentieth century.

stunt. An activity that is performed by a stuntman and sometimes by the actor himself that is outside the normal scope of acting. Riding a horse, falling down stairs, jumping from airplanes.

stunt coordinator. An individual who plans and choreographs stunts. He also oversees the execution of stunts to the director's satisfaction.

stunt double. A stuntman who resembles an actor and takes their place in scenes calling for stunts.

stylist. One of the production personnel. Coordinates fashions and accessories and checks fit of clothing.

sub-plot. A secondary storyline within the larger plot.

subtitles. Translation of the dialog into another language, shown as text at the bottom of the screen.

Sundance. Independent film showcase founded in 1981 by Robert Redford and held annually in Park City, Utah.

super. Abbreviation for superimposition; the technique of placing text over the image on the screen. Often used for credits and subtitles.

supervising producer. Typically works in TV and is involved on a continual basis with a particular show.

supervising sound editor. Oversees all postproduction sound work.

supporting. Describes a role that is big but not quite starring. An example would be Arnold Schwarzenegger's Mr. Freeze in Joel Schumacher's 1997 *Batman and Robin*.

swashbuckler. A movie about sword-carrying, ship-commanding, high-boot-wearing, good looking guys. Douglas Fairbanks and Errol Flynn epitomized the part.

swing gang. The members of the crew that build and take down a set.

syndication. The selling of a TV show for re-broadcast in multiple markets to individual stations.

T

table. Describes the act of gathering creative talent around a table to discuss a script and polish it as necessary.

Taft-Hartley. A federal statute that allows an actor to work on two union projects or for 30 days, whichever comes first, before having to join that union. In showbiz it is also the statute that automatically makes an actor eligible for membership in SAG if they work as a principal in a SAG signatory production.

tag. A short segment, attached to the end of a commercial, and providing additional information such as price of the product and where it can be purchased.

tagline. A catchy phrase that describes a movie in a memorable way. The tagline for Sergio Leone's *The Good, the Bad and the Ugly* (1967) is: "For Three Men The Civil War Wasn't Hell. It Was Practice!"

take. The continuous filming or taping of a scene. Most scenes require multiple takes to perfect.

talent. A general term that applies to actors and performers.

talkies. The early motion pictures which for the first time incorporated dialog. See also **silent movies.**

tearjerker. A sad movie.

tearsheet. Copy of a print ad that the actor keeps in their portfolio as proof of work.

telephoto lens. A lens that provides a close-up view of objects that are far from the camera.

teleprompter. TV-like screen that displays the cue card words.

tenpercenter. Hollywood-speak for a talent agent.

test shots, test photography. Photos used to build a beginning portfolio.

testimonial. Celebrity declaration as to the value of a product or service; improvisational endorsement of a product or service that the actor has officially tested, used and approved.

theme music. A song or melody that is used repeatedly in a movie or video program and is associated with it. "Lara's Theme" from David Lean's *Dr. Zhivago* (1965) is an unforgettable example.

Thomas Guide. A street-map guide in grid style that is invaluable for getting around any city, but especially Los Angeles.

three-quarters shot. A photo of an individual from the knees up.

three-shot. A shot in which three actors appear in the frame.

three-hanky. A very, very sad movie.

tie-in. A scheme for promoting a movie through related products and vice versa. *Star Trek* T-shirts, for example.

time cue. A cue given to on-camera talent, particularly in live television, to let them know how much time is left.

title role. Starring role after which a movie is named. For example, the role of the Pink Panther in the series starring the late Peter Sellers.

titles. The text that appears on the screen before and after a program and lists participants in the production as well as copyright and other information.

tracking shot. Describes a shot where the camera parallels the motion of the subject. See also **truck**.

trade shows. Industry promotional display of products and services usually in a hotel or convention center.

trades, trade papers. Publications that focus on a particular industry. For film and TV these include *Variety*, *Backstage*, *DramaLogue*, and *The Hollywood Reporter*.

trailer. A promotional production featuring the highlights of a film.

transition. Moving from one shot to another. Many techniques exist but the most commonplace is the simple cut. Dissolves, fades, wipes and very complex computer-generated transitions are also used.

transparencies. The slide forms of a photograph.

treatment. A summarized version of a screenplay used to pitch the project to prospective producers.

truck. A lateral movement of the camera. See also **tracking shot**.

turnaround. The time interval between the end of one day and the beginning of the next, from wrap to call time. Turnaround is required by unions to be no less than twelve hours. When it is shorter than that, the actors and crew involved are on a **forced call** and receive additional compensation.

twist ending. An unpredictable end to the action.

two-shot. A shot showing two actors in the frame, the typical dialogue configuration.

typecast. To pigeonhole an actor on the basis of other roles they've played in the past. For example, Bela Lugosi as a vampire.

U

undercrank. To run film through a camera at a rate slower than the standard twenty-four frames per second (fps). The resulting action appears to be in fast-motion. See **overcrank.**

union. An organization that represents its members in matters of compensation and workplace safety.

unit production manager (UPM). The ranking manager on a production. Often the person who hires production crews.

UPM. Unit production manager.

usage fees. A schedule of fees, varying by markets, that is used to compute an actor's residuals. An "A" city like Los Angeles, for example, will generate a higher residual payment per airing than, say, Modesto. These are based on population size.

V

Valley, the. The Fernando Valley, including Van Nuys, Burbank, and Glendale. It is home to many production companies. CBS, NBC, Universal Studios, Warner Brothers and Walt Disney Pictures all have large facilities here. The Valley is also known as a center for the porn industry. Hence the tongue-in-cheek moniker "San Pornando Valley."

visual effects. Postproduction manipulations of and additions to the actual footage. Often created with computers.

voice-over. The technique of recording human voice then overlaying it onto film or video images. Often the speaker is not shown, as in most historical narratives.

voucher. Triplicate or four-part form on which a production company records hours worked by an actor.

W

walkaway. A meal that the actor leaves the set to get. A meal that is not provided by the production company.

walk-on. Small role with no dialogue.

walla walla. Industry jargon for crowd noise. Also a small town in Washington State that is famous for its sweet onions and a concrete replica of Stone Henge. I couldn't make this stuff up.

wardrobe. The department that is responsible for designing and preparing costumes for actors and for fitting them before the shoot.

watermelon. The word repeated by extras everywhere when they are pantomiming conversation.

weather permit. A location job that is dependent on fair weather, may be canceled the day before or that morning.

WGA. Writers Guild of America.

whodunit. A suspense mystery movie in which the plot's purpose is to uncover the killer.

wide shot. See establishing shot and long shot.

wide-angle lens. A lens that provides a broad, panoramic view of a scene. Also fish-eye.

wild spot. A commercial that airs on an independent station.

wild track. Recording audio only to match up later with film footage.

wipe. A transition in which the image from one shot gradually slides onscreen while pushing the previous shot off-screen.

work print. A copy of the first complete version of a production. A work in progress that culminates in the rough cut.

wrangler. The individual responsible for dealing with animals on the set.

wrap. The end of production on a given day. Also used to let individual actors know that they are done for that day or for the project.

writer. The individual who creates the story and the screenplay.

Writers Guild of America (WGA). Represents television, radio and movie writers.

Z

zed card. See composite card.

z-film. An ultra-low-budget movie produced, directed and performed by amateurs. Many of legendarily bad director Ed Wood's films were z-films.

zoom. To zoom in is to go from a wide shot to a close-up. To zoom out is the reverse.

☆

BIBLIOGRAPHY

Work hard and, if you can't
work hard, be smart; and, if you
can't be smart, be loud.

— Sammy Glick in
Budd Schulberg's
What Makes Sammy Run

☆

Tears of love dry overnight in
Hollywood.

— Al Martinez

☆

☆

Adams, Cindy. *Lee Strasberg; The Imperfect Genius of the Actors Studio*. Garden City, NY: Doubleday & Company, 1980.

Altman, Robert. *The Player*. VHS. Directed by Robert Altman. Avenue Pictures Productions, 1992.

Asher, Joel. *The Actors at Work Series*. Vol. 4. "Directors on Acting." VHS. Directed by Joel Asher. Sherman Oaks: Joel Asher Studio, 1993.

Bacall, Lauren. *Lauren Bacall: By Myself*. New York: Ballantine Books, 1978.

Bacon, James. *Hollywood is a Four Letter Word*. Chicago: Henry Regnery Company, 1976.

Baker, Henry Barton. *English Actors: From Shakespeare to Macready*. New York: Henry Holt & Co., 1879.

Beard, Jocelyn A. ed. *The Ultimate Audition Book: 222 Monologues 2 Minutes & Under*. Lyme, NH: Smith and Kraus Inc., 1997.

Behlmer, Rudy, ed. *Memo From David O. Selznick*. New York: Viking Press, 1972.

Berland, Terry and Deborah Ouellette. *Breaking Into Commercials: the complete guide to marketing yourself, auditioning to win, and getting the job*. New York: Plume, 1997.

Bertolino, Angela, and Carla Lewis. *"Extra" Work For Brain Surgeons*. Vol. 23. Los Angeles: Hollywood OS, 2004.

Boller, Paul F. and Ronald L. Davis. *Hollywood Anecdotes*. New York: William Morrow & Company, Inc., 1987.

Brook, George. "Surviving the Roller Coaster: Worst and Best Practices in Project Management within the Television Production Industry." December 30, 2003. AllPM.com, The Project Manager's Homepage. http://www.allpm.com.

Broomfield, Nick. *Heidi Fleiss: Hollywood Madam*. VHS. Produced and directed by Nick Broomfield. 1996.

Brillstein, Bernie and David Rensin. *Where Did I Go Right?: You're No One in Hollywood Until Someone Wants You Dead*. New York: Warner Books, 2001.

Brouwer, Alexandra, and Thomas Lee Wright. *Working in Hollywood.* New York: Crown Publishers, Inc., 1990.

Buzzell, Linda. *How To Make It In Hollywood.* 2nd ed. New York: Harper Collins, 1996.

Callan, K. *The Los Angeles Agent Book.* 8th ed. Studio City: Sweden Press, Inc., 2003.

Chambers, Cullen. *Back to One, The Complete Movie Extra Guidebook, The Millennium Edition.* Hollywood: Back to One Publications, 2000.

Cini, Zelda, and Bob Crane with Peter H. Brown. *Hollywood Land and Legend.* Westport, CT: Arlington House, 1980.

Cole, Toby and Helen Krich Chinoy, eds. *Actors on Acting: The Theories, Techniques and Practices of the World's Great Actors, Told in Their Own Words.* New York: Crown Publishers, Inc., 1970.

Diderot, Denis. *The Paradox of Acting,* trans. W.H. Pollock. Hill and Wang, 1957.

Garrison, Lee, and Wallace Wang. *Breaking Into Acting for Dummies.* Hoboken: Wiley, 2002.

Gelman, Morrie and Gene Accas. *The Best In Television; 50 Years of Emmys.* Santa Monica: General Publishing Group, Inc., 1998.

Goldberg, Jan. *Careers for Extroverts & Other Gregarious Types.* 2nd ed. New York: McGraw-Hill, 2006.

Goldman,William. *Which Lie Did I Tell.* New York: Pantheon Press, 2000.

Hagen, Uta and Frankel Haskel. *Respect for Acting.* Hoboken: Wiley, 1973.

Harris, Fran. *Crashing Hollywood; How to Keep Your Integrity Up, Your Clothes On, and Still Make It in Hollywood.* Michael Wiese Productions, 2003.

Henry, Mari Lyn, and Lynne Rogers. *How to be a Working Actor; The Insider's Guide to Finding Jobs in Theater, Film, and Television.* 4th rev and exp. ed. New York: Watson-Guptill Publications, 2000.

Hochman, David. "Before I Was Famous." *Life,* 18 February 2005, 8.

Hunter, Cynthia. *Hollywood, Here I Come! How To Launch a Great Acting or Modeling Career Anywhere and Land in Los Angeles.* Hollywood: Yellow Deer Press, 2001.

Jones, Peter and A. Scott Berg. *Goldwyn; The Man and His Movies.* DVD. Directed by Peter Jones and Mark Catalena. Culver City, CA: 2001.

Kanin, Garson. *Tracy and Hepburn: An Intimate Memoir*. New York: Bantam Books, 1970.

Katselas, Milton. *Dreams Into Action: Getting What You Want*. Beverly Hills: Katselas Productions, 1997.

Katz, Ephraim. *The Film Encyclopedia, 4th Edition: The Most Comprehensive Encyclopedia of World Cinema in a Single Volume*. 4th rev. edition. New York: Collins, 2001.

LeRoy, Mervyn. *It Takes More Than Talent*. New York: Alfred A. Knopf, 1953.

Lewinski, John Scott. *The Screenwriter's Guide to Agents and Managers*. New York: Allworth Press, 2001.

Lodge, David. *Therapy*. London: Penguin Books, 1996.

Martinez, Al. *City of Angels: A Drive-By Portrait of Los Angeles*. New York: St. Martin's Press, 1996.

Mason, Paul, and Don Gold. *Producing for Hollywood*. New York: Allworth Press, 2004.

Merchant, Ismail. *The Courtesans of Bombay*. VHS. Produced and directed by Ismail Merchant. London: Merchant Ivory Productions, 1997.

Merlin, Joanna. *Auditioning: An Actor-Friendly Guide*. New York: Vintage books, 2001.

Miller, Henry. *Tropic of Cancer*. New York: Grove Press, 1961.

Mills, Thomas. *L.A. from A to Z: The Actor's Guide to Surviving and Succeeding in Los Angeles*. Portsmouth, NH: Heinemann Drama, 2002.

Morris, Eric, and Joan Hotchkis. *No Acting Please*. Los Angeles: Whitehouse/Spelling Publications, 1979.

Nemko, Marty, Paul Edwards and Sarah Edwards. *Cool Careers for Dummies*. 2nd ed. Hoboken: Wiley, 2001.

Newcomb, Horace. *Encyclopedia of Television*. 2nd ed. New York: Taylor and Francis, 2004.

Niven, David. *Go Slowly, Come Back Quickly*. New York: Doubleday & Company, 1981.

Obst, Lynda. *Hello, He Lied and Other Truths from the Hollywood Trenches*. New York: Little, Brown and Company, 1996.

O'Neil, Brian. *Acting As a Business: Strategies for Success*. 3rd ed. Portsmouth, NH: Heinemann, 2005.

Phillips, Julia. *You'll Never Eat Lunch in This Town Again*. New York: Random House, Inc., 1991.

Press, Skip. *Awesome Almanac California*. Walworth, WI: B & B Publishing, 1994.

Rawley, Donald. *The View from Babylon: The Notes of a Hollywood Voyeur*. New York: Warner Books, 1999.

Reid, David, ed. *Sex, Death and God in L.A.* New York: Pantheon Books, 1992.

Rensin, David. *The Mailroom. Hollywood History From the Bottom Up*. New York: The Ballantine Publishing Group, 2003.

Resnik, Gail and Scott Trost. *All You Need to Know About the Movie and TV Business*. New York: Simon & Schuster, 1996.

Robertson, Patrick. *Guinness Film Facts & Feats*. New ed. New York: Sterling Publishing Co., 1985.

Rush, Richard. *The Stuntman*. VHS. Directed by Richard Rush. Melvin Simon Productions, 1979.

Saint Nicholas, Michael. *An Actor's Guide: Your First Year in Hollywood*. Rev. ed. New York: Allworth Press, 2000.

Schulberg, Budd. *What Makes Sammy Run*. Reprint ed. New York: The Sun Dial Press, 1943.

Shaheen, Jack G. *Reel Bad Arabs: How Hollywood Vilifies a People*. Northampton, MA: Interlink Publishing Group, 2001.

Silva, L.D. *Hollywood Chronicles*. Manhattan Beach, CA: Starfish Press, 2002.

Smithee, Alan. *Burn Hollywood Burn*. DVD. Directed by Arthur Hiller. Los Angeles, 1998.

Stanislavski, Constantin. *Creating a Role*. New York: Routledge/Theater Arts Books, 1961.

Stanislavski, Constantin, and Elizabeth Reynolds Hapgood. *An Actor Prepares*. Reprint ed. New York: Theater Arts Books, 1991.

Stevens, George Jr. *George Stevens: A Filmmaker's Journey*. VHS. Produced, written, directed and narrated by George Stevens Jr. Burbank, 1984.

Strasberg, Lee. *A Dream of Passion: The Development of the Method*. Boston: Little, Brown and Company, 1987.

Torrence, Bruce T. *Hollywood: The First Hundred Years*. New York: Zoetrope, 1982.

Vater, Rachel. *Guide to Talent and Modeling Agents; the Best Source for Reaching 1000+ Agencies Looking for People Like You!* Cincinnati: Writer's Digest, 2002.

Waldie, D.J. *Where We Are Now: Notes from Los Angeles*. Los Angeles: Angel City Press, 2004.

Wilder, Billy. *Sunset Boulevard*. VHS. Hollywood, 1950.

Wood, Ed Jr. *Hollywood Rat Race*. New York: Four Walls Eight Windows, 1998.

Yager, Fred, and Jan Yager. *Career Opportunities in the Film Industry*. New York, Ferguson, 2003.

Young, Paul. *L.A. Exposed: Strange Myths and Curious Legends in the City of Angels*. New York: Thomas Dunne Books, 2002.

Zettl, Herbert. *Television Production Handbook*. 5th ed. Belmont, CA: Wadswirth Publishing Company, 1992.

Zollo, Paul. *Hollywood Remembered: An Oral History of Its Golden Age*. New York: Cooper Square Press, 2002.

The historical timelines, events and anecdotes throughout the text are synthesized from the following sources: *Encyclopedia Brittanica*, Wikipedia.com, Anecdotage.com, Filmsite.org, the Internet Movie Database (IMDB), *The Film Encyclopedia* and *Encyclopedia of Television*.

☆

INDEX

Hollywood does not
want to be revealed.

— Madam Alex
in Nick Broomfield's
Heidi Fleiss: Hollywood Madam
(1996)

☆

A

D

E

R

S

Strong Medicine, 229, 231
Struthers, Sally, 100
Studio Zone, 62
Submissions, 102-3
  agent, 102
  SAG, 104
  self, 103
Success, 56, 256
  bumpy road, 19
  ingredients, 56
Sum of All Fears, 233
2005 Sundance Film Festival, 237
Sunset Boulevard, 72, 152
Swanson, Gloria, 72, 223
  Sunset Boulevard, 223

T

Taft-Hartley Act, 160, 218
Tait, Charles, 20
talent, 29, 37, 50
  agency, 82, 83, 85
    federal regulations, 84
    laws relating to, 85
    studio divestiture, 84
  agent, 71, 84
    association of, 94
  and success, 51, 56
  experts, 40
  manager, 43
  pool, 88
  scouts, 40
  selecting, 77
Talent Managers Association (TMA), 90
Tandy, Jessica, 136
  Driving Miss Daisy, 136
Targeted: Osama bin Laden, 227
Tate, Sharon, 93
television
  9/11 coverage, 162
  agents, 88
  business hierarchy, 124
  CBS, 52
  Children's Television Act, 145
  day on the set, 122

FCC, 64
First color Academy Awards, 85
  interactive, 115
  JFK assassination, 85
  Lifetime, 231
  lunar walk, 89
  NBC, 56
  network, 66, 136
  Nixon resignation, 105
  organization, 124
  ownership, 75, 83, 110, 134
  roles, 99, 101
  sales, 66
  show production, 127
  stations, 66
  telecast firsts, 56
  unions, 55, 159
    extras quota, 134
  viewing habits, 151
    *M*A*S*H* finale, 118
Telstar I, 84
Temple, Shirley, 53
  Red-Haired Alibi, 53
Ten Commandments, The, 40
Terminator 3, 25
Texaco Star Theater, 65
The Actor's Roadmap of Essential Actions, 153
The English Patient, 149
The Lord of the Rings: The Return of the King, 164
the truth, 24
  John 8:32, 24
Thin Man Pictures, 193
Thomas Guide, 63
Thomas, Richard "John Boy", 188
Thomson, David, 21
Threat Matrix, 195
3D, 74
Three Mile Island, 110
THX, 118
THX 1138, 100
Tiger Child, 100
Time Inc., 136
Time Warner, 160
Tinseltown, 35

Y

Y2K, 153
Yahoo! Maps, 64
You Must Act!, 153
You'll Never Eat Lunch In This Town Again, 29, 176

Z

Zane Pillsbury, 178, 263
Zanuck, Darryl F., 72
zed card, 73, 172
Zenith, 75
Zollo, Paul, 155
　Hollywood Rememberd: An Oral History of Its Golden Age, 155

★

NOTES

NOTES

NOTES